AAU National Amateur
Horseshoe-Pitching Championships
1937–1977

AAU National Amateur

Horseshoe-Pitching Championships

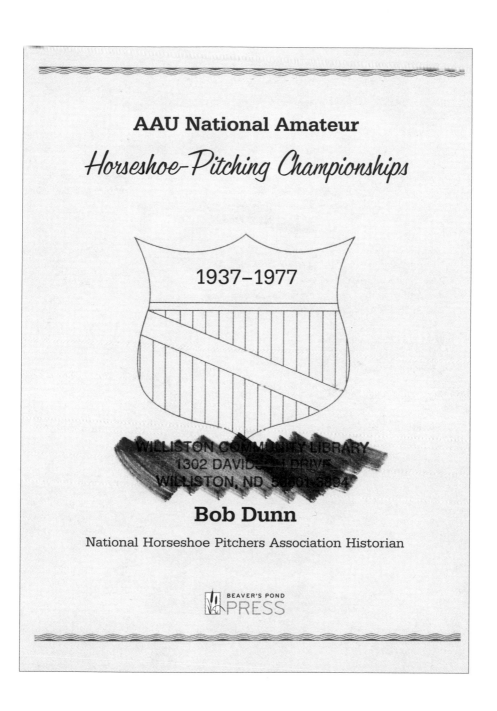

1937–1977

Bob Dunn

National Horseshoe Pitchers Association Historian

BEAVER'S POND
PRESS

ISBN: 978-1-59298-952-2
Library of Congress Control Number: 2013923174

Printed in the United States of America
Designed by Mayfly Design and Typeset in Whitman
First Printing: 2014

18 17 16 15 14   5 4 3 2 1

Beaver's Pond Press, Inc.
7108 Ohms Lane
Edina, MN 55439
(952) 829-8818
www.BeaversPondPress.com

To order, visit www.BeaversPondBooks.com
or call (800) 901-3480. Reseller discounts available.

TABLE OF CONTENTS

INTRODUCTION

Old newspaper clippings or even some issues of *Horseshoe World* magazines often refer to an "amateur" horseshoe-pitching champion. For years I wondered what that meant exactly, since the National Horseshoe Pitchers Association (NHPA) is, for the most part, an amateur organization. Finally I discovered that, while most of the members of the NHPA are viewed as amateurs in the sport, the Amateur Athletic Union (AAU) players were definitively nonprofessionals, so winners in AAU events were referred to as amateur champions. The distinction is rather narrow; the only players not allowed to enter AAU events were players who had won national or world titles in NHPA-hosted tournaments (or, in some cases, those who had played in a cash tournament). In reality, there were no true professionals in the sport other than Ted Allen and a handful of others who did performance exhibitions and were paid a fee for those performances. Essentially, someone listed as a national amateur champion was the winner of the National AAU horseshoe-pitching championship.

The issue of determining the difference between an amateur and professional horseshoe pitcher often crops up when reading accounts of the sport through the decades. In today's terms, any player who qualifies for a championship class in an NHPA-sanctioned event or wins a state championship is no longer an amateur. That definition offers a bit more clarity. Nearly all participating players played in AAU events as amateurs; several later pitched in the NHPA championship classes or won a state championship. A few even went on to be inducted to the NHPA Hall of Fame. In nearly all cases in which players were members of both organizations at the same time in their horseshoe-pitching careers, though, their activity in the AAU preceded their qualification for an NHPA event. When players earned championship-class status, they concluded their AAU involvement.

Horseshoe pitching in the AAU started in 1937. At the time, the sport was suffering mismanagement by the NHPA, the main symptom of which was a five-year gap in which no World Tournaments were held. The most recent World Tournament had been in 1935 in Moline, Illinois, and the next wouldn't be until 1940 in Des Moines, Iowa. One of NHPA's leaders, Raymond B. Howard, was highly involved in convincing the AAU to include the sport of horseshoe pitching in their annual calendar of events. The AAU's initial start and ability to hold a series of state tournaments and national contests was probably the result of their larger membership and more money.

At the time, Howard was serving as NHPA's secretary-treasurer. The reason for his mission to bring horseshoe pitching to the AAU is unclear. I could find no newspaper or *Horseshoe World* articles that address his purpose. Howard was immediately named Chairman of the National AAU Horseshoe-Pitching Committee. He was expending an immense effort to bring horseshoe pitching to the AAU. It's tempting to wonder why he didn't invest that effort in continuing the already established NHPA World Tournaments. Even though there was a lull in the World Tournaments, Howard did keep *Horseshoe World* magazine in operation, which is no doubt one of the reasons the sport and the NHPA are still around today.

Why should today's pitchers and followers of the sport have any interest in these early AAU events? In the 1930s, the AAU did a lot to promote the sport and contributed to an ongoing national interest in it. AAU events continued into the late 1970s, so their involvement was significant. It's also interesting to discover who crops up in the AAU events. In the very first event, for example, we find the name Arlo Harris, who served as NHPA president. In the 1940s we find the names Ralph Dykes, Bob Pence, and Lee Rose, all of whom went on to be officers in the NHPA and (except Harris) inductees into the NHPA Hall of Fame. And that's just to name a few of the interesting players and hall-of-famers. Did the AAU horseshoe-pitching program serve as a platform, or perhaps a catalyst, for several of these young men who went on to serve the NHPA so well? Or might that have happened anyway? It's impossible to be certain, but the 40-year affiliation with the AAU can't be ignored as a boost to many players' and promoters' careers.

The following article, which appeared on the inside front cover of the December 1936 *Horseshoe World*, announces the AAU's new involvement in the sport and gives a preview of what to expect:

The AAU Decision

The decision of the Amateur Athletic Union of the U.S. to embrace horseshoe pitching as one of its amateur sports, should be greeted with enthusiasm by many people—both amateur and professional, by playground and school athletic directors and by the manufacturers of horseshoe pitching equipment.

To the amateur it means an avenue of expression in the ancient and honorable game without the worry of being tainted with professionalism while engaging in amateur competition in other sports. To the professional, it means an opportunity to be of service to a great organization like the AAU and to have the knowledge that more pitchers are being developed, who eventually may become interested in the National Horseshoe Pitchers Association affairs. Playground directors and directors of sports in high schools and colleges will find much help from AAU leaders, as well as from the National Horseshoe Pitchers Association in promoting an amateur program that includes horseshoe pitching. Manufacturers of equipment will find a new class of pitchers coming on and new avenues for sales of shoes, stakes, carrying cases, etc.

To our mind it is a happy solution to the problem of how to satisfy all horseshoe pitchers—both amateurs and professionals.

The *Horseshoe World* pledges its fullest support to AAU leaders, as it has to the National Horseshoe Pitchers Association groups throughout the past several years. It will be a pleasure to serve both the amateur and professional horseshoe pitchers.

The unsigned article was written by none other than Raymond Howard, who wasn't just the NHPA's secretary-treasurer, but was also the publisher and editor of *Horseshoe World*, the longtime bimonthly official magazine of the NHPA. *Horseshoe World* was launched in 1922 and was published until 1943, with Howard as its editor for entire time. Howard was inducted into the NHPA Hall of Fame in 1966 as one of six charter inductees.

Raymond Howard

1937

It All Started in Cincinnati

The June–July 1937 edition of *Horseshoe World* carries this announcement:

National AAU Tournament July 25th

Arrangements were completed the past week to hold the National Senior AAU Horseshoe Pitching Championships at the Parkway Arena, Central Parkway and Findlay Streets, Cincinnati, by official notice of the Ohio Association, AAU, Sunday, July 25th.

The championships will consist of women's singles and doubles and men's singles and doubles.

This is the first year that the amateur end of the sport comes under AAU jurisdiction, the NHPA having relinquished control of that phase of the sport to the AAU at the latter's national convention in Houston, Texas, last December and Cincinnati was awarded the first annual tournament.

Any amateur horseshoe pitcher of the world will be eligible to compete for the National AAU title. All contestants must be registered with their respective district association before their entry is accepted.

The national amateur tournament will follow closely the professional rules of competition for the sport, with one important exception, the final competition instead of being a round-robin affair, with each final qualifier playing the other will be a strictly one-defeat-and-out tournament, with winners advancing to the next round of play and the losers eliminated. Sixteen contestants (or teams in doubles) qualify for the final competition, on a basis of highest ringer percentage in the qualifying competition. The top-flight qualifiers will be seeded in the pairings of the final competition in order to prevent their early meeting.

Winners in each competition will be crowned national amateur champion, receive the AAU gold medal and also special silver trophies. Runners-up and third-place winners will be awarded the AAU silver and bronze medals respectively. A special silver trophy will go to the contestant (man or woman) coming from the most distant point.

George D. Chumard, Secretary of the Ohio Association, AAU 644 Main Street, Cincinnati, is chairman of the entry committee and prospective contestants are requested to write him concerning information about the tournament.

That's a concise description of how it was all going to be handled, but there were some issues left open—most curious of all, no junior division was mentioned in the announcement. A women's division was specifically announced, which was significant since no national (or world) women's competition had been held since 1935. But no junior division competition had been held since 1924, when Minnesota's Frank Stinson beat Iowa's Emmett Mossman in a playoff.

We can only wonder about the players' reception to single-game elimination in the finals. The article offers no indication if the scoring was count-all or cancellation, or if the games would be played to 50 points.

The tournament was played as scheduled, as evidenced by this announcement article in the *Cincinnati Enquirer* on the day of the tournament, Sunday, July 25th, 1937:

Horseshoe Pitchers Will Battle Today
In National Senior AAU Championships

The National Senior American Athletic Amateur Union Horseshoe Pitching Championship, awarded to the Ohio Association, AAU, by the Horseshoe Pitching Committee of the National body at the Houston Convention last December, will get under way at the Parkway Arena today, starting at 9 a.m., bringing together many of the top-ranking amateur tossers of the country. Among the entries are three state champions and a number of metropolitan champions.

Competition will be held in both the singles and doubles with winners being crowned Nation Amateur Champion and will be recognized as such by the AAU as well as by the National Horseshoe Pitchers' Association. The winners will receive the National AAU gold medal and silver trophies and a leg on the John A. Gordon two-year trophy will also go to the singles victor. Runners-up and third place contestants will be awarded silver and bronze AAU medals.

Among outstanding contestants are John Lindmeier, Chicago metropolitan champion and 14-year-old Kenneth Hurst of Providence, Rhode Island state champion, with a ringer average of 54 percent. Ray Griffin of Atlanta, Ga., is another state champion entered, with a 60 percent ringer average. The Horseshoe Club of Greater Cincinnati will be well represented in the list of entries, headed by Alan Boles, 1936 champion of the city; Norman Henderson, Joe Clore, Ed Hull, Fred Wall and others.

The tournament will follow closely the professional rules, with one important exception, the final competition will be a one defeat and out affair, rather than a round robin. Contestants qualify for the final competition by pitching 100 shoes and count-all scoring.

R.B. Howard, London, Ohio, newspaper publisher and Chairman of the National Committee, also a member of the Executive Committee of the National Editorial Association and Secretary-Treasurer of National Horseshoe Pitchers' Association, will be in the city to toss the first shoe, officially starting the tournament.

Officials of the meet are: Tournament Referee, L. M. Moyer; Assistant, Roy Cahill; Announcer, Norman Henderson; Scorers, Gertrude Clore, E. A. Whitaker, N. Mathis, George Wiethoff, Harry Sokup, Ed Kinkel and R. Mertz.

Entries, Singles: Orville Harris, Arlo Harris, Indianapolis; Alan Boles, Norman Henderson, Louis Grant, C. Fred Weil Jr.; Joseph M. Clore, Ray Wright, Edward Hull, Harry J. Henn, Horseshoe Club of Greater Cincinnati; Charles Hill, Fred W. Kugler, Ralph Lackey, Hamilton, Ohio; Arnold Maki, Hibbing, Minnesota; Kenneth Hurst, Providence, Rhode Island; Ray Griffin, Atlanta, Georgia; Marion Morris, Pendleton, Ohio; Walter W. Lanes,

Hubert Trinkle, Anderson, Indiana; Guy Morgan, Middletown, Ohio; John Lindmeier, Oak Park, Illinois; Walter Lindmeier, Melrose Park, Illinois.

Entries, Doubles: J. R. Kirkpatrick – Clark Harlow, Deer Park, Ohio; Hubert Trinkle – Walter W. Lane; Charles Hill – Ralph Lackey; Alan Boles – Norman Henderson, Cincinnati, Ohio; C. Fred Weil Jr. – Joseph M. Clore; Arlo Harris – Orville Harris.

Members of the Horseshoe Club of Cincinnati, in charge are: Ed Hull, President and Norman Henderson, Secretary, will begin preparations this morning of laying our horseshoe courts at the Parkway Arena on Central Parkway, for the National event scheduled for tomorrow. Eight courts will be laid out, which would allow for completion of the preliminary qualifying competition, around mid-afternoon, with finals starting immediately after. Blue Clay from the Columbia Ave. viaduct excavation will be used in the pits.

The *Enquirer* reported on the singles finals in its Monday, July 26th edition:

ILLINOIS MAN HORSESHOE CHAMPION
Lindmeier Defeats Indianan 55-37, 51-18
Doubles Are On Tonight

John Lindmeier of Oak Park, Illinois, won the first annual national amateur horseshoe pitching championship, under AAU jurisdiction, at the Parkway Arena yesterday. He defeated Walter W. Lane of Anderson, Ind., in the finals 55-37 and 51-18. Rain marred the event, holding up play for several hours and the semi-finals and final tilts were played in rain.

Lindmeier's ringer average for the final two games was 67.5 percent. Third place in the tournament was won by Arlo Harris of Indianapolis.

Rain forced postponement of the double championships until 6 o'clock tonight, when eight teams will fight it out for the national doubles title at the Parkway Arena.

Alan Boles of Cincinnati was the highest scorer of the 16 final qualifiers, with a total of 236 out of a possible 300. Winning his first match in
the finals, he was eliminated by Charles Hill of Hamilton, Ohio.

Lindmeier received the John A. Gordon two year gold trophy and
the National AAU gold medal and also the Ohio horseshoe trophy.

Doubles pairing for tonight: A. Harris – O. Harris, Indianapolis vs. Kirkpatrick – Harlow, Cincinnati; Lackey – Hill, Hamilton vs. Trinkle – Lane,
Anderson, Ind.; Johnson – Johnson, Indianapolis vs. Clore – Weil, Cincinnati; Henn – Grant, Cincinnati vs. Boles – Henderson, Cincinnati."

The doubles finals were published the next day, July 27, 1937:

Hoosier Pair Best in Doubles Event
of Horseshoe Meet

Hubert Trinkle, Anderson, Indiana, state horseshoe pitching champion
and his partner, Walter W. Lane, also of Anderson, won the National AAU
doubles horseshoe pitching championship at the Parkway Arena last
night in a postponement from Sunday on account of rain. They defeated
Alan Boles and Norman Henderson. Boles was high qualifier in Sunday's singles. Third place went to Arlo Harris and his brother, Orville, of
Indianapolis.

Trinkle and Lane received the Ohio Horseshoe Company trophy and
the AAU gold medal. Boles and Henderson were awarded silver AAU
medals and the Harris brothers bronze medals.

The champions had a tough time beating the Harris boys in the
semi-finals, but found the Cincinnatians an easy match.

The August–September 1937 issue of *Horseshoe World* included only a short
summary of the event, but a very comprehensive review of the stats:

FIRST SENIOR AAU CHAMPIONSHIPS
ARE AWARDED

Qualifying Competition	Singles				Final Competition				
	Score	SP	R	DR	%	Games	SP	R	DR	%
Alan Boles, Cincinnati, Ohio	236	100	72	25	72	2	130	71	21	55
Arlo Harris, Indianapolis, Ind.	231	100	71	25	71	5	288	167	47	56
Hubert Trinkle, Anderson, Ind.	222	100	69	24	69	2	124	79	20	64
Ken Hurst, Providence, R.I.	219	100	67	25	67	1	68	39	12	57
Ray Griffin, Atlanta, Ga.	217	100	67	20	67	1	78	45	11	59
John Lindmeier, Oak Park, Ill.	214	100	59	17	59	7	408	265	95	65
Orville Harris, Indianapolis, Ind.	213	100	63	21	63	1	79	39	8	50
G. Johnson Sr., Indianapolis, Ind.	212	100	63	20	63	2	128	78	24	61
Arnold Maki, Hibbing, Minn.	206	100	58	16	58	1	64	30	7	31
Norman Henderson, Cincinnati	206	100	61	15	61	1	56	28	6	50
Charles Hill, Hamilton, Ohio	204	100	61	18	61	4	252	134	39	53
Ralph Lackey, W. Middletown, O.	203	100	61	17	61	2	112	58	15	58
Walter Lane Sr., Anderson, Ind.	201	100	59	15	59	6	412	236	70	57
Edward Hull, Cincinnati, Ohio	196	100	58	16	58	1	42	16	2	37
Ray Wright, Covington, Ky.	195	100	56	15	56	1	48	23	7	49
Myron M. Ferguson, Columbus, O.	190	100	57	16	57	1	74	38	9	52
Harry Henn, Cold Springs, Ky.	189	100	55	16	55					
Joseph M. Clore, Cincinnati, Ohio	189	100	52	12	52					
C. Fred Weil Jr., Cincinnati, Ohio	189	100	51	12	51					
Guy Morgan, Middletown, Ohio	182	100	50	15	50					
Marion, Morris, Pendleton, Ind.	181	100	51	13	51					
Louis Grant, St. Bernard, Ohio	179	100	52	16	52					
Walter Lindmeier, Chicago, Ill.	179	100	51	11	51					
Fred W.Kugler, Hamilton, Ohio	177	100	50	10	50					
Russell Spaulding, Cincinnati, Ohio	154	100	39	5	39					

Doubles

	Games	SP	R	DR	%
Walter W. Lane – Hubert Trinkle	5	324	205	63	63
Norman Henderson – Alan Boles	5	288	168	57	58
Orville Harris – Arlo Harris	3	212	121	30	52
Joe M. Clore – C. Fred Weil Jr.	2	118	59	28	30
Harry J. Henn – Louis Grant	1	50	24	7	48
J. R. Kirkpatrick – Clark Harlow	1	60	25	5	42
Ralph Lackey – Arthur Morgan	1	52	23	5	44

Highest number of consecutive doubles – Hubert Trinkle 6
Tournament Director – George D. Chumard

The event was referred to as a senior event. In contemporary sports terminology, the label *senior event* likely indicates an older group of players, maybe even 60 years old or older. But back in that day, *senior* merely indicated *not juniors*. Exact age guidelines for this period aren't available.

Some familiar names appeared at 1937 event in Cincinnati. Let's start with the winner—John Lindmeier. Just 19 years old for this early win, Lindmeier went on to become a four-time state champion in the competitive state of Illinois (1948, 1949, 1950, and 1955). Lindmeier's career also included qualifying for the World Tournament's men's championship class eight times, with top-ten finishes in five of those competitions, and a career ringers average of 73.63 percent. He first qualified at the World Tournament in 1946, nine years after this 1937 AAU event.

Arlo Harris, who was 26 years old at the time, finished third in singles and was part of the third-place team in doubles. He went on to a great career as a pitcher and a promoter. He was elected president of the NHPA in 1948 and may go down in history as one of the organization's most controversial presidents ever. He wasn't radical, he was just a few decades ahead of his time. Harris was a great promoter of league play and the count-all scoring system. His one-year term ended in turmoil and controversy, yet just 25 years later, Donnie Roberts wrote the guidelines of the NHPA Sanctioned League Program in the backseat of a car on the way to a weekend tournament. We all know the success of the league program today, which was the very thing Arlo Harris had supported. Harris was a good pitcher and a three-time Indiana state champion (1937, 1948, and 1949). He founded the American Horseshoe Pitchers Association (AHPA) in 1950, an organization based on league play that used the count-all scoring system exclusively. The AHPA still operates in Indiana and parts of Ohio. Harris also designed the Harris Professional Pitching Shoe, which was manufactured by Giant Grip of Oshkosh, Wisconsin. Today, shoe collectors prize his shoes.

The next name that should ring a bell for horseshoe pitchers is Ralph Lackey. At 32 years old he was a bit older than Lindmeier and Harris, but still a few years away from hitting his career highlights. Lackey was the Ohio state champion in 1948, 1950, 1951, and 1952. He never qualified at a World Tournament.

At age 42, Harry Henn was almost the most senior of the senior division in 1937. He was the state champion of Kentucky in 1934 and 1935. Of three attempts, 1949 was the only year Henn qualified for the World Tournament and he placed 32nd that year. For several years, his home club in Kentucky hosted an annual Harry Henn Memorial Horseshoe Pitching Tournament.

Arnold Maki was a Minnesota state champion, but he didn't know that while he was alive. No designated state tournaments were held in Minnesota between 1928 and 1935. In 1930, Maki won the White Bear Open, held in White Bear Lake, Minnesota, which was a large event that included all the top players of the time. In 1988, the executive board of the Minnesota Gopher State Horseshoe Pitchers Association (MGSHPA) sanctioned the 1930 event as a state tournament and awarded Arnold Maki a state championship. Maki passed away long before the tournament was sanctioned as a state championship event.

1938

Where Are the Youth?

From the July 1938 issue of *Horseshoe World*:

A Word About the AAU

The editor of the *Horseshoe World* has always been interested in amateur horseshoe pitching. This magazine has always contended that there is a place for the amateur, as contrasted with the professional, who has won cash awards in horseshoe events. Many college athletes would enter purely amateur horseshoe meets that could not attend meets sponsored by the National Horseshoe Pitchers' Association and its affiliate bodies.

That is why the editor of the *Horseshoe World* went to the American Amateur Athletic Union convention in Houston, Texas, in 1936, in an effort to get the AAU to become more interested in horseshoe pitching. As chairman of the AAU horseshoe committee for the following year, he worked hard, but for health reasons could not attend the AAU convention last year. Just how much interest the AAU showed in horseshoe pitching at the 1937 convention, the writer cannot say, as he was not present and was not reappointed by the AAU authorities, who have now turned to their own forces in other sports as leaders in the horseshoe game.

The fact still remains that amateur horseshoe pitching can still be made a big thing. The AAU will gain by it and when amateurs have become good pitchers they may want to join the NHPA, so the NHPA can look forward to amateur pitching acting as a "feeder" for professional pitching. Both groups can and should work in close harmony, although we fully realize that the AAU often looks with a great deal of misgivings toward a professional association. That may be the reason the AAU dropped the writer or it may have been because he was not present at the convention.

George Chumard is in charge of the horseshoe activity of the AAU He is a splendid chap and deserves the support of all horseshoe pitchers interested in amateur horseshoe pitching. Clubs should be warned, however, that some AAU groups are giving little regard to the membership lists of these clubs; signing up entire clubs under AAU rules when we have reason to believe that these clubs can be best served through the NHPA and its affiliates because members of these clubs want to play with professionals and undoubtedly have played in professional tournaments.

Why can't the AAU start from scratch and build up a membership of purely amateur horseshoe pitchers?

The NHPA, we are sure, extends a friendly hand to the AAU, but will be watching to see that the AAU players are not recorded on the National Association as having played in tournaments in which cash prizes were involved. The NHPA has shown a very unselfish attitude in this matter by even offering to share any of the field. Its leaders are really interested in amateurs and in seeing the AAU operate as a PURELY amateur horseshoe governing body—not that we care anything about how many 25 cent pieces it brings into the AAU coffers, but for the sake of giving the horseshoe pitcher who wants to be an amateur a chance to be one.

By the same token, however, the player who is known to be a professional should not be a "white-washed" by the AAU under the guise of getting a "starting point" for listing pitchers. The AAU can easily determine whether a player is an amateur or professional by his past activity!

It will be interesting to watch the development of amateur horseshoe pitching in America, if the AAU decides to do the right thing—and we think they will!

The writer of this piece was Raymond Howard, editor and publisher of *Horseshoe World* and the NHPA's secretary-treasurer. He certainly took a long time to comment on the AAU, and it's not entirely clear just what he was trying to say. His editorial suggests he may have been a bit sore about being relieved of his chairmanship. He also challenges the AAU on their selection of amateur horseshoe pitchers. How could the NHPA or the AAU determine a player's amateur status beyond what the player states his status to be, at least at the time of an event? A post-event research might uncover conflicting information, but at the event it would have been next to impossible to confirm or disprove a player's status. Perhaps Howard was telling the AAU that their participants should not include NHPA members, but that suggestion, either back in 1938 or today, doesn't mean much. It's difficult to view the vast majority of NHPA members as professionals, especially as compared to that classification in other sports. Howard's editorial implies there are some bruised egos, so is the new relationship between NHPA and the AAU getting off to a rough start? Not really, since National AAU tournaments continued into the 1970s. This article, if nothing else, piques our curiosity and reminds us to look for any "professionals" in the early AAU events.

The July 1938 *Horseshoe World* also announced that year's national event:

NATIONAL SENIOR AAU AMATEUR HORSESHOE PITCHING CHAMPIONSHIP

Under auspices of the Staten Island Pioneer Horseshoe Club and the Staten Island Horseshoe League and sanctioned by the Metropolitan Association AAU at Willowbrook Park, Victory Boulevard, Staten Island, New York, September 3rd, 4th and 5th, 1938, the National Senior AAU Amateur Horseshoe Pitching Championship will be held, consisting of women's singles, women's doubles, men's singles and men's doubles.

The contest is open to any registered or certified amateur horseshoe pitcher in the world and prizes will be awarded as follows:

National Senior AAU gold, sterling silver and bronze medals will be awarded to first, second and third, respectively, in each class of men's singles, women's singles, in all doubles. A trophy will also be awarded the contestant coming from the most distant point. The John A. Gordon trophy (two years) will also be in competition this year. Such additional trophies as are donated by local dignitaries and others will be awarded as determined by committee.

Registration
All contestants must have travel permits from their district association AAU.

Photographs
Send in your photo, suitable for newspaper work (snapshots will not do); also an outline of your past performances, for publicity purposes.

Rules
Rules as adopted by AAU Horseshoe Pitching Committee to govern.

Method of Competition
In the singles, each entrant shall be allowed to pitch two sets of 100 shoes each, contestants to have option of choosing either qualifying set as basis for entrance to final competition. The contestants will, insofar as necessary, be divided into various classes in accordance with the points obtained on qualification. The method of qualification for the doubles shall be at the discretion of the committee. The contests after qualification will be conducted on the round robin plan. Details and extent of said contests to be determined by committee.

Entry Fee
Entry fee, for singles $1.00; for doubles $2.00. Entries close with Leo Miller, 2272 Richmond Terrance, Port Richmond, Staten Island, New York, midnight, Saturday, August 20, 1938.

Miscellaneous
Qualifying competition will get under way promptly at 9 a.m. on September 3, 1938. Contestants unable to report at this time should notify chairman of the entry committee. If necessary, tournament will be completed under lights at night.

The right to reject any entry is reserved.

Entry closing date will be strictly observed. Entry fee must accompany entry blank. For additional entry blanks and any information concerning championships, communicate with Leo Miller.

Following is a copy of the official entry blank:

Dear Sir: Please enter me in the National Senior AAU Horseshoe Pitching Championships and I am enclosing $............ to cover entry fee. In consideration of your acceptance of same, I hereby, for myself, my heirs and assigns, waive any and all claims for damages which I might have against the Metropolitan Association Amateur Athletic Union, the city of New York or the Park Department, thereof, the committee in charge or any individual thereof, for any and all injuries suffered by me at such championships. I also certify I am a bona fide amateur athlete and eligible to compete.

Name (print) . . . .

Signature . . . .

Club . . . .

Address . . . .

City . . . .

AAU Registration No . . . .

Ringer Percentage. . . . .

The *Anderson Herald* of Anderson, Indiana, covered the story of their hometown heroes winning the 1938 National Championships.

Hubert Trinkle Wins National Title
Local Youth Whips Field of 15 Players

Trinkle-Lane Capture Doubles

Tossing ringers with the same unerring skill that has made him Indiana's greatest amateur flinger, Hubert Trinkle, 20-year-old hurler, ascended the throne of the nation's greatest in his class yesterday by winning the national Amateur Athletic Union senior singles crown at Staten Island, New York.

The slender willow-built boy who two weeks ago told home fans at Anderson Athletic Park that he and his partner Walter Lane Sr. were going to Gotham to do their best, defeated 15 contenders for the singles championship with 451 points total. He also helped defend the AAU doubles crown with his partner Walter Lane Sr., which they won the first time in 1937 at Cincinnati.

Second place in the singles event was won by Michael Dell of Peekskill, N.Y. and John Lindmeier of Oak Park, Illinois, 1937 singles champion, was third.

4 of 6 Places

Trinkle's feat gave the Madison County flingers four of the six places in the AAU event staged on the St. George Horseshoe Courts of Staten Island. Besides the champion's good work, Walter Lane Jr. and Marion Morris, Anderson's second doubles team, tied for second in the doubles along with Chet Morris, brother of Marion and fifth alternate flinger of the local group who paired with S. Rumley of Lexington, NC. The local flingers scored the distinction of a grand slam in the doubles.

1938 AAU Men's National Singles Championship Finals

Place	Name	City	W	L	%
1,	Hubert Trinkle	Anderson, IN	8	1	72.1
2.	Michael Dell	Peekskill, NY	6	3	50.9
3.	John Lindmeier	Oak Park, IL	5	2	60.5
4.	Walter Lane Sr.	Anderson, IN	3	4	50.6
5.	Marion Morris	Pendleton, IN	3	4	50.5
6.	Frank Lockwood	Montrose, NY	3	4	47.5
7.	Chet Morris	Anderson, IN	2	5	48.4
8.	James Sarullo	Montrose, NY	0	7	42.8

1938 AAU Men's National Doubles Championship Finals

Place	Name	City
1.	Hubert Trinkle	Anderson, IN
	& Walter Lane Sr.	Anderson, IN
2.	Marion Morris	Pendleton, IN
	& Walter Lane Jr.	Anderson, IN
3.	Chet Morris	Anderson, IN
	& S. Rumley	Lexington, NC

Makes Boast Good

It was a memorable night recently when Trinkle was introduced to Anderson's elite of sport fans from the boxing arena at Athletic Park. He was clad only in an old pair of overalls, hands dirty and hair disheveled after returning from an exhibition at Frankton.

His spirit sank and shoulders fell when the voice over the public address system called him from high in the bleachers on the south side. The contents of his impromptu talk were:

"Last year Walt Lane and I went to Cincinnati without the support of local people and won the National AAU senior doubles championship. This year we are going to New York with the support of the populace and hope to do even better."

Tourney Opens Friday

Success of the local crack shots in New York encourages the hopes of Anderson over their flingers in the coming AAU junior horseshoe tournament billed Friday, Saturday and Sunday, Sept. 9, 10 and 11 at the local fairgrounds. Several of the local pitchers that helped make horseshoe pitching history in Gotham will appear either in the singles or doubles competition or exhibition matches.

The stay-at-homes finished work on the Athletic Park Courts last night for the coming Junior classic which promises to draw hundreds of fans and onlookers in Athletic Park. New clay and six foot stakes were placed in the courts and 20-inch backboards behind the courts. Bleachers accommodating nearly 2,000 fans will be erected early Friday morning for the event.

Townsend Plays Baldwin

Interest is heightened in the tourney due to the forthcoming match billed between Governor M. Clifford Townsend of Indianapolis and Mayor Harry R. Baldwin of Anderson, on Friday afternoon or night. The match will be arranged to suit the convenience of both flingers.

This ad was placed in the local newspaper to show the town's interest in this junior tournament.

Tickets for the tourney are on sale at the three local sporting goods stores; Retz's, Decker's and Dobson's, beside the Anderson News.

On Friday afternoon, any horseshoe pitcher who uses the old-time horseshoes such as graces Ol' Dobbin is eligible to participate in an Old

Timers tournament starting at 1 o'clock. A prize will be given the winner and runner-up. Any flinger known to having pitched or is pitching the pen shoe will be barred from competition.

Qualification play will get under way Friday night and Saturday morning in both singles and doubles. The tourney will continue through Saturday afternoon and night and all day Sunday.

Plenty of talent is assured in the tourney as top-flight flingers from Cincinnati, Indianapolis, Muncie, Fort Wayne, New Albany, Bicknell, Frankton and Anderson are entered.

The Arlington Horseshoe Club has been invited to play the local flingers tonight under the lights at the municipal courts, starting at 7 o'clock.

Before we move on to a discussion of the 1938 junior event, there is still more coverage on the men's competition in New York. The *Staten Island Advance* printed some useful articles, including a big announcement on September 3rd:

HORSESHOE PITCHERS BID FOR AAU NATIONAL CROWNS

Final preparations have been made for the staging of the National Amateur Athletic Union's horseshoe pitching championships at Willowbrook Park over the Labor Day weekend.

Qualifications for the tournament, which will run over three days, got under way this morning, with the doubles tourney scheduled to start at 2 p.m. this afternoon. The singles matches carded for tomorrow, with 1 p.m. as the starting time, while the finals will be held Monday, starting at 1:30 p.m.

Aside from a large representation from Staten Island, including members of the Staten Island Horseshoe League, more than a dozen pitchers from scattered sections of the United States will also compete.

Champ Is on Hand

Heading the list is John Lindmeier of Oak Park, Illinois, who will defend the singles championship he won last year. Lindmeier is representing the Center Horseshoe Club of Chicago and is given a good chance of retaining his national title.

Walter Lane and Hubert Trinkle of Anderson, Indiana, are also entered. They won the doubles championship last year, and they are representing the Madison County Horseshoe Club of Indiana.

An eye-opening collection of awards has been gathered together by the committee in charge with the AAU National Championship medals holding down first place in the array of prizes, which will go to the most successful tossers.

With competition expected to be keen and with the attractive prizes up for claim, interest in the tournament is running high. Even those who have had no previous connection with the sport are getting enthusiastic about the tournament.

Stand Erected

Anticipating a large gallery at all the matches, the committee's request that grandstands be erected at the courts has been acted on by the Park Department. There is also a public address system at the pits, which will enable less informed spectators to keep abreast of developments.

The Park Department has installed 49 courts at the Willowbrook Arena and those who have inspected them report that they are in Class A condition.

Borough President Joseph A. Palma has been invited to toss out the first shoe this afternoon when the doubles competition gets under way at 2 p.m. and we understand that Palma has accepted the invitation.

Along with the National AAU champions, there are other titleholders entered. Louis A. Rumley, of Lexington, N.C., is included in the group. He holds the North Carolina state championship. Then there is Michael Bell of Peekskill, New York, the city champion, James Holtz, champion of Elizabeth, N.J., and Frank Leonard, New York City Park Department champion, are also on the list.

Jackson Heads Locals

Heading the Staten Island delegation is William Jackson, recent winner of the county championship. Jackson is expected to be given considerable assistance in his efforts to gain the championship for Staten Island by such tossers as Francis Hollywood, Tex Dawson, Joseph Santilli and Angelo Dusio.

Others who will seek the title are Harold Lockwood, Frank Lockwood and Vincent Doherty, all of the Montrose Club of Montrose, N.Y., James Sarullo, of the High Bridge, N.Y. Club, Emil Olsen, Tex Dawson Jr. Paul Coneti, Adolph Huth, Bernard Livingston, William Garrett, Charles Avaliotis, Daniel Belajac and Harry Robinson.

Walter Lane Jr. and Marion Morris, Chester Morris and Louis Rumley, and Joseph Santilli and Leo Miller are expected to press the claims of Lane and Trinkle for the doubles championship.

Numerous Awards

Among the prizes at stake are the National AAU Championship gold, silver and bronze medals for Class A, as well as corresponding medals for all classes below A.

Trophies include the John A Gordon Trophy, won last year by Lindmeier; the Joseph A. Palma Trophy; the Mark Allen Trophy, which will go to the Staten Island competitor with the highest ringer percentage; and the Community Councils of Greater New York Trophy, which will go to the Greater New York competitor with the highest ringer percentage.

Then there are the trophies donated by Jack's Idle Hour, Boeddinghaus Furniture Store, Weiseglass Dairy, Ohio Horseshoe Company and a set of horseshoes donated by the Giant Grip Manufacturing Company.

Anne K. Miller is acting director of the tournament, assisted by John J. Brady, Michael Carfero, Joseph Ryan, Leo Miller, Catherine Keller and Frances Ryan.

Lester L. Callan, Al Trigg and Walter Mullens are the referees.

The tournament's finals were covered in the *Staten Island Advance*'s September 6th edition:

TRINKLE WINS NATIONAL
AAU HORSESHOE TITLE

Big Crowds See Three-Day Event
at Willowbrook

Hubert Trinkle of Anderson, Indiana, is the 1938 National AAU singles horseshoe pitching champion. Trinkle took the honors yesterday after three days of pitching at Willowbrook Park. Mike Bell of Peekskill, N.Y., took second honors, with third honors going to 1937 champion, John Lindmeier of Oak Park, Ill.

Paul Conti of Greenridge, Staten Island, took first honors in Class B, with second place going to Frank Lockwood of Montrose, N.Y., and third place to Frank Parker of Port Richmond. At the end of the final round, Conti and Lockwood were tied for first place, with Edward Foggin, also of Port Richmond, tied with Parker for third place. In the pitch-offs, Conti won first place and Parker third place.

William Garrett of Thompkinsville, won Class C honors, with second place going to Fred Alff of Stapleton, and third to Frank Yasosky of Greenridge.

Fred Hansen of Bulls Head, took first honors in Class D, with Carl Johnson of Eltingville taking second place and third going to Leo Yasosky of Greenridge.

The tournament, run under the sponsorship of the Staten Island Horseshoe League and the Pioneer Club in conjunction with the Park Department Recreation Division exceeded the expectations of General Chairman Mark Allen and Richmond County AAU Commissioner Patrick J. Kelly.

Perfect Playing Conditions

The Park Department, under the supervision of James Mallen and Willard Williams, had arranged a wonderful set-up for the tournament. It presented a scene that was a picture that surprised the hundreds who attended the tournament on each of the three days.

The prizes were presented after the tournament last night at the Eltingville Shore Neighbor's Association, who through Roland Durkee, played host to the pitchers and those who conducted the tournament.

Mrs. Anne K. Miller directed the tournament, assisted by John J. Brady, Michael Carfero, Joseph Ryan, Leo Miller, Catherine Keller, Francis Ryan and Metropolitan Association AAU officials. Lester L. Callan, Al Trigg, Walter Mullens and A. O. Plummer were the referees.

Commissioner of Borough Works, George Allison opened the tournament on Saturday, in the absence of Borough President Palms. A total of 52 men qualified on Saturday, 20 more than competed in the same tournament last year at Cincinnati.

Wins Doubles Title

The team of Walter Lane Sr. and Hubert Trinkle successfully defended the doubles championship they won last year at Cincinnati. But there was a five-way tie for second place, necessitating a play-off yesterday morning. Walter Lane Jr. and Marion Morris took second place in the doubles, with third place going to Mike Bell and Harold Lockwood.

Great praise was heard throughout the three days for the Park Department and those who arranged the tournament, not only by the great crowd of spectators, but also by the contestants themselves. It was a genuine success.

The summaries:

Doubles Championship – 1938

		W	L	P	R	DR	Sp	%
1.	Walter Lane Sr. & Hubert Trinkle	9	0	470	281	80	474	60.0
2	Walter Lane Jr. & Marion Morris	6	3	400	231	51	518	45.7
2.	Michael Bell & H. Lockwood	6	3	441	264	56	634	41.0
2.	Chester Morris & Louis Rumley	6	3	417	238	56	538	45.0
2.	John Lindmeier & G. Lloyd	6	3	426	231	39	564	43.4
2.	Vince Doherty & E. Lockwood	6	3	413	219	38	530	41.3
6.	W. Jackson & D. MacQueen	2	7	348	206	36	616	33.5
7.	Joe Santilli & John Santilli	2	7	193	111	14	454	28.5
8.	J. Favata & E. Fox	1	8	218	122	14	496	23.4

Doubles Playoff

	W	L	P	R	DR	Sp	%
Walter Lane Jr. & Marion Morris	4	1	280	119	22	254	48.2
M. Bell & H. Lockwood	3	1	195	114	32	226	52.0
Chester Morris & Louis Rumley	1	3	159	107	20	234	48.3
John Lindmeier & G. Lloyd	1	3	126	87	21	218	41.2
Vince Doherty & E. Lockwood	1	3	132	72	15	220	36.9

Amateur Athlete, the AAU magazine, did not print an article on the 1938 seniors event, but the November 1938 issue lists the year's national champions for all sports, including horseshoe pitching. Of course, Hubert Trinkle was named men's singles champ and Trinkle and Walter Lane was listed as the doubles champs, but Florence Lockwood of Montrose, New York, was shown as the women's national champion. This is a major surprise, because despite the apparently thorough newspaper coverage, there's no mention of a women's competition in any of the newspaper articles.

How could that happen? We must remember in 1938 America was not so in tune with women participating in sports, or activities that were perceived as men's sports. It is possible that women's competitions were held and not reported in previous decades. In any case, it is rather surprising to see a women, Anne K. Hamilton, was the 1938 tournament director.

It's also possible that the women's competition was set up sometime during the progress of the tournament—when it was determined there were a sufficient number of lady pitchers on hand to hold a competition. In that case information couldn't have been provided in advance to the news media. And onsite reporters may have just missed it. Those circumstances might have been avoided, though, since the event used preregistration. But another look at the preregistration form indicates there was no line to declare division, or to separate the men from the women.

Although Florence Lockwood's hometown did not have a newspaper, the *Evening Star* of the neighboring town of Peekskill gave a rundown of the AAU Tournament in their September 7th edition, which included the following paragraph about Lockwood's women's national championship victory:

> In the Women's Class "A" finals, Miss Florence Lockwood, 18-year-old girl of Montrose, was declared Women's AAU National Champion, having won all her games and losing none. For her efforts she received a beautiful engraved gold medal. This fact is remarkable in as much as Miss Lockwood has only been pitching for the past three months under the guidance of her father and brothers, who are past masters in the art.

Here is *Horseshoe World*'s announcement of the 1938 junior tournament:

JUNIOR AAU MEET

Anderson, Ind. has been awarded the 1938 National Amateur Athletic Union Junior Horseshoe Championships for men and women and the event will be run off at Athletic Park Courts here, September 9, 10, and 11. A gala horseshoe celebration is being planned in connection with the three-day sport carnival and indications point to a successful event.

Three highlights of the tournament are planned to augment the regular completion in both singles and doubles events. Efforts are being made to have Governor M. Clifford Townsend, of Indiana, play Mayor Harry R. Baldwin, of Anderson, in the opening game of the tourney. This will take place on Friday, September 9, and will officially open the event. On Saturday, September 10, a horseshoe tournament for old-timers will be run off. No pitcher who has ever hurled the open shoe is eligible to compete in this attraction. On Sunday, September 11, Ted Allen, present national singles champion, will probably give a demonstration.

Each pitcher contemplating entering the national tourney at Anderson, must be registered with the AAU in their district and must have traveled permits issued by the AAU. The National Junior AAU gold, silver and bronze medal will be awarded to first, second and third place winners.

Each contestant will be permitted to pitch two sets of 100 shoes each, with the highest 16, based on ringer percentage plus one point for reach shoe six inches or less from the peg, qualifying for final competition. Contestants will have the option of choosing either qualifying set as a basis for entrance in final competition. The first 16 (or 8) final qualifiers will compete in a round robin to determine the tournament champion.

The entry fee for singles is $1, for doubles $2. Entries close with G. D. Chumard, Chairman, National AAU Horseshoe Pitching Committee, c/o O. W. Haven, 923 Jackson St., Anderson, Ind., midnight, September 3, 1938.

Qualifying competition will get under way promptly at 10 a.m., September 9. Contestants unable to report at this time should notify the chairman of the Entry Committee. The right to reject any entry is reserved. Entry closing date will be strictly observed. For additional entry blanks and any information concerning championships communicate with Mr. O. W. Haven, 923 Jackson St., Anderson, Ind. Contestants will be allowed to use their own shoes, provided they come within regulation dimensions. A junior in National AAU competition is defined as one who has not won a previous national junior or senior championship. There is no age restriction.

Lights have been installed for night pitching if necessary on the battery of 12 courts. Bleachers accommodating 1,500 fans will be erected in the park.

AAU took over jurisdiction of amateur horseshoe pitching two years ago and the sport may be included in the next program of the 1940 Olympic games. AAU has signed up hundreds of fair amateur pitchers this summer and unless one is an Allen or Nunamaker he can never hope to earn much, if any, pitching horseshoes. The attitude* AAU is taking relative to signing up new players, is this: If he has competed for money or merchandise prizes in the past, AAU is willing to overlook this phase of his past performances if he signs on the dotted line with AAU and walks the straight and narrow thereafter.

(*Editor's note—It was this "attitude" we have heard about that we hope the AAU doesn't take and about which this magazine complained editorially in the last issue. This article was sent to us by O. W. Haven, a fine booster for the sport, but if he is correct about the AAU, we are sure the AAU is wrong. We wish the AAU officials would clear this point.)

Anderson has a club of 35 active players and it is estimated that nearly 500 in this city play horseshoes. It is a common sight to see local crowds of 50 to 100 people assembled around one of the dozen lighted courts any evening watching Joe Smith play John Public in a 50 point game.

Now it seemed certain that a youth event was going to take place. But what was a *junior* player? The NHPA has always had an age guideline for junior players (in earlier years, 15 years old and younger). No similar policy was set by the AAU. One of the prerequisites was that the player had not won a previous national contest, so there will never be a two-time junior National AAU champion.

The sources reveal that the senior (men's) events would be single elimination, but the juniors would engage in a round-robin final. That is actually a very good decision. No reference is made about the pitching distance for junior players. The NHPA rules, as set in 1921, allow juniors (pitchers under the age of 16) to pitch from 30' rather than the 40' men (seniors) must pitch from. What would happen if a few youngsters were practicing from the 30' mark, but some participants insisted on a 40' competition?

The September 8th edition of the *Anderson Herald* printed this pretournament announcement:

TOWNSEND TO OPEN NATIONAL SHOE TOURNEY

Governor Matched With Mayor Baldwin
On Friday Morning

Trinkle and Lane, World's Doubles Champs
To Perform in Exhibition

Formal acceptance of Governor M. Clifford Townsend to play Mayor Harry R. Baldwin in opening the first National AAU junior horseshoe pitching championships on Friday morning at Athletic Park was received yesterday by Walter Jones of this city. The match will be called at 9:30 a.m. and a large delegation of officials from Indianapolis is expected to accompany Governor Townsend here for the Baldwin set-to.

The chief executive of Indiana, himself a horseshoe pitching devotee for several years, and the Anderson mayor are expected to engage in an interesting match. It is unofficially reported that the local executive is indulging in practice before the match. Mr. Jones is a member of the advisory committee of WPA recreation program of Anderson.

Appearance of these two celebrities to the fairgrounds is expected to attract a large throng of fans to the opening of the tournament. Tickets are reported in demand at the Retz, Deckers and Dobson Sporting Goods stores. Drawing out these two ranking civic officials should be the highlights of the 1938 horseshoe season, which has been its finest in history.

World's Amateur Champs Billed

In addition to the booking of the Townsend-Baldwin go, the world's amateur horseshoe doubles champions—Hubert Trinkle and Walter Lane Sr. of Anderson—will engage in an exhibition of 50-point games. They will meet all comers and demonstrate a few tricks in plain and fancy pitching.

Old-timers of the game will have their inning on Friday afternoon when they engage in a round robin tourney. No pitcher who has ever pitched or is pitching the open shoe will be permitted to participate. Action in this section of the tournament will start at 1 o'clock. A dozen pair of old horseshoes will be procured for the participants although each is invited to bring his shoes if he so desires.

Tourney qualification proper will get underway Friday night and continue Saturday morning at 9 o'clock. Championship play in the doubles and play in the singles title round is billed for Sunday all day.

A public address system will be used during the opening ceremonies of the three-day tourney, which will continue through Saturday and Sunday. The loudspeaker system will be donated by Claude L. Dobson Sporting Goods Store.

Reception Committee Named

Plans are going forward for a reception committee to meet Governor Townsend.

At the Hotel Stillwater at 9 o'clock on Friday morning. The reception group will include Mr. Jones, Jake Kuch and several intimate friends of the governor and officials of the horseshoe association including Walter Lane Sr., vice president; Marion Morris, secretary-treasurer; and O. W. Haven, president. Later the delegation will trek to Athletic Park.

One can't help notice the announcement's comments about the "old-timers" event. How would you like to be a judge or official for this event and be required to remove any player pitching an open shoe? If any player in the contest threw a ringer, he could be accused of pitching a so-called open shoe. Back in the day, a method of holding the shoe included placing your forefinger around the point down on the blade and then letting it rip. Those pitches may have turned out to be 5¾ turns. Flip shoes no doubt were allowed in the contest—it was the 1¼ or 1¾ turn shoes (then often called side shoes) that were banned. As it was, all the contestants were pitching shoes on the horse, so why put any limitation on a player's method or skill?

The September 10th, 1938, edition of the *Anderson Herald* hailed the opening of the national junior competition:

NATIONAL SHOE TOURNEY
OPENS TODAY AT PARK

Nine players, seven of which are from Anderson, opened qualifying play in the first annual National AAU Junior Horseshoe Tournament at Athletic Park Courts last night following the official tourney opening yesterday morning with the exhibition match between Governor M. Clifford Townsend and Mayor Harry R. Baldwin.

William Neilson of Jericho, stamped himself as one of the favorites for the single crown last night when he registered 258 points out of a possible 300 to qualify for the event.

Following the close of entries for the 1938 event this morning at 9 o'clock and the completion of qualifying play, participants will begin doubles competition at 1 p.m. in round robin play. Finals for the doubles playoff will probably be decided tonight and the singles title will be decided Sunday.

"Old-Timers" Event

Frank Lawrence defeated William Scouden in two straight games to take first place in the Old Timer's tournament, which was held yesterday afternoon. Both men are from Anderson. Other participants in the event, open to those not throwing the "open" shoe included: Jude Robert Smith, Lee Fidler, Gilbert Morris, Herman Grant, Herman Grant, Pete Hancock, Wilfred Dudley, Frank Young and Emory Childers.

In the Townsend-Baldwin clash yesterday morning, the Anderson mayor maintained the city's supremacy at the iron flinging game by besting the governor 30 to 22 after the state head had taken an early lead.

Playing under the good old rules whereby the closest shoes to the stake were given a count, Townsend ran up a 21 to 17 lead before the mayor got his shoes to working. After that it was a matter of how much the final count would be as Baldwin found the peg for several ringers.

Opening Scores

Qualifying scores, ringers and double ringers for the junior tournament include:

	Pts	R	DR
William Neilson, Jericho	258	83	33
M. Morris, Pendleton	214	65	21
Walter Lane Jr.	195	57	15
Louis Compton	188	52	14
E. Houldson, Jericho	188	45	11
Carl Hurley	152	42	9
Dwight Carter	151	41	6
O. W. Haven	151	39	4

The first national junior champion since 1924 is announced in the September 13th, 1938, *Anderson Herald*:

NEILSON CAPTURES SINGLES EVENT
OF SHOE TOURNAMENT

Twenty-five-year-old William Neilson of Dugger became the first National AAU junior horseshoe pitching champ Sunday afternoon when he defeated a field of twelve in the round robin finals at Athletic Park. Neilson, who hitchhiked 140 miles to participate in the tournament here, maintained the fast pace he set up in qualifying play on Saturday when over 80 percent of his shoe encircled the stake.

Pendleton shoes in the singles finals when Chet and Marion Morris, two of the county's classiest flingers, came in second and third.

The singles event Sunday followed the doubles competition, which was held on Saturday. Neilson paired with Everett Houldson of Sullivan to take his first title.

Orville W. Haven, president of the Madison County Horseshoe Pitchers Association, which sponsored the tournament, presented the winners with the AAU trophies. Neilson was awarded a statuette and gold medal; Chet Morris, a silver medal and his brother Marion, a bronze medal.

Marion Morris was adjudged third place winner in the singles when he bested Walter Lane Jr. and Paul Van Sickle in a playoff.

1938 AAU Junior Finals

Place	Name	City
1.	William Neilson	Dugger, IN
2.	Chet Morris	Anderson, IN
3.	Marion Morris	Pendleton, IN
4.	Walter Lane Jr.	Anderson, IN
5.	Paul Van Sickle	Anderson, IN

1938 AAU Junior Doubles Finals

1.	William Neilson	Dugger, IN
	and Everett Houldson,	Sullivan, IN

The hometown papers of the champions were searched for articles about the 1938 junior event, under the premise that the hometown hero would have garnered some coverage. But the local Jericho, Dugger, and Sullivan newspapers of 1938 revealed no articles about their junior champions. And information is definitely missing about the 1938 juniors doubles competition.

William Neilson went on to enjoy a highly successful career. He was the Indiana state champion in 1940 at the age of only 27, with a 9-0 record and an average of 76.4 percent ringers.

So in 1938, the first national junior champion in 14 years was crowned and the first-ever National AAU junior champion was five years older than the AAU senior men's national horseshoe pitching champion. No World Tournaments were held by the NHPA from 1936 through 1939, so this certainly is not meant as a criticism of the organization, but wouldn't age guidelines have made some sense? Surely they'd make tracking AAU horseshoe pitching events more interesting, as some of the participants were clearly old enough to enter the senior division.

1939

Indiana: Hot Spot for Amateurs

The year began with the announcement of the national junior event in the July 1939 issue of *Horseshoe World*:

HORSESHOE PITCHING CARNIVAL

A horseshoe pitching carnival featuring the 1939 National Junior AAU Horseshoe Pitching Championships, under the auspices of and sanctioned by the Ohio Association, Amateur Athletic Union, will be held at New Chester Swimming Pool Grounds, Spring Grove Ave. Route 4-W, Cincinnati, on Saturday and Sunday, August 19 and 20, 1939 at 2:00 p.m.

1. National Junior AAU Horseshoe Pitching Championship: singles and doubles.

2. Ohio Association AAU Horseshoe Pitching Championship: singles and doubles.

3. Greater Cincinnati Horseshoe Pitching Tournament: singles and doubles.

ELIGIBILITY—National Junior AAU (No. 1) open to any amateur horseshoe pitcher of the U.S. who has not won a previous national junior or senior title. Ohio AAU (No. 2) open to any bona fide resident of Ohio AAU territory (see official AAU handbook). Greater Cincinnati restricted to residents of Greater Cincinnati only. All contestants must be registered with their district association of the AAU. (Competitors in previous competitions where cash has been awarded as prizes, are not eligible for AAU amateur registration.)

RULES as laid down by the National AAU Horseshoe Pitching Committee to govern. Method of competition: Each contestant (or team in doubles) will be permitted to pitch 100 shoes, with the eight highest in each tournament qualifying for the final competition. All final competitions will be on a round robin basis.

ENTRY FEES—No. 1, singles $1.00; doubles $2.00; No. 2, singles 50c, doubles $1.00; No. 3, singles 25c, doubles 50c.

ENTRIES CLOSE with G. D. Chumard, 644 Main St., Cincinnati, at midnight, August 13th.

PRIZES—Gold, silver and bronze medals to first three in all tournaments. (In No. 1 the National Junior AAU medal will be awarded and in No. 2 the Ohio AAU medal. Trophy to winner of singles in No. 1 and No. 2. Trophy to contestant coming from the most distance point for the National Junior Tournament.)

MISCELLANEOUS—Qualifying competition will get under way promptly at 2:00 p.m. Saturday, the 19th and if necessary, resume at 9:00 a.m. Sunday. Entry closing date will be strictly observed. Entry fee must accompany entry blank. For additional entry blanks and other information communicate with G. D. Chumard, Cincinnati. Contestants will be permitted to use own shoes, provided they come within rules.

National Senior AAU Horseshoe Pitching Championships, Anderson, Ind. August 25, 26, and 27, 1939.

On August 19th, the local paper, the *Cincinnati Enquirer*, also announced the junior event:

TITLE AT STAKE TODAY

In National Horseshoe Pitching
Meet at Chester Park

National junior horseshoe pitching championship of the AAU will be contested this afternoon, starting at 2 o'clock at Chester Park. The meet brings twelve of the best amateur pitchers of the country.

Among out-of-town contestants are Marion Morris of Converse, Ind.; Paul M. Coss, Cambridge, Ohio; Clyde R. Claus, Tulsa, Okla.; Walter Lane Jr. and Lester Bagley of Anderson, Ind., all boasting ringer averages of 50 percent or better.

The winner will receive the National AAU gold medal, emblematic of the national junior championship pitching and also a trophy. The term junior has no age significance, simply the winner of this year's tournament will not be eligible for next year's tournament as a junior, but must, hereafter, compete as a senior.

The Ohio AAU and greater Cincinnati horseshoe pitching tournaments have been canceled, due to insufficient entries.

Anderson, Indiana, the site of the previous year's junior tournament, sent a good number of young pitchers on to Cincinnati. An August 12th *Anderson Independent Daily* article tells that story:

Local Pitchers Enter Tourney

Walter Lane Jr. and Lester Bagley, Anderson indoors singles champion, will leave late next week for Cincinnati, where they will participate in the second National AAU Junior Horseshoe Pitching Championships. Young Lane is the oldest son of Walter Lane Sr., city champion of Anderson for many years and who with Hubert Trinkle is defending national doubles champion.

1939

Lane and Bagley sent in their entries to G. D. Chumard, chairman of the event, early last week. Both pitchers have shown exceptional promise of developing into star performers in the past year.

Walter Lane Sr. will take his other two younger sons, Warner and Robert, both twelve, to Cincinnati, where they will put on a special exhibition for the national junior AAU event.

The Anderson paper also carried the junior event results:

Younger Lane Named Titlist
In Horseshoes

Walter Lane Jr., seventeen-year-old son of Mr. and Mrs. Walter Lane, residing on Raible Avenue, won the 1939 National AAU Junior Horseshoe Pitching Championship Saturday afternoon in the second annual national tourney held at Chester Park in Cincinnati.

The Anderson boy, playing in only his second major competition, proved the class of a field of 49 contestants in singles play and his triumph marked the seventh national horseshoe crown taken by Hoosiers since the AAU took over control of amateur horseshoe pitching two years ago.

Lane, paired with Marion Morris, formerly of Pendleton, won second place in the senior AAU doubles last year in New York City.

Young Lane's   father jointly holds the National AAU seniors doubles championship with Hubert Trinkle, also of Anderson. Trinkle is the national senior singles champion.

Succeeds Neilson

Young Lane succeeds William Neilson, of Dugger, Ind., as the junior titlist. The Dugger youth won his title last year in the initial junior tourney, which was held at Athletic Park in this city.

The Anderson boy qualified at Cincinnati along with his father and Lester Bagley, also of this city. Lane Jr., amassed a total of 314 points, 194 ringers, including 50 doubles, in 380 shoes tossed. His ringer average was 51 percent.

Bagley won third place in the singles, while Walter Lane Sr., came in fourth, and Paul Claus, of Tulsa, Oklahoma won second.

The new champion received a gold AAU medal and the Lattore-Levagood trophy and Bagley won a bronze medal. Claus won a silver medal award and a set of stakes and horseshoe given the pitcher coming the longest distance to participate in the meet.

Will Enter Meet

Young Lane will be among the entrants in the 1939 national senior AAU meet to be held Friday, Saturday and Sunday at the new horseshoe courts at Athletic Park.

Members of the Madison County Horseshoe Club, host to the national event, will practice each afternoon and night this week in preparation for the tourney. The Anderson Optimist Club will meet Heiney Produce Company in a special match Thursday night.

No explanation was offered about why no junior doubles competition was played. The Anderson paper had far better coverage than the Cincinnati papers, but neither reported doubles finals or any information whether the weather, low turnout, lack of time or some other factor caused that elimination from the tournament. It is possible, however, that there was doubles play late in the day and none of the papers picked it up.

Before moving on to the coverage of the senior meet, let's review an issue in the junior event. On a couple of occasions, announcements of AAU events have indicated that the winners of a national junior title will no longer be eligible to enter junior events. Since there were no age guidelines, that may be understandable, but it is less clear how the two-time senior doubles champion was allowed to enter the junior singles event. In fact, he was the father of one of the players, and father of the eventual champion. A shortage of entrants might explain how that could have taken place, but that's not the central issue. With that sort of practice, how can one expect any credibility in claiming that the entrants were limited to amateurs?

The Anderson *Daily Bulletin* announced the opening of the national senior tournament in its August 17, 1939, edition:

TOWNSEND APPEARS IN EXHIBITION

**Doubles Matches Scheduled Today
Lindmeier, Chicago Star Turns in
High Score in Qualifications**

With some of the outstanding horseshoe pitchers of the country converging on the city today to take part in the third annual National AAU Horseshoe Pitching Championships, qualifying rounds in both singles and doubles competition was held this morning and the first actual tourney matches were scheduled for this afternoon, when the doubles teams were to begin their matches. The play is being held at the new courts in Athletic Park.

Townsend Plays

As a feature of the opening of the tourney last night, Governor M. Clifford Townsend played an exhibition match with George D. Chumard, of Cincinnati, National AAU Horseshoe Pitching Committee Chairman. Prior to the game, Gov. Townsend made a short talk to the several hundred spectators who gathered for the contest. Chumard won the game, 50 to 32, scoring seven ringers to the Governor's five.

Prior to appearing in the exhibition game, Gov. Townsend was a guest at a reception at the Hotel Anderson. The committee, which was in charge of receiving the Governor, included: Rep. William J. Black, Sen. Walter Vermillion, Harry Muller, Albert McCoy, Mayor Harry R. Baldwin, Earl McCarel, Howard H. Brown, L. B. Duncan, Walter Jones and Orville W. Haven.

Champions Entered

Tonight and tomorrow have been reserved for playoff of singles competition. The host club has defending champions both in doubles and singles, Hubert Trinkle holding the solo crown and he and Walter Lane Sr., the doubles.

The Madison County Horseshoe Pitching Association is host to the tourney and Orville W. Haven, president, has been in charge of arrangements for the competition. Community Recreation Program officials have assisted with the tourney.

Qualifications Open

Following the exhibition match last night several qualifying trials were held with the following scores reported: John Lindmeier, Chicago 251; Dorne Woodhouse, Chicago 200; Warren Kellogg, Chicago 180; and Marion Morris, Converse 216 and 230.

Lindmeier's qualification provided the highlight of last night's pitching when he piled on 77 ringers and 31 doubles in 100 shoes pitched for his high score of the evening. Trinkle and Lane Sr., because they hold the present titles, are not required to qualify for the competition.

Anderson flingers who have entered in the contest include: Trinkle, Lane Sr., Walter Lane Jr., Lester Bagley, Louis Compton, Nick Carter, Bernard Vermillion and Cleatys, Arlo and Darrell Thomason.

Some of the pitchers most likely to lift the crown from the Anderson player's come from Chicago. Those entered from the city include: Lindmeier, Don Woodhouse, William Danhauer, Leonard Loerzel, Warren Kellogg, Frank Breen and Harry Durkee.

Trophies on Display

Headquarters for the officials and entrants have been established at the Anderson Hotel, through the courtesy of the manager, Harry Oldham. Trophies for the winners of the competition have been donated by the Anderson Free Fair Board and are on display at Deckers Book Store on west Eleventh Street. The Retz Sporting Goods Store has offered a pair of horseshoes to the pitcher coming the greatest distance.

Local public schools donated bleacher seats for use during the tourney and they were hauled to Athletic Park by a truck from Heiney Produce Company. Numbers for the courts were made by the Community Recreation Program and the Forkner-Manger Lumber Company furnished plywood.

Chicago Favored

Three members of the National AAU horseshoe committee met last night at the contest headquarters at the Anderson Hotel to discuss various business matters. An unofficial poll of the members showed that Chicago is favored for the 1940 national meet. The invitation to come to that city was extended by John Hogan, chairman of the Central AAU horseshoe pitching branch. Others attending the meeting last night included Mr. Chumard and Orville Haven.

The group discussed ways and means of increasing interest in amateur horseshoe pitching and indications were that a shakeup is imminent in the national committee.

The next meeting of the group will be held on Saturday, September 9, at Chicago and at that time Mr. Chumard will present a set of rules governing AAU horseshoe pitching tournaments. Members of the committee will make out rules and forward them to the chairman, who will condense them for a report at the meetings.

The August 28th *Anderson Daily Bulletin* gave a good review of the tournament's progress and the final standings:

NATIONAL HORSESHOE PITCHING TITLE WON BY TRINKLE

Anderson Duo Retains Two-Man Pitching Crown
For Third Straight Year

Hubert Trinkle of Anderson, is National Senior AAU singles horseshoe champion for the second successive year following the close of the annual Senior tournament yesterday afternoon at the new Athletic Park courts.

Trinkle, who first won the title at Staten Island in New York last year, annexed eleven straight matches without a setback to gain permanent possession of the John Gordon gold cup, valued at $150.00, as well as a statuette presented by the Madison County Horseshoe Pitchers Association, tourney host, and the AAU gold medal.

Breen Runner-up

Frank Breen, Elgin, Ill., city champion, who placed second with nine victories and two losses, fell before the Anderson star, 50 to 16.

Trinkle's hardest match was at the hands of Leonard Loerzel, Chicago. Loerzel had a 49 to 39 lead on the champion when Trinkle suddenly rallied to win by 50 to 49.

John Lindmeier, Chicago champion, who placed third in the singles rankings, also lost to Trinkle, 50 to 40. Lindmeier and Loerzel each finished the regular title series with eight victories and three losses apiece, and in the playoff to decide third, Lindmeier won from his fellow Chicagoan, 50 to 27.

Breen won the AAU silver medal and Lindmeier a bronze medal. Breen's only losses were to Trinkle and to William Danhauer, Chicago, 50-30.

Retain Doubles Crown

Trinkle's victory today closely followed his stellar performance of yesterday when he and Walter Lane Sr., also of Anderson, retained their national doubles title for the third successive year, winning five matches and losing none in round robin play. Trinkle and Lane first won the doubles at Cincinnati in 1937, then repeated at Staten Island last year. Walter Lane Jr., son the co-holder of the doubles crown, won the National Junior AAU singles title in Cincinnati last week.

Loerzel and Danhauer took second place with four victories and one loss. Lindmeier and Dome Woodhouse, Chicago, were third with three victories and two setbacks.

Fourth place in the doubles was captured by Louis Compton and Lester Bagley, both of Anderson, who dropped three matches. Warren Kellogg of Chicago, paired with John Riggle of Bicknell, took fifth, while Walter Lane Jr. and Bob Eutsler, took sixth.

1939 Senior Men's Singles Championship Finals

	Name	City	W	L
1.	Hubert Trinkle	Anderson, IN	11	0
2.	Frank Breen	Elgin, IL	9	2
3.	John Lindmeier	Oak Park, IL	9	3
4.	Leonard Loerzel	Chicago, IL	8	4
5.	Bill Danhauer	Chicago, IL		

1939 Senior Men's Doubles Championship Finals

	Players	City	W	L
1.	Hubert Trinkle & Walter Lane Sr.	Anderson, IN	5	0
2.	Leonard Loerzel & Bill Danhauer	Chicago, IL	4	1
3.	John Lindmeier & Dorne Woodhouse	Chicago, IL	3	2
4.	Louis Compton & Lester Bagley	Anderson, IN	2	3
5.	John Riggle & Warren Kellogg	Chicago, IL	1	4
6.	Walter Lane Jr. & Bob Eutsler	Anderson, IN	0	5

1939 was the second consecutive year in which the Indiana governor participated in the national tournament. That is really quite significant and certainly must have increased spectator attendance at the event. Think about all the state, national, and World Tournaments over the decades and how few could boast that a state governor attended, let alone pitched a complete exhibition game.

1940

Lindmeier Recaptures the Title

The 1940 senior event and its location site was previewed in the August 1940 issue of *Horseshoe World*:

National Senior AAU Meet at Anderson, Indiana

The Anderson Horseshoe Club of Anderson, Indiana, is busy preparing for the 1940 National Senior AAU Horseshoe Pitching Championships, which will be conducted on its spacious 14-court layout at Athletic Park. The three-day ringer event will be run off Saturday, Sunday and Monday, August 31, September 1 and 2.

Governor M. Clifford Townsend and Fred Bays, Chairman, Indiana Democratic Committee, have been invited to play the opening 50-point game at 8 p.m. Saturday night, August 31. Officials of the host club feel certain that both celebrities will accept the invitations. Governor Townsend helped open the 1938 and 1939 national amateur tourneys here and Mr. Bays has indicated a willingness to help in the opening ceremonies.

Any registered amateur pitcher is eligible to compete in the ringer classic. A pitcher who has participated in a cash prize tournament is not eligible as an amateur in this AAU tournament. The National Senior AAU gold, silver and bronze medals will be awarded winners of first, second and third places. Other prizes may also be distributed, depending upon the number solicited. All contestants must be registered with the AAU and out-of–town contestants must have travel permits from their district associations. Flingers intending [to enter] the tourney should send in a photograph suitable for newspaper work (snapshots will not do); also an outline of past performances, titles won, etc.

The defending champions are Hubert Trinkle, formerly of Anderson and now of Linton, Indiana, in singles and co-holder with Walter Lane Sr. of Anderson, in the doubles.

Rules governing the tourney are laid down by the AAU Horseshoe Pitching Committee. The method of competition: Each Pitcher will be permitted to pitch two sets of 100 shoes each, with the highest 8, 16 or 32, based on ringer percentage plus one point for each shoe six inches or less from peg, qualifying for the final competition; Each pitcher will be allowed the option of choosing either qualifying set as basis for entrance in final competition. The first 8, 16 or 32 qualifiers will compete in a round robin series to determine the tournament champion.

The entry fee for singles will be $2 for each player and $4 per team in doubles. The entries close with G. D. Chumard, Chairman National AAU Horseshoe Pitching Committee, care of O. W. Haven, P.O. Box 486, Anderson, Indiana, midnight, August 30, 1940.

The qualifying competition will get underway at 1 p.m., Saturday, August 31. Contestants unable to report at this time should notify chairman of entry committee. If necessary tournament will be completed under floodlights. The right to reject any entry is reserved. Entry closing date will be strictly observed. For additional entry blanks and any information concerning championships communicate with O. W. Haven, P.O. Box 486, Anderson, Indiana. Contestants will be permitted to use their own shoes provided they come within the rules. There is no age restriction.

The *Anderson Daily Bulletin* from August 30th published a pretournament announcement of the 1940 event:

ANDERSON AGAIN HOST FOR THE
NATIONAL HORSESHOE PITCHING TOURNAMENT

Trails To Be Opened Tomorrow

Qualification trials in the annual National AAU Senior Horseshoe Pitching Championships will open at 2:30 o'clock Saturday afternoon on the municipal courts in Athletic Park and indications today were that contenders from a number of different states of the Middle West and East will step up to the pegs when firing starts.

Judging from the caliber of the entries received so far, Orville W. Haven, of this city, vice-chairman of the National AAU Horseshoe Committee, believes that a higher ringer percentage will be necessary this year to qualify individuals and doubles teams for the senior title playoffs than was the case when the same event was held here last year.

Exhibition Match

An exhibition match will be staged at 8 p.m. Saturday at the local park to formally open the title competition. Gov. M. Clifford Townsend is slated to pitch, having as his partner, Fred F. Bays, Indiana Democratic chairman.

Competition in the doubles will immediately follow the exhibition. According to current plans, the doubles will be run off, if possible, Saturday night, while all the singles events will be completed on Sunday, thus making the event a two-day affair instead of three as originally planned.

Both of last year's titlists will be seen in action in the 1940 playoff. Hubert Trinkle, of Linton, is the singles champion and Trinkle and Walter Lane Sr. of Anderson, have held the senior doubles title every year since they first annexed it at Cincinnati in 1937. Trinkle first won the singles championship at Staten Island, N.Y., in 1938 and easily retained the diadem here last year.

The *Daily Bulletin's* evening edition from the next day, August 31, continued to build the hype. The follow-up article contained a bit more detail about the up-coming championship event.

HORSESHOE TOURNAMENT IS OPENED

More than Forty High-Ranking
Amateurs Here for Annual Playoffs

More than forty top-flight amateur horseshoe pitchers from a number of states participated this afternoon in qualification play preceding the start of doubles and singles matches of the 1940 National AAU Senior Horseshoe Pitching Championship tournament at the municipal courts in Athletic Park.

The trials started at 2:00 p.m. with Orville W. Haven of Anderson, vice chairman of the National AAU Horseshoe Committee in charge. Entries for the tournament closed today at noon.

Exhibition Match

Feature of tonight's program will be an exhibition match at 8 p.m. Immediately following the exhibition, actual doubles matches will start.

Singles matches will be played off Sunday morning and afternoon and presentation of awards will conclude tomorrow afternoon's program.

Following the tournament Sunday evening, a basket pitch-in dinner for contestants and guests will be held at a local park. The local committee in charge consists of Mr. and Mrs. Walter Lane Sr., Mr. and Mrs. Louis Compton, Mr. and Mrs. Raymond Gilpin and Mr. and Mrs. Dwight Carter.

Champions Return

Hubert Trinkle of Linton, the 1938 and 1939 singles champion, and Walter Lane Sr. of Anderson, who has shared with Trinkle the doubles championships of 1937, 1938 and 1939, are among the tournament entrants.

The complete list of entries received prior to last night was as follows: Anderson – Walter Lane Sr., Glen Austin, O. W. Haven, Louis Compton and Herbert Robinette. Linton, Ind. – Hubert Trinkle, Bob Malot, state CCC singles champion. Chicago – John Lindmeier, 1937 AAU singles champion, Leonard Loerzel and William Danhauer.

Parkersburg, W.V. – Arner Lindquist. New Albany, Ind. – Wilbur Cogswell, Louis Endris, Lawrence Kitterman and Arthur W. Endris. Toledo, Ky. – six entrants.

Awards Are Listed

Tourney awards include nine medals and five pairs of horseshoes. The awards will be presented as follows:

Singles Division

First place – AAU gold medal, donated by Dobson Sporting Goods Store; also Gordon Trophy donated by John Gordon, Los Angeles.

Second place – AAU silver medal, donated by the Coca-Cola Bottling Company.

Third place – AAU bronze medal, donated by Delco-Remy.

Fourth place – Pair of horseshoes donated by the Giant Grip Horseshoe Company.

Fifth place – Pair of horseshoes donated by the Ohio Horseshoe Company.

Doubles Division

First place – AAU gold medal, donated by Decker's Sporting Goods Store

Second place – AAU silver medal, donated by Anderson Free Fair Assoc.

Third place – AAU bronze medal, donated by O. V. Badgley.

Fourth place – two pairs of horseshoes donated by Marion Tool Company.

A pair of horseshoes, donated by the Diamond Horseshoe Company is to be presented to the player coming the greatest distance to the tournament.

The trophies will be presented to winners by A. O. Plummer of New York, vice-chairman of the AAU Horseshoe Committee.

The Marion Tool Company, of Marion, Indiana, made the Craftsman pitching shoe—no relationship to the Craftsman brand of tools sold by Sears & Roebuck. No doubt in 1940 they were gifting their latest model, the Craftsman

Ace, which was a beautiful shoe. The mold for the Craftsman became the mold used by Phoenix for their pitching shoes in the 1950s and 1960s.

The most unusual turns of events in the doubles finals were announced in the September 2nd edition of the *Daily Bulletin*:

TRINKLE AND LANE LOSE U.S. CROWN

Arner Lindquist and Leonard Loerzel
Set Pace for Singles Qualifiers
With Marks of 238 Points

The National AAU Senior Doubles Pitching Championship, which has been held since 1937 by Hubert Trinkle of Linton and Walter Lane Sr. of Anderson, was slated to pass into new hands in 1940 title competition at the municipal courts at Athletic Park after Trinkle, an entry in the matches here, failed to show up in time to join his local partner for competition.

Trinkle, the defending singles champion also, failed to put in an appearance despite the fact that officials delayed play in the event for more than an hour after matches started, he explained that he had been delayed in Indianapolis when his automobile caught fire.

Lane, meanwhile, had paired up with Arner Lindquist, of Morgantown, W. Va. and tied for third place.

Chicago was a cinch to take over the 1940 doubles crown, inasmuch as two teams from that city tied for first and second and a playoff was planned at the local park Sunday morning to decide the championship.

Leonard Loerzel and William Danhauer, of the Wells Park Club of Chicago, tied with John Lindmeier and Dorne Woodhouse of the Center Club, each with 6 matches won and 1 lost.

Lindquist and Loerzel, each with 235 points out of a possible 300, led in the singles qualifications Saturday. Competition was so keen that a mark of 195 or better was required to land in the championship flight of sixteen.

Among the qualifiers for singles matches on Sunday were: Lane, Louis Compton and Glen Austin of Anderson; Trinkle; Woodhouse, Danhauer, Lindmeier and Loerzel of Chicago; Kong and Stewart of Toledo;

Paul Reitdorf, Fort Wayne; Arthur Endris, Louis Endris, Wilbur Cogswell and Lawrence Kitterman, all of New Albany.

Only two players had claimed a National AAU singles title up to this time, and they each wanted to claim another championship as they forced the finals into a playoff:

CHICAGO PITCHERS WIN TOP HONORS
IN AAU SENIOR HORSESHOE TOURNAMENT

John Lindmeier is the new senior singles horseshoe pitching champion of the United States Amateur Athletic Union. Lindmeier took the measure of Hubert Trinkle, the 1938 and 1939 titleholder, in two straight games of a special playoff Monday afternoon at the municipal courts in Athletic Park after each had tied for top honors in round robin play with 14 victories and 1 loss.

Lindmeier, who won the singles title in 1937 at Cincinnati, took the first game by 50 to 48 and then clinched the diadem with a 50 to 32 victory.

The Chicagoan pitched 75 percent ringers in beating Trinkle in the first game, Lindmeier had 65 ringers, including 21 doubles out of 90 shoes pitched. Trinkle had 63 ringers and 21 doubles.

In the second game, Trinkle started strong, piling up a 12 to 0 lead before Lindmeier could get his range. At the end of the 27th inning Trinkle still led by 26 to 24. Then Lindmeier broke loose with 16 ringers in his next 18 shoes pitched. Lindmeier had 56 ringers and 22 doubles in the concluding battle, out of 72 shoes pitched, for a percentage of .777, while Trinkle had 50 ringers and 19 doubles for a figure of .694. The two men had four ringers on the stake eight times in the first game and 11 times in the second.

Cogswell Is Third

Wilbur Cogswell, of New Albany, won an extra-game series with William Danhauer and Arner Lindquist, to take third place in the singles. Cogswell defeated Lindquist 25 to 18 and Danhauer, 25 to 6. Danhauer then won fourth place and Lindquist fifth by the procedure of flipping a coin.

Doubles Decided

On Sunday morning in a special playoff, William Danhauer and Leonard Loerzel, both of the Welles Park Club of Chicago, won the doubles title, in a extra playoff with Lindmeier and Dorne Woodhouse. Third place went to Walter Lane Sr. and Lindquist.

AAU gold, silver and bonze medals presented by local sponsors went to winners. In addition, several pairs of horseshoe, donated by manufacturers, were presented. Orville W. Haven, of Anderson, AAU horseshoe commissioner, made the presentations. Ray Gilpin, of Anderson, was general chairman of the scorekeepers.

1940 National AAU Singles Championship Finals

	Player	City	W	L
1.	John Lindmeier	Chicago, IL	16	1
2.	Hubert Trinkle	Linton, IN	14	3
3.	Wilbur Cogswell	New Albany, IN	13	4
4.	Arner Lindquist	Morgantown, WV	11	5
5.	William Danhauer	Chicago, IL	11	5
6.	Glenn Austin	Anderson, IN	7	8
	Walter Lane Sr.	Anderson, IN		
	Leonard Loerzel	Chicago, IL		
	Dorne Woodhouse	Chicago, IL		
	Louis Compton	Toledo, OH		
	William Konz	Toledo, OH		
	Clinton Stewart	Toledo, OH		
	Paul Reitdorf	Fort Wayne, IN		
	Arthur Endris	New Albany, IN		
	Louis Endris	New Albany, IN		
	Lawrence Kitterman	New Albany, IN		

Not all the win/loss records of the players in the singles competition could be recovered, but the names of all who qualified are noted in the final standings, even if their actual ranking and win/loss record cannot be specified.

The playoff games in the singles matches were played to 25 points. That was a little detour from routine, but not a bad idea. The scores in the doubles playoff game was not given so we can't determine if the doubles playoff was played under the same change. Because the doubles playoff game was for the championship, it's likely it was held to the 50-point rule. The records don't mention if the games were played under cancellation scoring or the count-all scoring guidelines. An educated guess is that cancellation scoring is used—but in just a couple of years, we find mention that the games were played with count-all scoring.

In fact, the description of the Lindmeier and Trinkle playoff games indicate that the scoring had to be cancellation.

1940 National AAU Doubles Championship Finals

	Player	City	W	L
1.	Leonard Loerzel & William Danhauer	Chicago, IL	8	2
2.	John Lindmeier & Dorne Woodhouse	Oak Park, IL Chicago, IL	7	3
3.	Arner Lindquist & Walter Lane Sr.	Morgantown, WV Anderson, IN	6	3
4.	Clinton Stewart & William Konz	Toledo, OH	4	5

Apparently not all the doubles team players were named in the various newspaper articles, or the doubles competition was played through a triple round robin. That would be surprising, since there were plenty of players on hand to field more teams. The win/loss records listed above were taken from a short write-up in *Horseshoe World*.

Four National AAU championships had been held so far, and all those singles titles were won by just two individuals who were both only 22 years old in 1940.

This year's AAU tournament was Hubert Trinkle's final national championship event. In his short three-year career he earned five gold medals and one silver medal. He doesn't hold the record, however. Trinkle's five gold medals rank well, but Glenn Riffle earned seven and John Lindmeier won five.

The 1940 AAU junior event was held in Winston-Salem, North Carolina, in early August, as the event continued to work its way southward. The August 6th *Winston-Salem Journal* announced the tournament:

HORSESHOE MEET SATURDAY

Stars Gather Here
To Play In Tourneys

Horseshoe stars of the Carolinas and the nation will gather here Saturday to take part in the National AAU junior tournament and the annual Carolinas AAU event, slated for Fire Station One pits, starting at 9:30 o'clock.

This will be the first time a National AAU horseshoe tournament has been held in North Carolina and is expected to attract a large field of stars.

L. B. Hathaway, director of the playgrounds, is in charge of arrangements for the event.

Under the rules governing play, any horseshoe pitcher who has not won a junior or senior AAU championship may take part in the national event. This tournament was held at Cincinnati last year.

Luke Rumley, of Lexington, won the Carolinas AAU title held here last year and is expected to defend his laurels Saturday.

Entries for the tournament will close Thursday, August 8 and all horseshoe pitchers are requested to register before the deadline.

All pitchers will use one hundred pitches to determine the high eight to take part in the round robin play for the championship.

The same paper on August 8th published another piece before the big meet:

State Stars Enter Tournament

Eight outstanding horseshoe pitching stars of North Carolina have already filed entry for the National AAU Junior and the Carolinas AAU tournaments to be pitched at Fire Station One Saturday.

Four Winston-Salem stars, Luther Hine, C. R. Utt, Brice Barker and J. C. Masoncup, have entered the events, while Raymond Johnson and A. W. Wall, of Hamptonville; J. V. Garrison, of Shelby and Paul King, of Lenoir, are out-of-city visitors registered for the meets.

L. B. Hathaway, director of the playgrounds, who is in charge of the two major events, has requested that all players register by Thursday as entries will definitely close at this time. Winston-Salem players are expected to be registered, as well as visitors, by this deadline.

Hathaway also announced that a player may enter both doubles and singles events and take part in both National Junior and Carolinas AAU, while here.

Reports indicate that additional entries are expected from Lenoir and Shelby, as well as other North Carolina cities, for the two events.

The players will pitch one hundred shoes and the ten high will meet in a round robin for the championships. Pitching will begin Saturday morning.

The pretournament hype continued in the August 9th edition:

Horseshoe Stars Enter Big Tourneys Here on Saturday

Horseshoe stars continued to file entry this morning for the Carolinas AAU and the National Junior AAU tournaments to be pitched at Fire Station One Saturday morning.

Strong teams from Fieldale and Gastonia joined the field today while three players entered from Shelby to make it a four-man team from that city.

Entries for the two outstanding tournaments will close Thursday and all players are expected to be registered with the Recreation Office here by the deadline. Entries for the Carolinas and national singles follow:

Hamptonville – Raymond Johnson and A. W. Wall; Lenoir – Paul King; Shelby – J. R. Garrison, J. B. Cashion, D. Trammell and Newton; Gastonia – Alfred Bryant, M. Hughes, Olin Wilson, James Parker and Will Henson; Winston-Salem – Luther Hine, C. R. Utt, Brice Parker, J. C. Masoncup.

The entries for the doubles include the four men from Shelby and Luther Hine and C. R. Utt of Winston-Salem.

The entries for the National Juniors follow: Fieldale, Va. – Claude Padgett and Roy Ray.

The AAU final standings were listed in the August 13 edition of the *Winston-Salem Journal*, but clearly took second fiddle to the Carolinas tournament:

Final Results on Horseshoes

Luke Rumley, last year's Carolina AAU champion, won the national junior championship, with seven wins and no losses. Luke won the championship by defeating: Roy Ray 52-26; Claude Padgett 50-28; Audrey Ray 50-32; Paul King 50-9; J. P. Garrison 50-5; J. C. Masencup 50-23; J. H. Everhart 55-29.

J. H. Everhart won second place by defeating: Audrey Ray 55-26; Paul King 51-44; J. P. Garrison 51-44; Roy Ray 50-29; J. C. Masencup 52-49; he lost to Claude Padgett 26-50 and to Rumley 26-52.

Audrey Ray won third place. He defeated: J. C. Masencup 55-12; Roy Ray 53-43; J. P. Garrison by default; Claude Padgett 50-21; Paul King 50-43; he lost to J. H. Everhart 25-55 and to Rumley 32-50.

1940 National AAU Junior Championship Final Standings

	Player	City	W	L
1.	Luke Rumley	Lexington, NC	7	0
2.	J. H. Everhart	Lexington, NC	5	2
3.	Audrey Ray	Fieldale, VA	5	2
4.	Paul King	Lenoir, NC	4	3
5.	Claude Padgett	Fieldale, VA	3	4
6.	J. C. Masencup	Winston-Salem, NC	3	4
7.	Roy Ray	Fieldale, VA	2	5
8.	J. P. Garrison	Shelby, NC	0	7

1941

On to the Windy City for Lindmeier's Third Title

The April 1941 *Horseshoe World* announced that the 1941 senior national tournament event was to be held in Columbus, Ohio:

National AAU Horseshoe Pitching Tournament
At State Fair in August

The National AAU Horseshoe Pitching Tournament will be held in Columbus during the Ohio State Fair for the first time in history.

Little Rock, Ark., Des Moines, Ia. and Springfield, Ill., were outbid by Columbus to bring this tournament here. Columbus in the past has had many enthusiastic horseshoe twirlers and with the revival of the Franklin County AAU tournaments, it should be another sport to add to the pleasure of Central Ohio fans.

Win Kinnan, manager of the Ohio State Fair, has been contacted concerning the tournament. Governor John W. Bricker may pitch a horseshoe match against Governor James of Pennsylvania. If the Ohio State Fair authorities give permission, there is a strong possibility such a match could be arranged.

Trophies, medals and plaques will be awarded the winners in all events. Entries are expected from 18 states. Any other persons in Columbus who are interested in this event, should contact Jim Rhodes at City Hall. Mr. Rhodes was appointed last week to membership of the National AAU Horseshoe Committee by Daniel Ferris, executive secretary of the AAU.

Despite the apparently definitive announcement, the 1941 event was held in Chicago rather than Columbus. No announcement or information was located explaining the circumstance of the change of venue, so all information about the change and the new selected site had to be communicated strictly through AAU channels and publications.

The next bit of information uncovered was this pretournament article in the September 16th edition of the *Chicago Daily Times*:

Playground Star
Enters Ringer Meet

Making a bid for national honors, John Styler, 6637 Ellis, 1940 Board of Education playgrounds champion, today entered the National AAU horseshoe pitching championships, which open Friday morning on the Lincoln Parks courts at Clark Wells and Wisconsin.

The former playground star faces a strenuous weekend in the annual classic, which will be conducted by the Chicago Parks and the Center Horseshoe Club under the sponsorship of the *Chicago Times*. For the 1940 national champions in both singles and doubles play, all boasting an impressive list of victories, will be defending their titles in a star-studded field of the nation's greatest tossers.

Lindmeier Tops List

Leading the list will be John Lindmeier, representing the Center Club, who has been at the top in every major tournament for the past five years, taking the national singles title in 1937 and again in 1940. The champion doubles combination, Leonard Loerzel and William Danhauer of the Wells Park Club lately have displayed the same form that brought them the American crown last year at Anderson, Indiana.

The big tournament will start at 9:30 a.m. Friday with all contestants required to pitch a qualifying round of two sets of 100 shoes. They then will be rated on ringer percentage, plus one point for every shoe six inches or less to the stake and the top 16 paired off in a round robin for the singles championship.

Qualifying play will continue throughout the entire day on Friday and pitchers will resume their qualifying rounds Saturday morning and afternoon. Finals in the doubles will follow the singles preliminaries and tournament officials under the direction of Chairman John Mooney expect to have the 1941 doubles champions determined by Saturday evening.

Singles Finals Sunday

Sunday morning and afternoon will be devoted to the final round robin series in the singles competition.

The September 19th edition of the *Chicago Daily Times* built up the hype with an article by Marvin I. Thomas, director of the Chicago Times Athletic Association, that featured further pretournament announcements and a colorful preview:

Horseshoes Fly as Stars Pitch for National Titles

The 1941 National AAU horseshoe pitching tournament to determine the singles and doubles champions of the United States opened at 9:30 a.m. today on the Lincoln Park 12 court parlor at Wells, Wisconsin and Clark.

Conducted by the Chicago Park district and sponsored by the *Times* [Athletic Association], with the Center Club the host organization, the annual classic of glorified barnyard golf is scheduled to run from morning until dusk today, tomorrow and probably most of Sunday before the 1941 king tossers will have been determined.

Prominent in one of the classiest fields ever to compete in the national event are John Lindmeier, Center Horseshoe Club, the defending singles champion, state titleholder and member of the 1940 national doubles runner-up combination; Arner Lindquist of Morgantown, W.Va., who fans will remember as the gallant southerner mainly responsible for the fall of Hubert Trinkle, the Hoosier star and 1939 national champion at Anderson, Ind., last year.

Babusch a Threat

And Hubert Trinkle will be on hand—but on the sidelines, to watch proceedings in the game in which he dominated the field for a number of years. Anderson dispatches indicate he may not be able to compete. Chicago fans will not be surprised, however, if the Hoosier star decides to compete and again match shoes with his old rival, Lindmeier.

Up and coming and a constant threat to the title contenders will be Edward Babusch of Union Park, present Chicago league champion, whose ringer percentage of 65 definitely ranks him as a top player.

Marion Morris of Pendleton, Ind., Frank Breen and Edgar Schmoldt of the Watch City Horseshoe Club at Elgin, are other entrants with national ratings.

Top Doubles Field

In the doubles competition, defending champions Leonard Loerzel and William Danhauer of Wells Park and the 1940 runners-up, John Lindmeier and Dorne Woodhouse of the Center Club, lead the field. Walter Lane Jr. and his teammate Marion Morris will offer strong opposition.

Tournament officials under the direction of Chairman John A. Mooney were enthusiastic over the condition of the Lincoln Park courts. All voiced their appreciation of the splendid co-operation extended by the park officials, James Vanderbosch, James P. Gallagher and Joseph T. Moran and their staffs.

The 1941 championships got started and the qualifying round was high-lighted in the *Sunday Times* of September 21st:

John Lindmeier Defends
U.S. Horseshoe Title Today

Paced by Frank Breen of the Watch City Club in Elgin and Robert G. Pence of the Chicago Rowan Club, 16 of the nation's greatest tossers vie this morning and afternoon for the singles championship of the United States on the Lincoln Park courts, Clark, Wells and Wisconsin.

John Lindmeier, the defending champion who was qualified automatically for today's final round robin series, remains the unknown quality but there is little doubt in the minds of the horseshoe fans that crowded the Lincoln Park courts Friday and yesterday that Frank Breen will be exceedingly difficult to defeat.

Breen set a new world's record Friday in qualifying play by scoring 256 points with 80 ringers and was only a single point off Dorne Woodhouse's world's tournament mark made with the same number of ringers several years ago.

Robert G. Pence of the Rowan Club trailed Breen with a 250 score and 75 ringers. Edward Babusch of the Union Park Club, a local boy expected to do great things in this tournament, placed third in the 16-man field, scoring 248 points and 74 ringers.

120 Matches Today

Marion Morris of Pendleton, Ind., with a 237 and 70 ringers showing, occupied sixth place in the qualifying rounds, while Arner Lindquist of Morgantown, W.Va., landed in ninth place with 66 ringers and 226 points.

One hundred and twenty matches are on today's schedule and the winner will be determined on a percentage basis. Plenty of seats are available for the public and there is no admission charge.

The Qualifiers

	Name	Pts.	R	DR
1.	John Lindmeier	DC		
2.	Frank Breen	256	80	33
3.	Robert G. Pence	250	75	27
4.	Robert Babusch	248	74	28
5.	D. Woodhouse	242	73	27
6.	Marion Morris	237	70	24
7.	Leonard Loerzel	235	72	26
8.	John Fleming	230	69	26
9.	Arner Lindquist	226	66	24
10.	Ralph Dykes	225	66	23
11.	Henry Fleming	221	65	21
12.	Pete Markarian	218	62	17
13.	Leo Rollick	215	60	16
14.	Tyler Loy	213	60	16
15.	E. R. Zimmerman	213	58	18
16.	Gust Brock	207	57	14

A review of the qualifying scores reveals that there were some very capable pitchers in this championship class, but there are two names I'd like to concentrate on—Bob Pence and Ralph Dykes. This was the one and only AAU event for each player, and both went on to join the NHPA and serve with distinguished careers on the administrative side of the sport. Those of us who knew these two men will always remember them as older gentlemen of the game, but in 1941 Pence was only 32 years old and Dykes was just 28.

Bob Pence moved to Indiana where he served as the state association secretary-treasurer for more than 30 years and in the process built up the state membership to the largest in the country. He was elected NHPA's secretary-treasurer in 1958 and served in that role through 1971. During his years in office the NHPA Hall of Fame was established in 1966, a junior girls division was finally established for the World Tournaments beginning in 1967, World Tournaments were expanded to include classes C and D for the men (other divisions were also expanded), and the men's intermediate and senior classes were established. Pence was inducted to the NHPA Hall of Fame in 1969.

Ralph Dykes served as Illinois state association's president for more than twenty years, and was elected president of the NHPA in 1967, a position he held through 1973. Dykes was inducted to the NHPA Hall of Fame in 1973.

The 1941 doubles championship and the first round of the singles play was covered by the *Chicago Daily Times*:

Lindmeier, Woodhouse Win
Doubles Horseshoe Crown

Johnny Lindmeier, who yesterday teamed up with Dorne Woodhouse to win the National AAU doubles championship, today goes after his third U.S. horseshoe pitching crown when he competes in the singles competition on the Lincoln Park courts.

Lindmeier and Woodhouse swept through the two-man final round in the championship tourney being conducted by the Chicago Park District and Center Horseshoe Club under the sponsorship of the *Times* [Athletic Association].

Sixteen of the nation's greatest tossers vie for the singles title. Lindmeier, defending champ, Arner Lindquist of West Virginia and Henry Fleming of Hi-Way Club led the field with four straight victories each after yesterday's competition. Eleven more games remain for each player making a total of 88 games for today's card. Play opens at 9:30 a.m.

Close to Leaders

Three other players are close upon the leaders. Frank Breen of Elgin, Leonard Loerzel of Wells Park and Woodhouse chalked up three victories apiece while dropping one. Breen, the most colorful player in the tournament who set a world's record of 256 in Friday's qualifying round, suffered his lone defeat at the hands of Champion Lindmeier in a match which took almost an hour to run off. Fifty-nine innings were required and 139 ringers were tossed before Lindmeier won out, 50-46.

Woodhouse gave notice to all that he was still very much in the running as indicated by his sparkling match in the second round against Robert Pence of the Rowan Club, Woodhouse tossed 31 ringers out of 38 shoes for a percentage of 81.5 to take the game from Pence, 52-11.

How They Stand

Standing at the end of the fourth round:

	Won	Lost
John Lindmeier	4	0
Arner Lindquist	4	0
Henry Fleming	4	0
Dorne Woodhouse	4	0
Frank Breen	3	1
Leonard Loerzel	3	1
E. R. Zimmerman	2	2
Ralph Dykes	2	2
Pete Markarian	2	2
Marion Morris	1	3
Gus Brook	1	3
Leo Rollick	1	3
Edward Babusch	1	3
Tyler Foy	1	3
John Fleming	0	4
Robert Pence	0	4

Lindmeier and Woodhouse, runners-up in last year's meet at Anderson, Ind., won five matches and dropped one in winning the doubles title. Their lone loss came at the hands of the Fleming boys, John and Henry.

A three-way tie developed for second place, between the teams of Breen and Edgar Schmoldt, the Fleming boys and Tyler Loy and Robert G. Pence at the end of the regulation playing session. Extra matches were played and Breen and Schmoldt climbed to second place with Pence and Loy third and Henry and John Fleming landing fourth.

Doubles Finals

Round 1
Breen-Schmoldt beat Loerzel-Danhauer 53-40;
Woodhouse-Lindmeier beat Lane-Morris 51-18
Fleming-Fleming beat Lindquist-Rollick 50-17

Round 2
Pence-Loy beat Loerzel-Danhauer 51-35;
Breen-Schmoldt beat Fleming-Fleming 53-13
Lindquist-Rollick beat Lane-Morris 50-6

Round 3
Woodhouse-Lindmeier beat Pence-Loy 52-30;
Fleming-Fleming beat Loerzel-Danhauer 40-42
Breen-Schmoldt beat Lane-Morris 50-18

Round 4
Pence-Loy beat Fleming-Fleming 50-17;
Woodhouse-Lindmeier beat Lindquist-Rollick 52-26
Loerzel-Danhauer beat Lane-Morris 51-32

Round 5
Lindquist-Rollick beat Pence-Loy 50-28;
Fleming-Fleming beat Lane-Morris 50-22
Woodhouse-Lindmeier beat Breen-Schmoldt 51-28

Round 6
Pence-Loy beat Lane-Morris 50-28;
Breen-Schmoldt beat Lindquist-Rollick 52-47
Woodhouse-Lindmeier beat Loerzel-Danhauer 50-31

Round 7
Pence-Loy beat Breen-Schmoldt 50-43;
Loerzel-Danhauer beat Lindquist-Rollick 51-46
Fleming-Fleming beat Woodhouse-Lindmeier 50-44

Second Place Playoff
Breen-Schmoldt beat Fleming-Fleming 51-47;
Breen-Schmoldt beat Pence-Loy 51-36
Pence-Loy beat Fleming-Fleming 52-47

1941 National AAU Doubles Championship

		Won	Lost
1.	Woodhouse-Lindmeier	5	1
2.	Breen-Schmoldt	6	2
3.	Pence-Loy	5	3
4.	Fleming-Fleming	4	4
5.	Loerzel-Danhauer	2	4
6.	Lindquist-Rollick	2	4
7.	Lane-Morris	0	6

The singles championship finals were reported on Monday, September 22nd by the *Chicago Daily Times*:

Lindmeier Retains Horseshoe Crown

Fresh from his victory in the doubles with teammate Dorne Woodhouse, Johnny Lindmeier of the Center Club successfully defended his singles title in the National AAU horseshoe pitching tournament at Lincoln Park yesterday in a thrill-packed series that was not decided until the final game. The tournament was conducted under the sponsorship of the *Times* [Athletic Association].

Although chalking up an impressive mark of 14 victories and one defeat, the Chicago star was hard pressed throughout the day and a half battle by husky Frank Breen of the Watch City Club of Elgin. Not until the final shoes of the tournament had been tossed was the big fellow counted out.

67 Percent Ringers

Breen, with 13 victories and two defeats, was the runner-up, while Dorne Woodhouse, at 12 and three, took third place. In the 15 game final series, the champion tossed 964 shoes, 646 of which were ringers for a ringer percentage of 67. Breen threw 1074 shoes with 750 ringers, good for a 69.5 percentage. Woodhouse had a 67.5 percentage with 631 ringers out of 935 shoes.

The break in the series occurred in the third round when Lindmeier defeated Breen, 50-46. The game lasted almost an hour, fifty-nine innings were required and 139 ringers were tossed.

From this point on Breen trailed the champion. Lindmeier stumbled in the eight round, bowing to Pete Markarian of Union Park, 51-23, for his sole defeat but Breen was unable to gain on the champion when he lost a close battle to Leonard Loerzel of Wells Park in the following round, 51-44.

The tournament was one of the most successful contests ever held in amateur competition and veteran pitchers were loud in their praise of officials, experts from Chicago's well-known shoe clubs and outstanding AAU men for the excellent manner in which the tournament was conducted.

Park officials James P. Gallagher, Jim Vanderbosch and Joseph T. Moran, who conducted splendidly in staging the championships, were especially pleased with the enthusiastic reception accorded the Lincoln Courts. The subway clay proved to be "tops" for horseshoe pitching. Both Breen and Lindmeier, veterans of many tournaments, remarked that the courts were the best they have ever played on.

To John A. Mooney, the tournament director, to our many officials and contestants and to all who helped make the tournament such a grand success, the *Times* A.A. extends congratulations and sincere thanks.

1941 National AAU Men's Championship Finals

	Name	City	W	L	%
1.	John Lindmeier	Chicago, IL	14	1	67.01
2.	Frank Breen	Elgin, IL	13	2	69.83
3.	Dorne Woodhouse	Chicago, IL	12	3	67.56
4.	Arner Lindquist	Morgantown, WV	9	6	61.23
5.	Marion Morris	Pendleton, IN	9	6	60.30
6.	Leonard Loerzel	Chicago, IL	8	7	61.22
7.	Pete Markarian	Chicago, IL	8	7	60.30
8.	John Fleming	Chicago, IL	7	8	62.50
9.	Ralph Dykes	Lombard, IL	7	8	60.43
10.	Edward Babusch	Chicago, IL	7	8	60.24
11.	E.R. Zimmerman	Chicago, IL	7	8	57.76
12.	Henry Fleming	Chicago, IL	7	8	57.54
13.	Tyler Loy	Chicago, IL	6	9	59.52
14.	Lee Rollick	Chicago, IL	5	10	55.38
15.	Gust Brock	Chicago, IL	2	13	49.41
16.	Robert G. Pence	Chicago, IL	1	14	47.43

This was John Lindmeier's final National AAU event and he went out a champion. Throughout his career, Lindmeier accumulated 11 medals: five gold, one silver and five bronze.

In addition to the AAU senior event in Chicago, a junior event was held in the North Carolina and South Carolina area. Winston-Salem will later demonstrate they were a leader in sponsoring the AAU events.

Coverage of the 1941 junior event began with this pretournament announcement:

AAU HORSESHOE TOURNAMENT HERE

National Meet To Be
Combined with Carolina's Play

The National AAU Horseshoe Tournament, which will be held in Winston-Salem August 16th with the Carolina's horseshoe tournament, was announced yesterday by L. B. Hathaway of the City Recreation Department.

Horseshoe pitchers from all over the United States are eligible for the tournament, said Hathaway, although entrants will probably not compete except in the Southern area.

The Carolinas meet and the national meet will be held so that those who may wish will be able to participate in both, Entrance fee for the national tourney is one dollar for the single and two dollars for the double. Entrants must be members of the AAU or they may join by August 14th by payment of initiation fee of 25 cents.

All registrations for both tournaments must be in by August 14th.

Many local pitchers are expected to enter the tournaments. All are eligible who have not won a national or state tournament previously.

Winner of the national horseshoe contest last year was Luke Rumley of Lexington and the Carolinas winner was Paul King of Lenoir.

The contest will take place at Fire Station No. 1.

The August 17, 1941, *Winston-Salem Journal* provided the event's final standings:

Naylor Wins Two Trophies
in Horseshoes

Southpaw Ed Naylor of Lexington, made his shoes do practically everything but talk yesterday as he captured both the national junior AAU and Carolinas AAU singles horseshoe titles at the No. One Fire Station.

The Twin Cities pitching wizard, who could land nothing better than runner-up position in the city tournament, topped star-studded fields of 18 juniors and 32 in the Carolinas—twice the number that entered the 1940 tournaments. Naylor, whose 199 was points off John Higgins pace in the junior qualifying and also second in the Carolinas qualifying to Louis Rumley, failed to drop a single game in the round robin play that followed. Hot as a firecracker, he demonstrated his skill and defeated each of the other seven qualifiers in both events.

Wins Handsome Trophies

The bespectacled Twin Citian carried away two handsome trophies for his day's work and also AAU medals for each victory.

Luke Rumley of Lexington, winner of the national junior tourney last year finished second to Naylor in the Carolinas and won a medal. R. A. Long, of Forest City, captured third place and a medal. Woodrow Stone and Fred Duncan, of Richmond, Va. finished second and third, respectively in the Juniors event to win AAU medals.

Last year's Carolina's junior champion, Paul King of Lenior, failed to qualify for he national as the competition was the toughest ever seen here.

John Higgins, Lexington, rolled up the highest qualifying score of the day, 225 for the Juniors. Louis Rumley's 201 qualifying score in the national topped the field. Records were complied on the basis of 100 pitched shoes.

A trophy was awarded the entrant from the most distant city. However, four men—C. O. Jones, W. H. Stone, Fred Duncan and Benny Jenkins—were from Richmond and the trophy went to the one with the highest ringer percentage, which was Jones with 57 ringers.

Only two teams entered national doubles tournament and Fred Duncan and Woodrow Stone. Richmond, won the crown from Charles Jones and Benny Jenkins, Richmond, two games to one.

Luke Rumley and R. B. Kennedy, Lexington, took the Carolina's doubles championship, which had only nine teams entered, three games won and no losses.

The Results

Qualifying scores for the national junior tournament, eight highest scorers gained place in the round robin finals:

John Higgins, Lexington 225; Ed Naylor, Winston-Salem 195; J. C. Masencup, Winston-Salem 191; Charles O. Jones, Richmond 187; Woodrow H. Stone, Richmond 197; Fred Duncan, Richmond 179; Chester Utt, Winston-Salem 178; A. J. Schuyer, Roanoke 170; Paul King, Lenoir 169; Benny Jenkins, Richmond 166; J. B. Darnell, Roanoke 152;

Spencer Warren, High Point 154; Bootsie Williams, Mayodan 141; Claude Badgett, Fieldale 129; E. F. Cundiff, Roanoke 124; Jesse W. Richardson, Mayodan 104

1941 National Junior Championship Finals

	Player	Home	W	L
1.	Ed Naylor	Winston-Salem	7	0
2.	Woodrow Stone	Richmond	6	1
3.	Fred Duncan	Richmond	5	3
4.	J. S. Higgins	Lexington	4	4
5.	Charles Jones	Richmond	3	4
6.	J. C. Masencup	Winston-Salem	3	4
7.	Chester Utt	Winston-Salem	1	6
8.	A. J. Schuyer	Roanoke	0	7

Duncan and Higgins played a playoff game to decide third place.

1942

A New Men's Champion and a Home-State Hero

One of the most unforgettable personalities and characters ever to grace the sport of horseshoe pitching is NHPA Hall of Famer Lee Rose. He first pitched in a World Tournament in 1928, was a three-time Michigan state champion (1934, 1944, and 1955), and was elected NHPA's secretary-treasurer in 1939. Rose, who passed away in 1998 at the age of 92, was a pure student of the game, a strong promoter of the sport, and eventually he owned and operated the Lattore Horseshoe Company.

Besides being an NHPA officer, he also served as the Michigan secretary-treasurer of the Michigan association from 1935 to 1960. He was inducted to the NHPA Hall of Fame in 1984, and he is also a member of the Michigan Horseshoe Pitchers Hall of Fame.

Rose also proved to be one of the sport's best historians, though he never held that title officially. He published *The Horseshoe Compendium*, a fine history of the sport, in 1940 and recorded his personal experiences in hand-written journals dating from 1924 to about 1955. *The Horseshoe Compendium* has been scanned and is available in its entirety on the NHPA website, horseshoepitching.com.

The wildest part of Rose's story is that halfway through his journals, we find out that he wasn't Lee Rose after all. His given name was Lee Jacobs. As a teenager, his father forbade him to play in horseshoe-pitching tournaments, so for over 20 years he played under an assumed name. (But that is another story, perhaps even another book.) For now, here is an account of the 1942 AAU tournament from the journals of one of its participants, Lee Rose:

On September 11, Sunny and I took off in the "Escritoire" for Cincinnati, Ohio and we arrived there after an all-day and not very eventful trip. We landed at Schuster's in Deer Park and I warmed up at a court a block down the street. That night Sunny went to a show and I went to the Old Dutch Mill.

Afterward we went to the Club Melody. I certainly didn't feel very good in the morning but Sunny and I went downtown and crossed the free bridge to Newport, Ky., where I qualified for the finals of the National AAU Tourney.

After a show, eats, drinks, etc., we went to bed and arose the next morning to go back to Newport for the finals. It was held at the Northern Kentucky Horseshoe Club.

Finals were held on a basis of 50 shoe games with a count-all system! Phooey!!

I met Walter Lindmeier of Chicago in the first game and led nearly all the way to best him, 95-84. Then I beat Harold Lange, 108-85. I lost my next start to Dorne Woodhouse, 105-104.

Disgusted with that one-point defeat and the whole crazy system of playing, I lost to Harry Henn, 107-84. Then I lost to Stan Manker, 96-88.

Then my natural instincts got the better of me and I started to click. I defeated Martin, 112-95, and Eha, 100-90. Then I met the defending champion John Lindmeier and I battered him down 114-91 with 72%. My next game with Frank Breen was my best of the day; I beat him 129-119, shooting 42 ringers for 84%, winding it up with 8 straight doubles.

Then I met the very slow pitching Arner Lindquist, who was leading the event. I had only 1 ringer out of the first six shoes and he led 12-4. From then on I pulled up on him but due to the game only lasting 50 shoes, I didn't have time to catch him and lost out 110-106. I wound up the day by nosing out Johns 112-111 and tied for 3rd place.

Rose does a fine job of telling about his experience at the 1942 AAU championships. Without ruining the suspense, so we can still follow though the media's coverage. From the September 8th *Cincinnati Times Star*:

Horseshoe Pitching

Among early entries for The National Senior AAU Horseshoe Pitching Championship Tournament scheduled for Saturday and Sunday at the Northern Kentucky horseshoe courts, located on Riverside Drive, Newport, are those of the defending singles champion and his doubles partner, John F. Lindmeier and Dorne Woodhouse, representing the center Horseshoe Club of Chicago.

Harold Lange and Frank Breen of the Watch City Horseshoe Club of Elgin, Ill., also are early entrants. Breen is the holder of the National AAU high qualifying score of 256 points out of a possible 300 score, which he set last year in the national tournament at Chicago. He averaged 69.8 percent ringers for the entire tournament.

Over a dozen Greater Cincinnati pitchers also will compete in the tournament, representing the northern Kentucky, Fort Thomas and Norwood horseshoe clubs.

Qualifying play will get under way Saturday at 1 p.m. and the final round robin in singles and doubles will be played Sunday.

Joe Clore, veteran local horseshoe pitcher, has been selected to referee the tournament.

Saturday night. Lindmeier and Woodhouse will compete in exhibition matches at the Fort Thomas Horseshoe Courts against Pete Wallace and Tom Luck, top-ranking pitchers of the Fort Thomas Horseshoe Club. Included on the program will be Tommy White, the sensational 13-year-old Norwood boy pitcher.

The start of the event was covered by the *Cincinnati Enquirer* on September 13th:

Champ Equals Record

Scoring 79 ringers out of 100 shoes pitched, John Lindmeier, Chicago, defending champion, equaled the National AAU high qualifying score with a total of 256 points in the national senior AAU horseshoe pitching tourney at the Northern Kentucky Horseshoe Club courts, Newport, yesterday. The mark was set by Frank Breen, Elgin, Ill., at the national meet at Chicago last year.

Lindmeier and Breen were tied in two new National AAU horseshoe records, with 21 consecutive ringers and 10 consecutive doubles, beating the old marks of 12 and 6, set by Hubert Trinkle of Pendleton, Ind., at Anderson Ind., in 1939. Lindmeier's 256 score came in the early minutes of the qualifying round and was threatened only twice, when Arner Lindquist of Morgantown, W.Va., turned in a 249 score and James H. Johnson, Ludlow, Ky., made a 238 score. Lindmeier's 79 percent ringer average was one less than Frank Breen's National AAU record of 80 percent pitched in 1941.

Final round robin contest between the survivors of the qualifying competition will get under way at 9 o'clock this morning at the Northern Kentucky courts. The doubles competition is also scheduled.

Results of the qualifying competition:

Score	Contestant	City
256	John Lindmeier	Chicago, Ill.
249	Arner Lindquist	Morgantown, W.Va.
234	Dorne Woodhouse	Chicago, Ill.
233	Frank Breen	Elgin, Ill.
221	Harry Henn	Cold Spring, Ky.
219	Harold Lange	Elgin, Ill.
218	Harold McPherson	Newport, Ky.
217	Charles Eha	Bellevue, Ky.
214	Lee H. Rose	Detroit, Mi.
218	Stanley Manker	Chillicothe, Ohio
200	E. L. Martin	Norwood, Ohio
191	Walter Lindmeier	Chicago, Ill.

The contest's winner, a participant in previous years, but a first-time AAU senior champion, was announced by the *Enquirer*:

NEW CHAMP CROWNED

West Virginian Best in
Horseshoe Pitching Tourney

Averaging 66½ percent ringers, forty-six year old Swedish-born glasscutter and engraver, Arner Lindquist, Morgantown, W.Va., became the new national senior AAU horseshoe pitching champion yesterday, displacing John F. Lindmeier at the Northern Kentucky Horseshoe Club courts. Lindmeier and his partner, Dorne Woodhouse, however, retained their national doubles title.

Lindquist won 11 of the 12 games in the round robin. His only defeat came at the hands of Lindmeier, who lost four other games in the final competition, which put him in a four-way tie for third place.

Mr. Lindquist won the A.A.U. National Championship at Newport, Ky., winning 11 out of 12 games. He qualified with 78 ringers our of 100 shoes and 249 points out of a possible 300. His best ringer average on his home courts this summer was 92 our of 100 tosses.

Lindmeier had the highest ringer percentage for the final competition with 68 percent. Second place went to Woodhouse in the singles and Lindmeier was awarded third place, due to having the highest ringer percentage over the other three tied for the third place position.

1942 National AAU Men's Doubles Championship Finals

		W	L
1.	John Lindmeier & Dorne Woodhouse	3	0
2.	Arner Lindquist & Stanley Manker	2	1
3.	Frank Breen & Harold Lange	1	2
4.	Tom Luck & J. R. Kirkpatrick	0	3

1942 National AAU Men's Championship Finals

	Name	W	L	%
1.	Arner Lindquist	11	1	66.5
2.	Dorne Woodhouse	9	3	65.0
3.	John Lindmeier	8	4	68.0
4.	Stanley Manker	8	4	67.0
5.	Lee H. Rose	8	4	64.0
6.	Frank Breen	8	4	63.0
7.	James "Pops" Johnson	7	5	55.0
8.	Harold McPherson	5	7	54.0
9.	Everett L. Martin	5	7	52.0
10.	Harold Lange	4	8	52.0
11.	Harry Henn	3	9	53.0
12.	Charles Eha	1	11	52.0
13.	Walter Lindmeier	1	11	44.0

A 1942 national junior AAU event was held in Richmond, Virginia. The formal announcement for the national junior tournament appeared in the June-July 1942 issue of *Horseshoe World*. The article largely repeats the previous year's announcement, so only an excerpt is quoted here:

Amateur Athletic Union
National Junior
Horseshoe Pitching Championships

Sponsored by
Virginia Association, AAU and
Richmond Division of Recreation
Fonticello Park, Richmond, Virginia
Saturday August 22, 1942

Events:

1. Junior National AAU Horseshoe Pitching Championship – Singles and
   Doubles.
2. Virginia AAU Horseshoe Pitching Championships – Singles and Doubles.

Method of Competition:
Each contestant shall pitch 100 shoes for qualifying and the eight highest scores qualify for the final round robin competitions.

Tournament Committee:
William A Bryson ....Chairman
Harry T. Woodfield...Tournament Director
George C. Patterson....Chief Clerk
M. J. Barr, George Charland, Harris A. Brightly, Pembroke Thomas

It's surprising to see is the name of Harry Woodfield as the tournament director. No better name could be put in that role, though. Woodfield was a long-time promoter and organizer in the sport and to add to the situation, he had been elected NHPA president in 1939 so 1942 would have been his third of eight years in office. He was an active and productive leader and was inducted to the NHPA Hall of Fame in 1968. One of his notable achievements for the NHPA was his relationship with the Truman White House; he assisted President Truman in constructing horseshoe-pitching courts on the White House lawn. Woodfield's efforts to publish the NHPA newsletter by mimeograph machine after *Horseshoe World* was discontinued were also a significant contribution to the sport. His interest and active involvement in the AAU events must have strengthened the relationship between the two organizations.

The *Richmond Times Dispatch* gave a pretournament announcement on August 22nd:

'Shoe Tourney Will be Held
Here Today

Harry T. Woodfield of Washington, D.C., president of the National Horseshoe Pitchers Association, will confer with tournament directors and officials of the Virginia State Association in regard to today's state and national tournaments to be held at Fonticello Park, it was announced yesterday. Woodfield will meet with the local officials at 9 a.m. and qualifying will continue this morning at 9:30 a.m.

Four Richmond pitchers qualified last night at Fonticello. J. O. Gulbranson notched high score with 205 points out of 100 shoes, 58 percent ringers. Charlie Jones tallied 196 points, 55 percent; W. H. Stone, 187 points, 48 percent, and C. N. Thompson, 154 points, 38 percent.

Woodrow Stone, of Richmond, will defend his state title, but is expected to receive a stern challenge from Charlie Jones, another Richmonder, who holds the 1942 city title. Stone, runner-up in the Junior Nationals, is seeded top place as the 1942 winner.

Round robin matches today will start at 1 p.m. following the morning qualifying. Eight participants will play a round robin championship final.

William A. (Bill) Bryson, tournament official, said yesterday that "Boo" Henson, Metropolitan Washington champion, had wired that he had officially accepted the match with Private Vito Feliccia, New York titleholder now stationed at Camp Lee, and Bryson scheduled this exhibition at 8 p.m. as a windup to the full day.

Well, now! Exhibition games had been held at previous AAU events, but mainly between politicians and other dignitaries. This game between champions, one of whom was a soldier, is a truly great exhibition and a statement to the times. On the same page of the *Richmond Times-Dispatch* this article that tells a bit about Vito Feliccia appeared:

Feliccia Winner of Camp Lee Horseshoe Title

Private Vito Feliccia, three-time winner of the New York state horseshoe pitching championship, notched another title when he bested seven of Camp Lee's flinging contestants in the horseshoe finals.

Feliccia gained entry by out-pitching all opposition in his own 10th Regiment Training Center and then proceeded to eliminate the top tossers of camp by slapping ringer after ringer around the pegs.

Feliccia's score of 68 ringers out of 94 deliveries in the quarterfinals, semifinals and finals proved too much for all opposition and the champion from New York emerged victorious as undisputed king of the camp shooters.

In addition to the New York State wins, Private Feliccia won the New Jersey open championship in 1936, '37 and '40 and the Island championship in '39, '40 and '41.

Feliccia is a member of Headquarters Detachment of the 10th Regiment while his finals opponent Private John Miller is in Company C of the 10th.

Vito Feliccia was a indeed a star of the game at a young age. He won two New York state championships, in 1936 and 1949, and he won hundreds of open tournaments during his 40-year career. He was inducted to the New York State association's hall of fame.

Boo Henson, 30 years old at the time, was also a star on the East Coast, winning 15 Virginia state championships, the first in 1930 and the last in 1949. He won the Washington, D.C., championship 34 times. His friendship with

Harry Woodfield led to many invitations for exhibition matches—besides this match with Feliccia, he played against Jimmy Risk and Blair Nunamaker. He is a member of the Virginia state association's hall of fame.

The finals were reported in an unusual article that contained a lot of general information about the sport and not much about the final play. The context suggests the writer had more input from an NHPA person than an AAU person, as was usually the case:

Horseshoe Pitching Has Left
The Old General Store Stage

Harry Woodfield of Washington, D.C., president of the National Horseshoe Pitchers Association of America, believes that day of the country gentleman horseshoe pitcher is over. Those gatherings behind the gen'l store on a Sunday afternoon for the purpose of a hot shoe contest are finished.

Interest is being manifested in the tournaments such as was conducted under the auspices of the Virginia State AAU and the Richmond Horseshoe Club here yesterday at Fonticello Park. Woodfield believes and he is attempting, through carefully prepared publicity, to interest the nation in pitching Dobbin's footwear around a stake some 40 feet away.

The war has interfered with Woodfield's plans. Manufacturers have stopped making regulation shoes. Oh, yes, just any old shoe won't do. They are made especially for pitching, balanced just right. Old Dobbin, you see wears his shoes down, either on one side or the other. That upsets the balance and the expert shoe pitcher can't have that happen, particularly when there is a little at stake.

Millions of Throwers

There is not any way to tell just how many Americans are pitching shoes. Woodfield says. "Just say that there are millions upon millions, not only in America, but all over the world," he declared. In an effort to get horseshoes established the world over, Woodfield says that he has written over 4,000 letters to various parts of the globe on which we live.

"Probably I won't receive but a hundred or so replies," he asserted, "but I will have a contact." He is expecting to hear from both England and Australia. His contacts are already firmly established in Canada.

Thirteen members of a Canadian team, from all over Canada, were scheduled to participate in a tournament in upper New York State recently. This was of course before the gas shortage. They traveled down, not only to New York, but also to Washington, D.C., to visit President Woodfield of the United States organization. While in the nation's capital, Woodfield says, they visited and played with a senator, who is an ardent follower of the game. The senator was planning to attend a social function that night but put it off and played a match with one of the Canadians from the far northern part of our neighboring country.

Mexican is United States Champ

Fernando Isais, a Mexican, strangely enough, is champion of the United States. He won the title two years ago at Des Moines, Iowa, in the national tournament. The Iowa city usually is the site of the national tournament because of its central location. Pitchers from all parts of the United States are present. The national convention is held concurrently with the tournament. However, because of the war, the convention and the tournament have been postponed until better times.

To qualify for a national tournament, a pitcher must have a ringer average in the 80's. This means, according to horseshoe slang, a man must pitch 80 ringers out of 100 shoes. "Any dub can pitch an 80 percent game," Woodfield says, "but he can't do it consistently."

Nelson Triple Winner

Private Grant Nelson, who learned how to pitch 'em on a farm in Indiana, was the individual star of the day. The Camp Lee soldier won both the national junior and state singles titles and paired with Private J. H. Miller to take the state doubles title from Charles O. Jones and J. O. Gulbranson, 50-40, in the finals last night.

The junior national doubles title went to Jones and Gulbranson, both Richmond entries, as they defeated Privates Nelson and Miller, 50-46.

Private Vito Feliccia, of Camp Lee, former New York State titleholder, scored an upset by defeating "Boo" Henson of Washington in an exhibition match. Henson is seeded eighth among the amateurs of the nation, while Feliccia the titleholder at Camp Lee, is a professional.

Other results, showing round robin scores in games won and lost and the ringer percentages follow:

Exhibition Match

Vito Feliccia defeated "Boo" Henson three games to one: 28-50, 50-31, 50-42, 50-25.

1942 National Junior Doubles

Charles O. Jones and J. O. Gulbranson defeated Private Arthur St. Jean and Private Wayne Adkins, 50-18 and 54-22.

Private Grant Nelson and Private J.H. Miller, bye.

Jones and Gulbranson defeated Privates Nelson and Miller, 51-44.

1942 National AAU Junior Singles Championships

	Player	W	L	%
1.	Grant Nelson	7	0	62.1
2.	F. B. Duncan	6	1	47.4
3.	Charles O. Jones	4	3	50.6
4.	J. H. Oyler	4	3	44.5
5.	A. J. Schuyler	4	3	41.8
6.	J. H. Miller	2	5	34.9
7.	Woodrow Stone	1	6	39.6
8.	J. O. Gulbranson	0	7	45.2

1943

Start of Michigan Prominence

Our discussion of the 1943 AAU tournament begins with another section from the Lee Rose journals:

The National AAU Tournament was held at the Lincoln Park courts in Chicago on Sat., Sun. and Mon., September 4-5-6. Lundgren and I attended.

We left on Friday night, being lucky to get on a crowded bus and got to Chicago at 4:30 a.m. on Saturday. We got a room at the Bancroft Hotel and after 3 hours of sleep, arose and went to Lincoln Park on the streetcar. We both qualified for the finals in singles and doubles both.

On Sunday, Lundgren and I played in the doubles tournament "just for the fun of it." We played 7 games and we won our first 5 games to be the only undefeated team at that point. Then we lost to Arner Lindquist and his partner and then lost to Lindmeier and Woodhouse to tie for 2nd. We won the 3-way tie for second place by slaughtering Lindmeier and Woodhouse and then Danhauer and Loerzel.

We played two rounds of the singles that day also and Lundgren and I each won our two games easily.

On Monday, we resumed our play. We each won our first game in the morning, then we played each other. Lundgren won a nip and tuck struggle from me, 50-46. I lost another to Breen and later, one to Lindquist and one to Henn. Lundgren went through everybody until the second to last game, when he was upset by Burkhalter.

Lundgren tied for first and defeated Lindquist for the title in a single game playoff.

So that's Rose's account of the action. He gave away who won the championship, so there's no suspense on that front, but here's how the *Chicago Daily Times*, in article by Glenn Fairall, announced the event:

Shoe Stars Launch
U.S. Title Drive

National doubles and singles championships went on the block when the cream of the nation's horseshoe crop opened hostilities this morning in the three-day National AAU-*Times* [Athletic Association] horseshoe championships at the Lincoln Park courts, Clark and Wisconsin.

Equal interest centered on the two divisions of the meet as Arner Lindquist, Morgantown, W.Va., stepped out in defense of his 1942 crown and the Chicago doubles team of John Lindmeier and Dorne Woodhouse went after its third straight national two-man crown.

Blocking the paths of these title incumbents were a baker's dozen of Chicago's ablest tossers together with other noted flingers from Ohio, Indiana and points east. Lindmeier, recent winner of the state AAU [event] stood forth as a staunch challenger for Lindquist's singles crown and his doubles partner, Woodhouse, also was well backed in the one-man scramble.

The national singles champ was expected to encounter strong opposition from a soldier boy, Corp. Frank Breen, a member of the military police in the Chicago area. Breen finished runner-up to Lindmeier in the recent state tournament. Then there was William Danhauer of Chicago, third place finisher in the state and a member of a nautical championship doubles team three years ago.

Qualifying play started at 9:30 a.m. today and will continue throughout the day. Sixteen qualifiers in the singles class will start championship action tomorrow afternoon. Title play in both divisions will close on Monday.

And then they offered an update on the qualifying round:

Breen Cracks Shoe Record, Ties One

Soldier boy Frank Breen, a corporal in the military police, cracked one world's record qualifying [score] and tied another as he set the pace for early qualifiers in the National AAU–*Times* [Athletic Association] horseshoe pitching championships, which got underway yesterday at the Lincoln Park courts, Clark and Wisconsin.

The new record was entered in the books when Corp. Breen, in tossing 100 shoes, wrapped 25 consecutive ringers around the peg. He shattered his own world's record qualifying record of 23 perfect tosses in a row.

The military policeman also compiled 256 points with his 100 shoes to tie another world's record. Then, too, he engineered another rarity when he notched 43 ringers with his first 50 shoes. He failed to maintain the pace over the last half of the qualifying route, but finished with the enviable mark of 79 ringers in the 100 tosses.

Because of his brilliant display of qualifying shots, the corporal moved up among the leading challengers for the national singles crown now worn by Arner Lindquist of Morgantown, W.Va. He will also be in the thick of the firing for the U.S. doubles title held by the Chicago pair of John Lindmeier and Doran Woodhouse. Each member of the defending champions trio was included in the field which set off yesterday in the three-day event.

Qualifying play started at 9:30 a.m. yesterday and continued throughout the day. Sixteen qualifiers in the singles class started championship action at 10 a.m. today and doubles play will get under way this afternoon. Title play in both divisions will close tomorrow.

This next article includes some very interesting information, including a mention of the Central AAU junior tournament and updates about the senior event:

Shoe Hysteria Hits
Lincoln Courts

Horseshoe hysteria hit the Lincoln Park locality today and will linger in that vicinity until a national horseshoe tossing champion is crowned in the *Times*-sponsored National AAU tournament sometime Monday.

Today's excitement in the ringer-flipping business centered around the 17 and under novices—both boys and girls. Thirty-eight of these eager kids took over the Lincoln courts today to apply championship touches to the Central AAU–*Times* [Athletic Association] tournament, which opened last week.

Champions in four divisions will be crowned in the novice competition this afternoon and tonight. Exactly 20 district qualifiers in the junior boys' and girls' divisions started the fireworks at 2 o'clock today and 18 qualifiers in the intermediate boys' and girls' divisions will take over at 6:30 tonight.

A two-day lull in activities will follow today's showdown matches to be followed by the start of the National AAU title competition on Saturday at the same courts. Approximately 35 of the finest ringer-tossers in the nation will go after the national title now held by Arner Lindquist.

Lindquist will be here himself seeking to repeat in the role he earned last year at the national meet held in Kentucky. Disputing his right to the crown will be numerous foemen, including about 15 of the best shooters now operating in the Chicago vicinity.

Qualifying play on Saturday will be followed by play in singles and double on Sunday. The meet will close on Monday with the winner of the round robin event to be determined on a won-and-lost basis.

So thanks to this article we learn that an AAU junior tournament was being held and girls were to be included. It would have been nice if the article had been more specific and stated if some girls did actually participate (and, if so, how many). The winners of the junior competition were not announced in the *Chicago Daily Times* and I could find no other mentions. The description of it as a Central AAU junior event suggests it was larger than an Illinois state competition—it's likely there were competitors from a number of states involved. If that indeed was the case, it sure would have been helpful if the article had indicated that the event was a prelude to the National AAU junior tournament and had said where the national tournament would be held. Or if the national junior event had already happened, it might have stated that. To date, I have not been able to confirm whether or note there was a national junior tournament in 1943.

The senior championship, though, was won by a new and rather unknown pitcher who just happened to be Lee Rose's travel companion:

Detroiter Takes *Times*
National Horseshoe Title

The National AAU–*Times* [Athletic Association] national horseshoe meet closed yesterday in Lincoln Park with Carl Lundgren of Detroit besting the defending champion, Arner Lindquist, in a single game playoff, 50-27. They had been tied with 14 wins and a single loss after the regulation 15 games. While his opponent could gain no more than 30 ringers out of 62 tries, Lundgren threw 38.

However, in the 15-game round robin, Lindquist came up with an average percentage of 67.4 by tossing 473 perfect shoes in 789 attempts. In this competition, Cpl. Breen averaged 65.5% on 545 ringers out of 832 shoes thrown. The new singles champ's 520 ringers in 824 shoes pitched was good for an average percent of 63.8.

Military policeman Cpl. Frank Breen, whose record setting play set the pace early in the meet, was third.

In the doubles championship completed Saturday, Lindquist and his partner, Charles Grosselin also from Morgantown, emerged with the crown. John Lindmeier and Doran Woodhouse, the Chicago pair and defending titlist, could do no better than third, with Carl Lundgren and his shooting mate, Lee Rose of Detroit, finishing in second.

The following final results for the competition are incomplete, but are list the best information that research allowed.

1943 National AAU Men's Championship

	Player	City	W	L	%
1.	Carl E. Lundgren	Detroit, MI	15	1	63.8
2.	Arner Lindquist	Morgantown, WV	14	2	67.4
3.	Frank Breen	Elgin, IL			65.5
	Lee Rose	Detroit, MI			
	Dorne Woodhouse	Chicago, IL			
	Burkhalter				
	Harry Henn	Cold Spring, KY			

1943 National AAU Doubles Championship

	Player	City	W	L	%
1.	Arner Lindquist-	Morgantown, WV			
	Charles Grosselin	Morgantown, WV			
2	Lee Rose-	Detroit, MI			
	Carl E. Lundgren	Detroit, MI	7	2	
3.	John Lindmeier-	Oak Park, IL			
	Dorne Woodhouse	Chicago, IL	5	3	
4.	Wm. Danhauer-	Chicago, IL			
	Leonard Loerzel	Chicago, IL	5	3	

1944 was the final national tournament appearance by John Lindmeier, who garnered five gold medals in his six-year AAU career. He didn't appear in an NHPA-sponsored World Tournament until 1946, when he qualified for the men's championship class and placed tenth in the World with a winning record of 13 wins and 10 losses. He continued on to have a distinguished NHPA career, qualifying for the men's finals eight times. He earned a career ringer average of 73.63 percent, with five top-ten finishes. Lindmeier finished in fourth place in 1953 on 30-5 record, and in 1951 earned a fifth-place finish on a 25-10 record. In total, Lindmeier won 168 games, which means he still ranks 46th in all-time wins. He won four Illinois state championships: 1948, 1949, 1950, and 1955. Lindmeier has not been inducted to the NHPA Hall of Fame, but he deserves to be; he is on the ballot and hopefully in time he will receive that honor.

A final side note for 1943. On the August page of the 1943 *Amateur Athlete* calendar, the following appears: "Everett L. Martin, chairman of Ohio AAU Horseshoe Pitching reports he has a six-team league of girl horseshoe pitchers at the Norwood Municipal Courts. The National Junior Championship is scheduled for August 28–28, 1943, at the 12 Norwood Horseshoe Courts." My research has recovered no further details or results.

1944

The Flower of Detroit

Michigan, at this time, was a very competitive area for horseshoe pitching, so it's unsurprising that the 1944 National AAU event would be held in Detroit. Pitchers from Detroit won consecutive national amateur titles—Carl E. Lundgren in 1943 and Lee Rose in 1944. In fact, the next chapters we will read about three different Michigan pitchers winning three titles in a four-year period.

This is a most unusual chapter, not only do we have a participant's firsthand account of the event, but the participant was the event's champion, Lee Rose (aka Lee Jacobs). He may not have been well liked by his fellow players. Though, perhaps he might have been easier to get along with on days when he was winning rather than the days he lost. His journals reveal his extreme desire to win. He had a tremendous self-confidence. He even called himself the "Flower of Detroit," a derivative of his assumed surname. One of the reasons Michigan was a pitching powerhouse at the time was Rose's effort to promote horseshoe pitching at all levels of the sport. Even in the 1920s he made clear efforts to establish teams and league competition at a local level and then to expand local league play into local and state competitions.

A careful read of Rose's journals, which detail the tournaments he participated in, the question of what criteria determine amateur status arises again. By 1944, he was a nearly 20-year veteran of the sport who had earned the Michigan state championship in 1933 and again in 1944 and 1955 and twice qualified for the men's championship class at World Tournaments (1927 and 1928). At the 1935 World Tournament, he missed the cut off for the championship class, but qualified for class B (which was known as the dispatch tourney) and earned $5.00 for eleventh place. That $5.00, or any other prize money he may have won, doesn't make Rose a professional or nonamateur any more than any of the other talented pitchers of the day. There were very few trophy-only tournaments and most of pitching events needed to a small cash purse to draw any good pitchers—but that's another issue that will crop up later in this chapter.

There are a couple of brief newspaper articles tacked into his journal, but most of this chapter come from Rose's journal:

National AAU Tournament
Held at Northwestern Field Sept. 16–17

On September 15, the evening before the big meet, I went over to Northwestern Field for some practice and there was Sgt. Breen warming up. I played him 2 practice games and really poured it on him. I hit around 90% to drop him 50-18 and overcame him in another game 50-33, which must have gone 140 shoes, with me still crowding 90%.

September 16 was the qualifying and the doubles. I warmed up a while and then qualified with a 256, 80 ringers to tie Breen's national record. Latzko hit 79 ringers and 255 points.

Koppitch and I teamed up in the doubles, and only bad luck stopped us from taking the title! We just couldn't get started against Yorkison & Fagan and lost out. (Games were 50 shoes, count-all system.) After beating Breen and Manker, we lost a hard-luck game to Middletown & Sheppard. Then we went to town and knocked off 4 good teams—Lundgren & Otto, Lindquist & Grosselin, Latzko & Woodward and Kelly & Getz. We wound up tied for 1st with Latzko & Woodward. The playoff game was played under the lights and Koppitch and I were beaten.

Several of the pitchers were entertained by me at my house that evening, and most of the night.

Everything was set for the big finals on Sept. 17. Sixteen pitchers faced the barrier in 50-shoe count-all games. The day was hot and almost no wind at all—just perfect for the "tiger." A large crowd was on hand, even before play opened and heated speculation ran rampant as to who would win the meet. Chief choices were Latzko, Rose (or Jacobs, as he is known in AAU circles) and Lundgren, Breen and Lindquist.

Rose opened with Sheppard and had no trouble in coming out ahead. The second game with Manker of Ohio was just as easy. In the third game against Yorkison, Rose hit the high game of the entire day, scoring 133 points with 43 ringers out of 50 shoes. Grosselin was easy and then Rose struck his first snag in Middleton. Rose trailed most of the way. The game was played on the first court with people running through and interfering, making it very hard to rally. Rose tied the score on the last throw by hanging a double ringer over Middleton's leaner. The game went four extra innings. Rose galloped away with 4 straight doubles and finally won.

An hour of rest for lunch was called here and only Rose and Latzko were undefeated.

We came back from a light lunch, Rose had to face Arner Lindquist! Lindquist jumped right off in front and his slow way of pitching made it difficult to rally against him. Rose however, never wavered and even when things looked almost beyond recall, he kept bearing down. Then, near the end, Lindquist weakened and the Detroit ringer machine was quick to slip ahead and squeeze out a win, 103 to 101.

The 7th game, against Hirschman, was easy after 20 shoes and then came Breen. Rose tore into Breen early and ran up a lead and then sat back and defended it stoutly against the soldier's desperate rallies. Breen fell just a little short. Lindquist upset Latzko in this round and Rose stood alone at the top.

Kelly was the next victim of Rose, being powered under early by a flood of doubles. Rose was really going to town as he scented a national title in the offing. He met Getz in the 10th game and Getz jumped off to a lead at the start. Photographers were trying to snap pictures of Rose as he tried to catch up and that made things almost bad enough to cause Rose to blow up. But he didn't blow—instead, he came on with a consecutive drive of doubles that soon caught Getz and snowed him under.

Lundgren fired a broadside at Latzko in this round and bounced him down. This left Rose 2 games in front and 5 to go.

An immense crowd surrounded the courts. Persons who hadn't been around for years were to be seen. Harold Arnold, Joe Galesky, Ed Levagood and Sherer showed up. Stanley David and Johnny Schultz were there.

Fitzgerald and Konz of Toledo were there. Greenfield, Goodell, Ingraham and others from Clark Park were there. Even E. L. Holmes, a schoolteacher back in Western High in 1921–25, came around to say hello.

Pekkala was easy in the 11th game and then came the Rose-Latzko clash. Latzko pitched a very good game, the game of a man who is very desperate and getting an early lead over Rose, he clung to it all the way and won out.

This enlivened the situation to a great extent as Rose now had Miller, Lundgren and Otto to play and had to win them all to keep out in front. The story of these last three games Rose played cannot adequately be put into words! With an immense following crowded around his court and following his every pitch, the "Flower of Detroit" put on a show that has few equals in history.

Rose showered on 40 out of 50 to run a hard-fighting Miller to the ground, then hit 39 out of 50 to swamp Lundgren. Then back to the hazardous 1st court, he tossed a thunderous barrage of 41 out of 50 to smash down Otto and become the NATIONAL CHAMPION!!!

In all these last games, Rose was the perfect horseshoe machine and indeed all through the tournament, never once gave vent to any temperamental outburst that had distinguished him in the past.

His manner was outwardly a cool, collected, icy-cold, machine-like attitude, fortified by a never-say-die quality that kept him coming over the rough spots. Mechanically, his pitching was beautiful, a high wobbly shoe that just seemed to adore the stake.

A just reward for a great pitcher!

Wow! We'd be hard-pressed to find an event account any more personal than that. One could safely say that Lee Jacobs was a competitive soul and rather proud of his accomplishments. A newspaper clipping included in his journal reads:

'Shoe Title Stays Here

Lee Jacobs, who began pitching horseshoe 25 years ago when he was 13 years old, finally crashed the elusive national championship circle yesterday, winning the AAU singles title at Northwestern Field.

A lathe operator at the Ford Motor Co., Jacobs triumphed in 14 of his 15 matches, edging out Joseph P. Latzko, of Flint, by a margin of one match. The latter, who handed the new champion his lone setback, won 13 and lost two.

Third place went to Arner Lindquist, while Carl Lundgren, last year's titleholder, took fourth place from Sgt. Frank Breen, after the two had finished in a tie.

Sixteen contestants out of a field of 23 qualified for the finals. The competition was staged under the direction of George D. Chumard, Cincinnati, AAU horseshoe chairman.

Championship medals were presented to the first three place winners.

While the issue of eligibility for amateur play may have arisen for the occasional player, there are no accounts of a specific challenges about a player's amateur status before this news clipping included in Rose's journal that reports a challenge to our newfound hero:

Horseshoers Called Pros

Professionalism charges were brought against Lee Jacobs of Detroit and Joe Latzko after they placed one-two in the National AAU horseshoe pitching tournament at Northwestern Field Sunday.

It was charged that Jacobs, who won 14 and lost 1 yesterday, had played in a tournament in Port Huron a month ago. Latzko is second with 13 and 2 was in the same meet, it is said.

Arner Lindquist of Morgantown, W.Va. and Frank Breen, of Elgin, Ill., were tied for third with 11 and 4 and will play off for the title if Jacobs and Latzko are disqualified. Jonas and Carl Lundgren, both of Detroit were next with 11 and 4.

Joe Kelly of Saginaw and Otto Woodward of Flint also are charged with playing in the pro meet.

Similar charges may have been leveled after contests or events in future years, but this is the first and only documented case that has turned up in my research. It's intriguing that Rose thought enough of the article to clip it out and tack it in his journal. Who brought the charge forward? It's unlikely that it was a player who had participated in the event, because they no doubt would have brought the charge forward when Rose entered the contest. It's unlikely that it was any of the leading players; they were from out of the area and wouldn't have been aware of which tournaments Rose or any other Michigan-based players had participated in. Regardless of the source, nothing must have come of the challenge since Rose is still the recorded winner, and he was allowed to participate in other AAU tournaments. Latzko not only played in other events, he won the national championship in 1946. The article doesn't accurately report the final standings, but that information will be clarified in the official final standings report.

Here is how Lee Rose recorded the tournament results in his journal:

1944 Senior AAU Horseshoe Pitching Championship Tournament—Singles and Doubles, under the auspices of the City of Detroit, Department Parks and Recreation, at Northwestern Playfield, Grand River & Wreford, Detroit, Mich., Saturday and Sunday, September 16–17, 1944.

1944 National AAU Singles Final Standing

Place	Player	Qual	R	Pts	SP	R	%	W	L
1.	Lee Jacobs, Detroit	256	80	1728	750	520	69	14	1
2.	Joe Latzko, Flint	255	77	1666	750	511	68	13	2
3.	Arner, Lindquist, W.Va.	245	74	1634	750	462	62	11	4
4.	Cark Lundgren, Detroit	DC		1490	750	435	57	10	5
5.	Frank Breen, Elgin, Ill.	237	73	1433	750	421	56	10	5
6.	Jonas Otto, Ann Arbor	220	64	1497	750	434	58	10	5
7.	Andrew Yorkison, Detroit	210	60	1464	750	403	54	9	6
8.	Ed Woodward, Flint	204	58	1522	750	439	59	9	6
9.	Joe Kelly, Detroit	219	63	1432	750	399	53	8	7
10.	Stanley Manker, Ohio	238	72	1518	750	443	59	7	8
11.	Charles Grosselin W.Va.	222	64	1345	750	356	48	6	9
12.	Norris Shepard, Flint	219	63	1262	750	348	46	6	9
13.	Alfred Pekkala, Detroit	208	58	1300	750	344	44	3	12
14.	B. Hirschman, Saginaw	203	53	1288	750	336	45	3	12
15.	B. Getz, Ferndale	202	53	1291	750	341	45	2	13
16.	Roy Middleton, Flint	206	59	931	600	247	41	1	14
					11,850	6,439	54.34%		

(Note: Middleton withdrew after 13th round of play.)
(Jacob's 256 qualifying score equals the National AAU record. 133 high individual score for one game, set by Jacobs, 3rd round.)

Non qualifiers as follows:

Ed Wall, Detroit	250	76

(3rd high qualifier—failed to show up in time for finals)

Harry Henn, Cold Spring, Ky.	198	57
Frank Koppitch	187	53
Harley Rizor, Toledo, Ohio	185	49
Henry Zessin, Saginaw	182	
Joe W. Fagan, Detroit	162	42
Lin Roberts, Detroit	102	15

Doubles Competition – Final Standing

Place	Players	Pts	SP	R	%	W	L
1.	Ed Woodward – Joe Latzko	863	350	239	68	6	2
2.	Lee Jacobs – Frank Koppitch	788	350	230	66	6	2
3.	Frank Breen – Stan Manker	783	350	215	61	5	3
4.	Jonas Otto – Carl Lundgren	794	350	228	65	5	3
5.	Arner Lindquist – C. Grosselin	715	350	175	50	3	5
6.	Joe Fagin – Andrew Yorkison	641	350	168	48	3	5
7.	Ray Middleton – N. E. Shepard	648	350	191	55	2	6
8.	Joe Kelly – B. Getz	699	350	196	56	2	6

(Note: Finals standings in doubles listed as result of playoffs to break ties.)

1945

Back to Ohio with a Hometown Hero

Lee Rose did not write much about the 1945 National AAU tournament, but journal records that he did attend. His entry doesn't command much interest, but his single paragraph does indicate that the tournament was held in Norwood, Ohio. Other research failed to turn up either the dates or site of the 1945 event. The Cincinnati newspapers carried good coverage. The first announcement was on September 2nd:

Tourney at Norwood

Entry blanks have been mailed for the Senior National AAU horseshoe pitching championships at Norwood Municipal Horseshoe Courts, Allison and Sherman Aves., September 22–23. The tourney will be conducted in connection with the Ohio AAU championship meet. Defending singles champion is Lee Rose, Detroit. Jim Johnson, Ludlow, Ky., is the defending Ohio AAU champion.

Then on September 19th:

Horseshoe Meet Opens Saturday

Norwood Municipal Horseshoe Courts will be the scene of the National Senior AAU horseshoe pitching champion tournament Saturday and Sunday.

A crew of men, under Norwood City Engineer Al Ellis, Recreation Director H. C. Dillion and Leo McGrath, president of the Norwood Horseshoe Club, have been putting the courts in shape for the feature horseshoe attraction and they compare favorably with any court in the country, according to those who have seen the best. Ten courts comprise the Norwood layout.

The entry of Sgt. Frank Breen of the U.S. Military Police, Chicago, was received for the national tournament Tuesday, G. D. Chumard, chairman of the national committee, stated. Breen's civilian address is Elgin, Ill., where he is a member of the Watch City Horseshoe Club, one of the leading clubs of the Mid-West. Breen is co-holder with two others for the high qualifying score in the national tournament. The mark is 256 points out of a possible 300.

Missing from the list of entries will be that of 79-year-old George Everhard of Linwood, who qualified last year for the final round robin competition of the state tournament. Everhard will be on hand as a spectator and may pitch a few games but the tough tournament grind is a little too much for his age, he contends.

The entries include the 1943 and 1944 singles champions, Carl Lundgren and Lee Jacobs. Arner Lindquist, the 1942 champion, has also entered.

The double tournament schedule calls for qualifying competition in both to get underway Saturday at 1 p.m. Saturday, doubles in both at 4 p.m. Saturday, final round robin in the state tournament 9 a.m. Sunday and final round robin in the national at 1 p.m. Sunday.

The mention of Leo McGrath is a surprise in the coverage. Those who knew Leo McGrath personally can attest that he was always involved in the sport, working and helping. McGrath was born in 1903, so he would have been 42 years old in 1945. He was part of the NHPA scene in the 1960s and 1970s as a very active worker and he was a strong promoter of the sport for over 50 years. He served as president of the Buckeye Horseshoe Pitchers Association of Ohio for 27 years, from 1955 until 1982. That alone is an extraordinary service accomplishment. McGrath was elected NHPA's vice president in 1969. He is a charter member of the Ohio HPA Hall of Fame and was inducted to the NHPA Hall of Fame in 1974. McGrath passed away in 2000 at age 98.

The September 23rd edition of *Cincinnati Enquirer* reported on the start of the tournament:

West Virginian High in Qualifying Round of Horseshoe Pitching Tournament

Arner Lindquist of Morgantown, W. Va., was the high qualifier in the National Senior AAU Horseshoe Pitching Tournament yesterday at Norwood Municipal Court with a score of 235, one point more than Jim Johnson of Ludlow, Ky., which gave the latter the high qualifying score for the Ohio AAU championship tournament. In third place was Joe Latzko of Flint, Michigan, with 232 and Ralph Lackey of West Middletown, Ohio, fourth, 228.

In the finals of the doubles championships there was a four-way tie at the completion of sixth rounds of play: Joe Latzko and Ed Woodward of Flint, Michigan, Charles Grosselin and Arner Lindquist of Morgantown, W. Va., Jim Johnson and H. MacPhearson of Covington and Carl Lundgren, Detroit and Jonas Otto, Ann Arbor, Michigan.

And then the announcement of the new champion for 1945:

Ludlow Man Wins Title

Jim Johnson, Ludlow, Ky., won the National Senior AAU Horseshoe Pitching Championship at Norwood Municipal Courts Sunday. The matches were held under the auspices of the Norwood Horseshoe Club and the Norwood Recreation Commission.

Johnson also retained his Ohio AAU singles title and with Harold MacPhearson, Covington, won the Ohio AAU doubles championship. The two finished third in the national senior doubles. Johnson was also second high qualifier in the national tournament and high qualifier in the Ohio AAU.

He won 14 out of 15 games in the final round, his only loss coming at the hands of Lee Jacobs, Detroit, 1944 champions, who finished second this year. Jacobs, who had two losses, outscored Johnson on total points and ringer percentage.

Stanley Manker, Chillicothe, in third place and Joe Latzko, Flint Mich., also outscored Johnson on Ringer percentage, but in the final analysis the winner had most games won, which is what counts.

Arner Lindquist and Charles Grosselin won the doubles title in a three-way playoff. Charles Hills, Hamilton, and 74-year-old Guy Morgan, Middletown, were dethroned as Ohio AAU doubles champs by Johnson and MacPhearson.

It was estimated approximately 2,000 spectators drifted in and out during the 11 hours of play Sunday morning, afternoon and night.

The winner, James "Pops" Johnson, has an interesting story. He had a Kentucky address in 1945, but the AAU still allowed him to participate in the Ohio state competition. He was probably a long-time member of the Norwood Club—Ludlow, Kentucky, and Norwood, Ohio, are border towns. I wonder how the other Ohio players felt about the situation. Perhaps they felt he was one of their own rather than an opportunist. In 1964, he Johnson relocated from Kentucky to Cincinnati, Ohio. Before moving, Johnson won four consecutive state championships in Kentucky, 1947 through 1950.

Johnson went on to play in NHPA events, qualifying ten times for the men's championship class finals from 1948 through 1966. In his first year, 1948, he averaged 78.2 percent ringers and won 19 games, placing eleventh in the world standings. Johnson had just one top-ten finish, when he placed sixth, averaging 77.4 percent. In 1974, Pops was the intermediate men's world champion, going undefeated (7-0) in the finals with a 67.7 percent ringer average.

Pops Johnson was elected NHPA's vice president in 1961 and served on the hall of fame committee for ten years. Johnson was inducted to NHPA Hall of Fame in 1985, is a charter member of the Kentucky Horseshoe Pitchers Hall of Fame, and is also a member of the Ohio Horseshoe Pitchers Hall of Fame.

1945 National AAU Singles Final Standings

Place	Player	City	W	L	%
1.	James "Pop" Johnson	Ludlow, Ky.	14	1	58.5%
2.	Lee Jacobs	Detroit, Mich.	13	2	
3.	Stanley Manker	Chillicothe, Ohio			
4.	Joe Latzko	Flint, Michigan			
5.	Ralph Lackey	Middletown, Ohio			
6.	Arner Lindquist	Morgantown, W.Va.			
7.	Frank Breen	Elgin, Illinois			
	Mulroy				

1945 National AAU Doubles Final Standings

1. Arner Lindquist & Charles Grosselin, Morgantown, W.Va.
2. Carl Lundgren, Detroit & Jonas Otto, Ann Arbor, Michigan
3. James Johnson Ludlow & Harold MacPhearson, Covington, Ky.
4. Joe Latzko & Ed Woodward, Flint, Michigan

The final standings are incomplete, but reflect all the information that has been recovered. At least Rose's journal provided the event location. That information was the only lead that allowed me to find this much data on the event. His journal recounts just how close he came to winning for a second consecutive year: "I lost the National AAU title in Norwood, Ohio, to James Johnson. I was the only one to defeat him, but I lost to Manker and Mulroy, each by one point. The games were 50 shoe count-all."

This was the final AAU event for Arner Lindquist, the 1945 sixth-place singles finisher and half of the first-place doubles team. In all, Lindquist won three gold medals, two silver medals and two bronze medals. In 1942, at the age of 46, Lindquist became the oldest national champion to that point. He went on to win five West Virginia state championships: 1949, 1950, 1953, 1956, and 1957. His career continued with his participation in NHPA World Tournaments. From 1946 to 1965, Lindquist qualified 11 times for the men's championship finals, winning 154 games which still ranks 52nd on the list of all-time wins. His highest finish was in 1946 when he placed seventh on a 16-7 record. He had another top-ten finish in 1950, when he placed ninth. His best overall season record was in 1957, when he averaged 74.28 percent ringers, had a record of 17-13, and placed twelfth.

Lindquist worked hard to promote horseshoe pitching. In 1955, the NHPA initiated its program of having regional directors lead the promotion of the sport, and Lindquist was one of the original seven regional directors. His wife Anna was the women's world champion in 1948 and 1949 and she was elected NHPA's vice president in 1953. Arner Lindquist has not been elected to the NHPA Hall of Fame, but he is on the ballot and hopefully in time he will get the nod and the public recognition he deserves.

1946

Ohio Again, But a New Champion

We can let the words of Lee Rose set the tone for the 1946 AAU event:

> The 1946 National AAU Tournament was held at Norwood, Ohio. Intermittent rain and cold weather made things bad.
>
> I didn't do so good in the meet, but had the pleasure of knocking off the defending champion Jimmy Johnson after he had won 13 straight games. This put him in a tie with Joe Latzko and when Joe nosed out Johnson, he became the new champ!
>
> So much for 1946.

The *Cincinnati Times-Star* provided thorough coverage starting on September 18, 1946:

West Manchester Youth
In Horseshoe Tournament

The entry of 12-year-old Jacob Hoff of West Manchester, Ohio, was received for the National Senior AAU Horseshoe Pitching Championship Tournament to be held Saturday and Sunday at Norwood Horseshoe Courts, under the auspices of the Norwood Recreation Commission and the Norwood Horseshoe Club. Hoff consistently has been averaging over 60 percent ringers.

Another entrant in the national event is that of Carl Smith of Deer Park, who will also compete in the Ohio AAU Championships, to be held simultaneously with the national event.

Qualifying competition will get under way at 1 p.m. Finals in the doubles start at 4 p.m. Saturday, September 21st.

And then on September 20th, the *Cincinnati Times-Star* printed:

Norwood Mayor to Open Tourney

Mayor Frank J. Ward of Norwood will welcome the contestants and pitch the first shoe opening the 1946 National Senior AAU Horseshoe pitching Championships Saturday and Sunday at the Norwood Horseshoe courts.

The national championship tournament was first held in Cincinnati in 1937 and since then New York, Anderson, Ind., Detroit; Chicago and Louisville have been scenes of this event.

The program of events call for qualifying competition to get under was Saturday at 1 p.m., finals in the doubles Saturday at 4 p.m. and the top 16 qualifiers will play the singles round robin all day Sunday starting at 9 a.m.

It is estimated a total of 20,000 shoes will be pitched before nightfall Sunday night and considering the caliber of the contestants over 50 percent of the shoes pitched will be ringers.

National AAU horseshoe pitching records are: High qualifying score, 256 points held by three players, John Lindmeier, Frank Breen and Lee Rose; most consecutive ringer, 21 held by John Lindmeier; high score single 50 shoe game, 133 out of possible 150 held Frank Breen

Lee Hayes will serve as tournament referee; Chester Dumford, official scorer; Al Keller, Ed Sullivan, J. Hayes and George Grainger, judge of disputed shoes; Art Reno and Ben Hagedorn, statisticians.

And then, from the September 23rd edition of the *Cincinnati Post*:

Shoe Champs Are Crowned

Joseph P. Latzko of Flint, Michigan, won the 1946 Senior National AAU Horseshoe Pitching Championship Sunday at Norwood Municipal Horseshoe Courts from a field of over 30 entrants. The Michigan boy won 17 of his 19 final round robin games.

In qualifying Saturday for the finals, Latzko set a new National AAU mark of 262, exceeding the old mark of 256 held by jointly by three pitchers. He also set a new mark of 36 ringers, in a 50-shoe game.

Jim Johnson, 1945 winner, was second, winning 16 of 19 games. Stanley Manker was third and Ralph Lackey fourth. Tied for fifth place were 12 year old Jacob Hoff and his father Charles Hoff. However, on ringer percentage basis fifth place went to the elder Hoff and sixth place to the youngster.

Action of the 1946 Event

Scoreboard for the 1946 Event

Officials of the 1946 Tournament; Leo McGrath is on the right.

Ralph Lackey and June Marcum of Hamilton won the National AAU doubles title, finishing in a tie for first place with Latzko and Ed Wood-house, [and then] winning in a play-off. Johnson retained his Ohio AAU title, with the Ohio AAU doubles title going to Lackey and Marcum.

1946 National AAU Singles Championship Finals

Place	Player	City	W	L
1.	Joe Latzko	Flint, Michigan	17	2
2.	James Johnson	Ludlow, Kentucky	16	3
3.	Stanley Manker	Chillicothe, Ohio		
4.	Ralph Lackey	Middletown, Ohio		
5.	Charles Hoff	West Manchester, Ohio		
6.	Jacob Hoff	West Manchester, Ohio		
	Lee Rose	Detroit, Michigan		

1946 National AAU Senior Doubles Championship Finals

Place	Player	City
1.	Ralph Lackey & June Marcum,	Hamilton, Ohio
2.	Joe Latzko & Ed Woodward,	Flint, Michigan
6.	Harry Henn,	Cold Spring, Ky.
	& Guy Morgan,	Hamilton, Ohio

The available records listed only seven of the players in the singles finals, but by the win-loss record for Latzko, we can surmise that there was a 20-player class. The photo shown in this chapter lists all the 20 players as of the fourth round. So here are the other 13 players so they can be part of the AAU history: H. Seibert, H. Henn, Jonas Otto, N. Thompson, Harold McPherson, E. Tishock, Paul Focht, June Marcum, L. Reuther, C. Smith, H. Wolfe, J. Gouvenal, and Ed Woodward.

Amateur Athlete magazine, a publication of the AAU, had a small article about the event with no final standings or stats. The article, written by George D. Chumard, vice chairman of the Horseshoe Pitching Committee, provides some additional information:

> Seventy-five-year-old Guy Morgan of Hamilton, Ohio, was a contestant but failed to qualify for the final round robin, but with his partner Harry Henn, placed sixth in the doubles. Incidentally, Johnson, the 1945 winner, had the high ringer percentage for the tournament at 68%.

How unfortunate that the remaining teams in the doubles competition weren't noted in any of the newspaper articles or in *Amateur Athlete* account written by Chumard, who as vice chairman surely had record of all the pitchers. A central goal of the research for this book was to be able to at least list all the players involved, even if the finals stats might be unavailable. The incomplete records for 1946 fall short of that goal.

The first five years of the National AAU Horseshoe Pitching Championship were dominated by two players—John Lindmeier and Hubert Trinkle. Now, in the last five consecutive years, a new champion has emerged and three of the last four champions hailed from Michigan.

The 1946 tournament was Ralph Lackey's second and final appearance in an AAU tournament. Lackey was one of the better Ohio pitchers to ever participate in the AAU games. He won four Ohio state championships: 1948 on an 18-1 record, while averaging 76.2 percent ringers; and 1950, 1951, and 1952, in which he averaged over 70 percent ringers in each event. In 1962, in his only appearance at an NHPA World Tournament, at age 57, Lackey tied with Floyd Toole for the 36th and final qualifying position with 492 points, but lost out on qualifying in a playoff game. In future years, Floyd Toole went on to win a couple of National AAU championships and was inducted to the NHPA Hall of Fame in 1981.

Stan Manker also played his final AAU event in 1946 and went on to have an illustrious NHPA career, both as a pitcher and promoter. His achievements were recognized with his induction to the NHPA Hall of Fame in 1977. Manker qualified 11 times for the World Tournament men's finals from 1955 through 1970. His pitching feats include the state championship of Ohio in 1955. His best tournament was in 1968 when he averaged 75.1 percent ringers, though he still had a losing record in this highly competitive event, ending up with a 16-19 record and placing 20th overall. His career highlight was winning the senior men's world championship a record five times, the last one in 1979 after a playoff. Five titles remains the all-time record for the senior men's division; Manker shares that record with John Paxton.

For several decades, the Ohio Horseshoe Company produced a popular style of tournament pitching shoes, and Stan Manker was the official national distributor of the Ohio horseshoes.

1947

No Event Information Available

In my research so far, I have been unable to locate results for a 1947 AAU event. The November 1947 issue of the AAU's *Amateur Athlete* includes a list of 1947 national champions and horseshoe pitching singles and doubles are on the list, but with no entries. If a scheduled event was canceled due to weather, there was no indication on the list. There is a chance that no event was scheduled, but then horseshoe pitching probably wouldn't be on the list at all. There is the possibility that the event was on the calendar and was held, but no results were turned in for reporting in *Amateur Athlete*. If that's the case, it's unfortunate that the tournament's intended site wasn't printed on the calendar. In that case, a search of the host city's newspapers might have filled in many of the missing details.

1948

No Tournament Held

I could find no explanation given as to why no tournament was held in 1948, but generally this type of development boils down to the event being cancelled due to inclement weather, a lack of event organization, or no event chairman to schedule and conduct the tournament. Occasionally through the years, tournament plans have been made and put into motion, but the venue suddenly becomes unavailable and no time remains to locate a new event site. We probably will never know the actual reason for lack of a 1948 AAU tournament.

1949

The Start of a String in Baltimore

1949 was the beginning of a five-year period in which four National AAU championships were held in Baltimore. These circumstances could have served East Coast pitchers well. It's likely the reason for the repetition was that "C. W. Doc" Ashley, the AAU chairman for horseshoe pitching, was a Baltimore resident. He didn't see that the event circulated to various locations around the country, as had been the case previously. The unfortunate consequences of this circumstance become clear when you review the home cities of the participants, most of whom were from Maryland. The statistics show that the skill level of the entrants was lower than most previous events and certainly than the events that follow. A summary of the 1949 championship, held on August 27th and 28th of that year, was printed in the AAU's *Amateur Athlete* and the *Baltimore Sun* provided more of the details. From *Amateur Athlete*:

Dale Carson Wins
Horseshoe Crown

Dale Carson, representing the 21st Ward Democratic Club of Baltimore won the National AAU Singles Horseshoe Pitching Championship held at Gwynn Oak Park, in Baltimore on August 27 and 28.

Carson tossed 166 ringers, 59 double ringers and scored 369 points in eight games. Having pitched 228 shoes, he had a ringer percentage of 72.8%. Elmer Swartz of Annandale, Va., was second and Jene Durham of the United Democratic Club of Baltimore wound up in third position.

The doubles crown was captured by Clarence Stem and Albert Reinbold of the Forest and Stream Club of Westminster. Their teammates Harry Flohr and Oliver Spencer, were second with Edward Perrott and Earl Grace of the Berkshire Ringer Club of Baltimore, were third.

Arthur Price, President of the South Atlantic Association, presented trophies to Dr. Hugh Stephenson, of St. Louis, Mo., the contestant coming from the most distant point; Minor D. Donnell, 15 years old, of Hagerstown, Md., the youngest pitcher and Oliver Spencer, Westminster Forest & Stream Club, 68 years of age, the oldest player.

Dale Carson put on the most dominating performance ever in an AAU finals. Not only did he go undefeated, five opponents of his opponents never exceeded four points and only two players scored in double figures against him. One player scored 10 and the other scored just 16 points. He outscored his seven opponents 369 to 36. The scores of Carson's games follow:

Carson's score	Opponent & score
52	Perrrott, 4
50	Dr. Stephenson, 10
55	Schwartz. 4
54	Minor C. Donnell, 1
52	Durham, 16
55	Biderbrook, 1
51	Minor D. Donnell, 0
369	36

1949 National AAU Senior Championship Finals

	Player	City	W	L	%
1.	Dale Carson	Baltimore, MD	7	0	72.9
2.	Elmer Swartz	Annandale, MD			
3.	Jene Durham	Baltimore, MD			
	Dr. Hugh Stephenson	St. Louis, MO			
	Edward Perrott	Baltimore, MD			
	Minor D. Donnell	Hagerstown, MD			
	Pete Biderbrook	Baltimore, MD			
	Minor C. Donnell	Hagerstown, MD			

1949 National AAU Senior Doubles Championship Finals

	Players	City
1.	Clarence Stem & Albert Rumbold	Westminster, MD
2.	Harry Flohr & Oliver Spencer	Westminster, MD
3.	Edward Perrott & Earl Grace	Baltimore, MD

1949 marked Dale Carson's first appearance in a national championship, but he certainly was not new to the game. He was Pennsylvania's state champion in 1936. Starting in 1950, he earned the Maryland state championship 20 times, 1950–65 and again from 1967–77. These statistics are impressive, but they become even more amazing when you consider that at the 1949 AAU meet, Carson was already 45 years old. Carson played against all the great players of his day and even pitched exhibitions in front of President Harry Truman. He did not participate in many NHPA World Tournaments. In fact, only one time did he qualify for a championship class final—in 1969, when he finished 25th overall while pitching 71.8 percent. Carson was inducted to the NHPA Hall of Fame in 1976.

Another rookie pitching in his first AAU Championship was Elmer "Dutch" Swartz, at age 38. Swartz was active in World Tournaments, but not until around 1976, when he was well over 50 years old. No doubt the highlight of his pitching career was winning a world championship by capturing the 1984 intermediate men's crown. At that time, the intermediate division was for pitchers between the ages of 60 and 65. Swartz qualified for the championship class as the ninth seed, but survived the two days of competition and won the title on a 9-2 record while pitching 55 percent ringers, the lowest average to ever win the title in that division. Swartz didn't have the highest average of the group (in fact, three other players had a slightly higher average), but Dutch won more of his games.

This is a good spot to take a look at what was going on in the NHPA. This was a significant time for the organization and the World Horseshoe Pitching Tournament. The NHPA's World Tournament was being held in Murray, Utah, in 1950 for the third time in four years. It was held in Murray for 11 consecutive years, from 1949 through 1959. Not only was Murray one of the most beautiful settings for the annual horseshoe-pitching spectacle, during these years, the competition seemed keener than at any point in the sport's history. Stronger than the National AAU events? Most definitely. A couple of the AAU graduates were making their mark at the NHPA's tournaments in Murray, too— John Lindmeier and Arner Lindquist.

There was a difference in the skill levels of the AAU and NHPA members. While the National AAU had hosted annual events from their start in 1937 to the present (with the exception of 1948 and, possibly, 1947), the NHPA was finally showing a renewed sense of stability and a much stronger field of competition. For example, the AAU had had only one player average 70 percent ringers in a complete tournament until Dale Carson's 72 percent performance in 1949. At the World Tournament in 1949, three players averaged over 80 percent out of the 36-player championship class and another seven averaged 75 percent or better. In the 1950 World Tournament, three players averaged over 80 percent ringers while another 11 pitchers averaged more than 70 percent.

Was there competition between the two organizations? Not in the least. Of the 36 finalists in the 1949 World Tournament, only six players were from states east of the Mississippi River. Since all of the AAU events were east of the Mississippi, it was good for the sport that the AAU continued to host the national amateur championship. The national amateur championships weren't held in a state west of the Mississippi until 1962. Another important aspect of the compatibility of the AAU and the NHPA was the AAU's commitment to junior events, which cultivated the next generation of pitchers. The NHPA did not reestablish a junior division until 1951.

1950

Hall of Famer Retains Title

Much of the 1950 National AAU championship remained the same as the previous contest: same city, same champion. The *Baltimore Sun* gave a preview of action on the tournament's opening day, September 17th:

National Crowns at Stake Today
at Carroll Park

Singles and doubles championships will be decided today when the annual National AAU horseshoe pitching tournament concludes on the Carroll Park courts. Starting time is at 1 p.m.

Dale Carson of the Twenty-first Ward Democratic Club is defending champion in the singles division and will be favored to keep the crown he won in the tournament here last year. Al Rumbold and Clarence Stem, of Westminster, will attempt to keep the doubles title.

A number of prize awards are to be presented after competition is concluded. The singles titlist receives the Governor of Maryland's trophy, the doubles winners the Mayor D'Alesandro Trophy, plus a number of other medals which the second and third place finishers will be given.

Other awards, already listed for presentation, include the "Doc" Ashley Trophy to Dr. Hugh Stevenson, Jr., of Columbia, Mo., for the man coming the greatest distance; the George Miller Trophy to Kenneth W. Nichols as the youngest contestant and the Hon. Elmer Thater Trophy to the oldest participant.

In addition, the Charles Buckley Trophy goes to the contestant who makes the highest ringer percentage.

This finals coverage is from the October 1950 issue of *Amateur Athlete*:

Dale Carson Retains Horseshoe Crown

Twelve singles entrants and 5 doubles teams appeared at the newly built Carroll Park Courts in Baltimore, Maryland, Saturday, September 16 to qualify for the National AAU Horseshoe pitching championships. Thirteen individuals won the right to play in the round robin tournament on Sunday, and from 1 p.m. to 7:15 p.m., these men tossed a total weight of 10,600 pounds of steel when they threw 4,240 horseshoes, each weighing 2½ pounds.

Dale Carson retained his title won in 1949 by winning all seven of his games and added another record to his last year's ringer percentage record for all games of 72.5% when he tossed 38 ringers, 10 doubles ringers out of 46 shoes for a single game record in AAU competition of 82.6%. In the seven games this year Carson made 358 points and threw 205 ringers, 68 double ringers out of 284 shoes for a ringer percentage of 71.8% for the tournament.

Mr. Albert Wheltle, president of the Amateur Athlete Union of the United States, on behalf of Governor William Preston Lane, presented Dale with the Governors Trophy and the AAU gold medal. Then Mr. Walter R. Wilson, Metropolitan Club, Washington, D.C., received the second place medal and his teammate Willard Nellis, received the bronze medal.

"Doc" Ashley, AAU Horseshoe Pitching Chairman, then presented the Mayor Thomas D'Alesandro Trophy to the winning doubles team of Clarence Stem and Albert Reinbold. West A.A. of Westminster, Md., who retained their title. This doubles championship was very close and required a play-off game to decide first place and another to pick the third place winner. For example, after all the games were completed, Westminster "A" team had scored 231 points, 127 ringers, 24 double ringers out of 308 shoes pitched and the Washington, D.C. "A" team has 227, 127 ringers, 26 double ringers out of 308 shoes. Westminster "B" team won third place when they won the playoff game, although the Washington "B" team had a total score and ringer percentage higher than Westminster in all games.

"Pop"Woodfield, chairman of the District of Columbia Horseshoe Pitching Committee, entered the tournament and won the Hon. Elmer Thater trophy for the oldest contestant—73 years of age. Dale Carson also won the Charles Buckley trophy for scoring the highest percentage of ringers.

Scores of the individual games:

Round One –	Carson 50 – Nellis 5	Wilson 53 – Perrott 14
	Clift 53 – Stephenson 16	Jones 50 – Cotton 14
Round Two –	Carson 50 – Jones 14	Clift 50 – Perrott 18
	Wilson 50 – Stephenson 8	Nellis 55 – Cotton 41
Round Three –	Wilson 50 – Cliff 29	Perrott 52 – Stephenson 20
	Carson 50 – Cotton 1	Nellis 52 – Jones 22
Round Four –	Carson 55 – Perrott 4	Clift 50 – Jones 29
	Wilson 51 – Nellis 47	Cotton 50 – Stephenson 32
Round Five –	Jones 53 – Perrott 27	Carson 52 – Stephenson 3
	Nellis 52 – Clift 33	Wilson 51 – Cotton 3
Round Six –	Nellis 50 – Perrott 26	Jones 50 – Stephenson 21
	Clift 52 – Cotton 8	Carson 50 – Wilson 19
Round Seven –	Nellis 50 – Stephenson 9	Wilson 50 – Jones 46
	Carson 51 – Clift 13	Perrott 52 – Cotton 6

Dale Carson didn't have as dominating a tournament experience as in 1949, though he did dominate the finals, outscoring his opponents 358 to 59:

1. Carson 50 – Nellis 5

2. Carson 50 – Jones 14

3. Carson 50 – Cotton 1

4. Carson 55 – Perrott 4

5. Carson 52 – Stephenson 3

6. Carson 50 – Wilson 19

7. Carson 51 – Clift 13

358   59

1950 National AAU Senior Singles Championships

	Player	City	W	L	Pts	R	DR	SP	%
1.	Dale Carson	Baltimore, MD	7	0	358	205	68	284	71.8
2.	Walter Wilson	Washington, D.C.	6	1	334	202	52	402	50.2
3	Willard Nellis	Washington, D.C.	5	2	311	167	32	400	41.7
4.	Everett Clift	Washington, D.C.	4	3	263	168	35	380	44.2
5.	Charles O. Jones	Richmond VA	3	4	268	171	39	388	44.0
6.	Edward Perrott	Baltimore, MD	2	5	192	107	12	340	31.4
7.	John Cotton	Baltimore, MD	1	6	123	68	8	336	20.2
8.	Dr. Hugh Stephenson Jr.	Columbia, MO	0	7	107	70	10	304	23.0

						R	DR	SP	%
Best single game (singles) – Dale Carson					51	38	10	46	82.6%
Next best single game – Charles O. Jones						38	14	48	79.2

1950 National AAU Senior Doubles Championships

	Player & City	Pts	R	DR	SP	%
1.	Albert Rumbold & Clarence Stern	231	127	24	308	41.2
	Westminster, MD					
2.	Willard Nellis & Woodely	227	127	26	308	41.2
	Washington, D.C.					
3.	George Nichols & Oliver Spencer	202	104	19	282	36.8
	Westminster, MD					
4.	Hoffman & John Cotton	90	51	8	232	24.5
	Baltimore, MD					

	Pts	R	DR	SP	%
Best single game (doubles)	50	31	10	58	53.4
(The team who posted the best game was not named.)					

This is the final year we will find Pop Woodfield listed as a participant in a tournament write-up. Two years before this September 1950 AAU event, in 1948, he had concluded an eight-year stint as the NHPA's president. Woodfield passed away in December 1950.

1951

Still in Baltimore – New Champion

A new National AAU singles champion would be crowned at the conclusion of the 1951 tournament, held again in Baltimore, on September 1st through the 3rd.

On the tournaments opening day, the *Baltimore Sun* printed:

AAU Meet Starts Today

The National AAU Senior Horseshoe Pitching championships begin today on the courts at Carroll Park at 12 noon for the entrants to qualify for play tomorrow at 12 noon to decide the National Amateur Champion in singles and doubles.

Entries have been received from Richmond, Va., New Freedom, Pa., Westminster, Md., Glen Burnie, Md., and Baltimore.

Defend Doubles Title

Albert Rumbold and Clarence Stem, Westminster, will defend their doubles title but the singles crown is open due to the former champion, Dale Carson, entering the professional ranks this year.

The winner in singles will receive the Mayor Thomas D'Alesandro trophy and AAU gold medal. Second place and third place winners will receive silver and bronze medals. The doubles champions will receive a trophy apiece, the George Leithauser trophy and Hon. Carl Bacharach trophy, plus AAU gold medals.

Trophies To Be Given

The player making the highest ringer percentage in the round robin tournament in singles will receive the Harry J. McGuirk trophy, the Mr. and Mrs. C. M. Struven trophy will be awarded to the youngest player entered, and the Charles Buckley trophy to the oldest contestant. To the player coming from the most distant point will go the Leon Yarneth trophy.

The *Baltimore Sun* then gave an update on the qualifying pitchers on September 2nd:

Rumbold with 216 Points Leads Qualifiers
in Horseshoe Championship
Lutter Gains Second Place

Albert Rumbold, of Westminster A.A., scored 216 points to lead ten other entrants in the qualifying round of the National Senior AAU horseshoe pitching tournament yesterday at Carroll Park. Rumbold registered 59 ringers and 17 doubles ringers in compiling his total while Fred Lutter, of New Freedom, Pa., dropped in 61 ringers, including 17 doubles, to place second with 214 points.

100 Best Count

Each player pitched 200 horseshoes, with the best 100 counting. Three points were scored for a ringer and one point for any shoes within six inches of the stake. Of the eleven who entered, eight players were qualified to compete in the round robin for the title today. Doubles matches were not held, as only six teams entered the competition.

Dale Carson, of the Twenty-first Ward Democratic Club, was the 1950 champion, but he turned pro, making him ineligible to compete again this year. His winning total included 205 ringers and 63 doubles for a .718 percentage.

Two Top Meet

The pairings for today bring together yesterday's top two in an opening match and the winner will be favored to capture the title as next highest score to Rumbold and Lutter was Robey Spencer's 180. Spencer is also from Westminster A.A.

Results of Qualifying Round

1. Albert Rumbold – 218   2. Fred Lutter – 214
3. Robey Spencer – 180   4. Charles Jones – 174
5. Edward J. Perrott – 158   6. Jene Durham – 157
7. George Nichols – 145   8. M/Sgt. Stanley Hyzy – 145

Singles Pairings For Today

Rumbold vs. Lutter   Durham vs. Perrott
Spencer vs. Hyzy   Jones vs. Nichols

Doubles Pairings

Nichols & Spencer vs. Harmon & Hammerbacher
Rumbold & Stem vs. Harry Flohr & E. R. Killner
Durham & Clift vs. Perrott & Means

Amateur Athlete magazine also provided coverage of the event:

Durham Wins Horseshoe Pitching Crown

Jene Durham of the United Democratic Club of Baltimore captured the AAU Horseshoe Pitching Singles Championship at Baltimore, Maryland; on September 3rd. Albert Reimbold and Clarence Stem of Westminster, MD, retained their doubles title for the third straight year.

Durham pitched 432 shoes in 7 games to score 361 points. He tossed 224 ringers and 35 double ringers for an average ringer percentage of 51.1 percent. His best game was 54 points, 29 ringers, 10 double ringers in 48 shoes pitched, making a percentage of 60.4.

Durham received the Mayor Thomas D'Alesandro trophy for winning the singles plus the Harry J. McGuirk trophy for making the highest ringer percentage. Reinbold and Stem received the George Leithauser trophy and the Hon. Carl Bacharach trophy. Kenneth W. Nichols received the C. M. Struven trophy for being the youngest player entered, while Charles Jones, 59, of Richmond, Va., received the Charles Buckley trophy for being the oldest player and the Leon Yarneth trophy for coming from the most distance.

It's worthy of remark that if Charles O. Jones, recipient of the award for being this tournament's oldest player, was 59 years old in 1951, then he was 49 years old when he played in the 1941 National AAU *junior* championship.

Jene Durham, at age 23, was playing in his second AAU championship in 1951 and to his, and everybody else's, good fortune, Dale Carson had decided not to participate. Durham was a good pitcher in his own right, though; he was the Maryland state champion in 1961.

1951 Singles Individual Game Scores

Round One
Rumbold 52 – Stem 36   Spencer 55 – Perrott 45   Durham 50 – Nichols 46

Round Two
Durham 55 – Stem 30   Rumbold 53 – Nichols 23   Spencer 52 – Hyzy 36

Round Three
Stem 52 – Perrott 42   Durham 50 – Spencer 28   Nichols 50 – Hyzy 42

Round Four
Durham 53 – Hyzy 9   Spencer 50 – Stem 38   Rumbold 51 – Perrott 20

Round Five
Durham 52 – Perrott 21   Spencer 51 – Nichols 40   Rumbold 51 – Hyzy 18

Round Six
Stem 52 – Nichols 48   Perrott 52 – Hyzy 36   Rumbold 52 – Spencer 37

Round Seven
Durham 53 – Rumbold 39   Stem 52 – Hyzy 32   Nichols 50 – Perrott 32

1951 National AAU Senior Singles Championships

Place	Player	City	W	L	%
1.	Jene Durham	Baltimore, MD	7	0	51.8
2.	Albert Rumbold	Westminster, MD	6	1	44.2
3.	Robey Spencer	Westminster, MD	5	2	40.9
4.	Clarence Stem	Westminster, MD	4	3	43.1
5.	George Nichols	Westminster, MD	3	4	36.7
6.	Edward Perrott	Baltimore, MD	2	5	39.0
7.	M/Sgt Stanley Hyzy	Camp Mead	1	6	32.9
8.	Frederick Lutter	New Freedom, PA (withdrew)			57.6

1951 Doubles Individual Game Scores

Round One –   Rumbold/Stem 52 – Flohr/Killinger 49;
              Nichols/Spencer 54 – Harmon/Hammerbacher 31
Round Two –   Rumbold/Stem 50 – Harmon/Hammerbacher 32;
              Flohr/Killinger 53 – Nichols/Spencer 19;
              Flohr/Killinger 50 – Means/Perrott 25
Round Three – Rumbold/Stem 50 - Means/Perrott 9;
              Nichols/Spencer 53 – Means/Perrott 19;
              Flohr/Killinger 50 – Harmon/Hammerbacher 23
Round Four –   Rumbold/Stem 51 – Nichols/Spencer 18;
              Harmon/Hammerbacher 51 – Means/Perrott 15

1951 National AAU Senior Doubles Championships

Place	Player	City	W	L	%
1.	Albert Rumbold & Clarence Stem	Westminster, MD	4	0	51.8
2.	Harry Flohr & E. R. Killinger	Westminster, MD	3	1	50.0
3.	George Nichols & Robey Spencer	Westminster, MD	2	2	32.9
4.	E. Harmon & G. Hammerbacher	Baltimore, MD	1	3	30.9
5.	Robert Means & Edward Perrott	Baltimore, MD	0	4	21.5

1952

A Visit to Richmond

Richmond had two newspapers that covered the 1952 event, which was held from August 30th to September 1st. The *Richmond Times Daily* carried this pretournament announcement in its August 28th edition:

National Horseshoe Tourney
Open Saturday at Byrd Park

Over 25 horseshoe enthusiasts from all over the United States are expected to participate in the National AAU Horseshoe Pitching Championships, scheduled for Bryd Park this Saturday and Sunday.

According to Marshall Rotella, director of the matches for the City Department of Recreation and Parks and Virginia AAU Chairman, applications have already been received from Atlanta, Winston-Salem, Baltimore, Fredericksburg and Roanoke. And inquiry into the matches has been received as far away as Indiana, Rotella said.

Registration blanks are still available for men and women of all ages at the Department of Recreation and Parks, located in the Mosque. All contestants must be registered with the AAU. An entry fee of $2.00 will be charged for singles and $4.00 for doubles entrants.

Registration will close midnight August 29. Tournament hours will be from (a.m. to 10 p.m. on Saturday and from 2 to 10 p.m. on Sunday.

The National AAU Senior gold, silver and bronze medal swill be awarded to the first, second and third place winners respectively.

Trophies will be given as follows: one each to the contestant with the highest ringer percentage for the tournament in round robin play, winners of singles and doubles championships, oldest contestant, youngest contestant and player coning from the most distant point.

Chauncey W. Ashley, chairman of the National Horseshoe Tournament from Baltimore, Maryland will be present at the Richmond tournament.

The public is invited to participant or be spectators at the tournament.

And in the same paper's August 30th edition, this short article appeared:

Mayor Will Pitch First Shoe

Mayor Haddock will be on hand tomorrow a 1 p.m. to pitch out the first shoe in the National AAU horseshoe tournament scheduled tomorrow and Sunday at Byrd Park.

Round robin singles play will begin tomorrow at 1 p.m., following a morning qualifying round. Doubles are scheduled Sunday beginning at 2 p.m.

Local interest will center on the entries Charles (Racehorse) Jones, Sam Ukrop, Farl Gilpatrick, F. B. Duncan, Jr. and Herbert Burnette.

The final results and the winner were announced on August 31st:

Georgia "Pitcher" Wins
Horseshoe Championship

Ray Griffin, of Atlanta, who left Georgia because he could not find a challenger, yesterday captured the National AAU horseshoe pitching championship in the meet at the Byrd Park pits.

Griffin, today will team up with Robert Shytle, a North Carolina pitcher who received a thorough trouncing from his partner in singles play yesterday, for the doubles championships starting at 2 p.m.

Griffin for many years has monopolized the Georgia championships to the extent that he quickly found that he had no challengers when horseshoe pitching time came around. When the tournament dates are posted, the Georgia pitchers ask if Griffin has entered. If he is an entry, no one bothers to enter.

This year the Georgia championships fell on the same date as the AAU championships. When Griffin announced that he would pass up defense of his Georgia title to enter the Richmond tournament, Georgia officials were not surprised to find more than 80 pitchers entered in their tournament this weekend.

Frank Garrison of South Carolina and Albert Rumbold of Westminster, Md., finished in a second place tie, each with seven victories as against four defeats in yesterday's round robin. Garrison the defeated Rumbold in a playoff to take second place.

1952 National AAU Singles Championship Finals

	Player	City	W	L	%
1.	Ray Griffin	Atlanta, GA	11	0	59.6%
2.	Frank Garrison	Cramerton, NC	8	4	50.1
3.	Albert Rumbold	Westminster, MD	4	5	44.6
4.	J. J. Dove	Roanoke, VA	6	5	43.3
5.	James Garrison	Cameron, MD	5	6	45.5
6.	Clarence Stem	Westminster, MD	5	6	44.6
7.	Herbert Burnett	Richmond, VA	5	6	42.8
8.	G. B. Darnell	Roanoke, VA	5	6	39.6
9.	Robert Stytle	Lexington, NC	4	7	37.5
10.	W. G. Epperly	Roanoke, VA	4	7	47.1
11.	Charles O. Jones	Richmond, VA	4	7	39.2
12.	Charles Lynch	Charleston, SC	3	8	43.9

Georgian Pitches "Double Ringer"

Ray Griffin, 47-year-old railroad worker, captured the national amateur horseshoe pitching tournament here over the weekend and then teamed up with Robert Shytle of Lexington, N.C., to take the doubles title with a 59 percentage. Frank Garrison won a playoff for second place in the singles and with James Garrison took a playoff for runner-up spot in the doubles. Albert Rumbold and Clarence Stem, defending champions were third.

1952 National AAU Doubles Championship Finals

Players	%
Ray Griffin & Robert Shytle	48.6%
Frank & James Garrison	46.4
Albert Rumbold & Clarence Stem	42.5
Charles O. Jones & Herbert Burnett	38.0
W. G. Epperly & Harris	33.3

For a number of years, the coverage has offered no information about the junior events. Whether none were organized or some took place but were not reported, we don't know at this time. That is not the case for 1952, however.

Up to this point, the NHPA and the AAU had not collaborated on any events, and there's little evidence of mutual assistance or a shared effort to promote the good of the sport. The exceptions to that rule were when the NHPA's secretary Raymond Howard served as the AAU's horseshoe-pitching committee chairman in 1937, the first year the sport was included in the AAU's programming, and NHPA's president Harry Woodfield's attendance at a couple of events in the 1940s (once as a participant).

1952 was different, although there are scant records. The NHPA's World Tournament was held at Murray, Utah, in the period, and a junior competition was reestablished there in 1951. The 1952 World Tournament also included a junior competition and it was conducted by the AAU.

Now remember, no age guidelines had been established by the AAU, but the NHPA had strict age guidelines—competitors were only eligible as juniors through the year of a player's sixteenth birthday. That divide created turmoil as competitors showed up for the competition. The NHPA's junior members were competing for a world championship while the AAU's junior members were competing for a national championship. (Players for both organizations were mixed in the same events.)

I was unable to locate newspaper coverage of the 1952 combined junior event, and neither the NHPA or AAU publications contained reports or coverage. The only accounting available at this time is a letter, written some 57 years after the event, from tournament participant Gary Backer. Though letter was solicited as part of a previous book project, *The World Champions of Horseshoe Pitching*, I feel confident Backer would willingly share his account in this similar context. Shortly after he sent me this letter, he passed away.

While it's problematic to recognize a letter from an event participant written almost six decades later should become the official record. But since there are no period sources, Backer's letter plays that role and we're fortunate to have a participant's firsthand account as the only remaining description of the 1952 junior event:

Junior Championship—1952

The event sponsored by the AAU was advertised as the Junior World Horseshoe Pitching Championships at Liberty Park in Salt Lake City, Utah, and was held at the same time and in conjunction with the World Horseshoe Pitching Championships in Murray, Utah.

It was very disappointing when the officials let several boys play that were older than Junior age. Clive Wahlin was 24 years old and others were even older.

The tournament started with 16 players—about half were Junior age. About 10 games of a round robin were played the first day. The second day we finished the singles. I was the only one to beat Wahlin; Wahlin beat Dave Loucks; Loucks beat me; an older man beat me and someone else beat Loucks. So Clive won the tournament with a 14-1 record; Loucks was 13-2 after regulation play and so was I. Loucks and I were asked to play each other again in a playoff game for 2nd place. I started slow, Dave started with almost all ringers and I wasn't able to catch up.

Then the players teamed up and played a meaningless doubles tournament.

Dave Loucks later claimed to be the rightful 1952 Junior World's Champion with a 7-0 record, plus a playoff game win. Considering about half of the 16 players were of Junior age and he beat me in the playoff I agreed with him completely. I believe that I should have credit for second place on a 6-2 record.

Backer was entered as an NHPA member, and his letter clearly comes from that perspective. Backer goes on to relate:

Per the NHPA records, Dave Loucks is credited with the 1952 Junior Boys World Championship on a 7-0 record and pitching 50.0 percent Ringers. The *Horseshoe Pitcher* did not publish a single word on the Junior competition. Even though there was decent coverage of the 1952 World Tournament in the *Murray Eagle*, and the Junior competition was announced as being scheduled, there were no results of the competition published in the *Eagle* or any other newspaper. And Dave Loucks made this comment,

"The Junior event was sponsored and run by the AAU. As I remember, it was pitched at a different park and play included some doubles games. My trophy does say AAU Champion. Arch Stokes told me at the time that since the AAU was running the tournament, they set the format. The pitching records would be accepted by the NHPA and I would still be considered NHPA Junior Champion which has been the case over all the past 57 years."

Dave Loucks was declared the junior world champion, based on having the tournament's best win-loss record among the NHPA's junior members. This was his second junior title, and he went on to earn his third consecutive title in

1953. Loucks became one of the NHPA's most valuable and productive members. He served for 19 years as president, and for nearly as many years as editor of *Newsline*, the organization's newsletter. Loucks was inducted to the NHPA Hall of Fame in 1991 and he currently heads up the National Horseshoe Pitchers Foundation (NHPF), the NHPA's charitable arm.

Gary Backer's younger brother, Bill Backer, missed winning a world junior championship after losing a playoff in 1957. The following year, Bill beat his younger brother Richard in a playoff to win the World Tournament junior title. Their father, Reinhard Backer, served one term as president of the NHPA beginning in 1959; received the NHPA's 1966 Stokes Memorial Award for his efforts to promote, foster, and build the sport; and was inducted to the NHPA Hall of Fame in 2005.

Clive Wahlin, the AAU member Gary Backer mentions in his letter, was indeed 24 years old at the time—and he was the National AAU junior champion in 1952. After a request for information, he sent me a copy of his gold medal. At the age of 83, Wahlin is alive and well, and still resides in Murray, Utah. He kept no records of the event and at this late date, he does not recall his partner in the doubles competition. Wahlin went on to win 16 Utah state championships between 1956 and 1981. Wahlin qualified for the men's championship finals in nine World Tournaments between 1954 and 1966. He had four top-ten finishes—the highest of which was fourth place in 1958, pitching 79.7 percent ringers. He is not presently in the NHPA Hall of Fame, but is on the ballot and is a likely candidate for induction.

1953

Another Champion From Illinois

After 14 competitive years in National AAU championships, Frank Breen finally brought home a title in 1953. Up to this point, he had achieved three runner-up finishes and one third-place finish. He had also come close to wins in doubles competitions. But he finally won a championship in 1953. His achievement was earned in Baltimore, where the tournament was held on September 12th and 13th. The *Baltimore Sun* covered the action:

Mid Westerner Wins
in Horseshoe Contest

Frank Breen, a steady smooth southpaw from Elgin, Ill., squeezed through seven rounds of horseshoe pitching without defeat yesterday to win the National AAU Championship at the Carroll Park pitching courts.

In the doubles tournament, the Sykesville Fish and Game Club of Sykesville, Md., with a winning team of Irving J. Ruby and Leslie Holman, scored an upset by taking the national crown over the favored Burlington Mills team from Cramerton, N.C., which dropped to a disappointing third. In perfect cool weather the pitchers threw more than 20,000 pounds of steel during the eight hours of competition.

The Illinois pitcher, however, was the main attraction of the day for the small group of enthusiasts who stared at the consistent arcing of shoes and listened to the click of shoe against stake. "He is the best lefthander I've ever seen, amateur or professional," declared singles runner-up Ray Griffin, the defending champion, who came all the way from Atlanta, to defend his title.

Tie Broken in Playoff

"There was no competition for the man," Mr. Griffin said, adding "Frank Breen is just in a class by himself."

A play-off, held to break a three-way tie for third place among James Garrison, Irving Ruby and Scott Bennett, was won by Garrison. Garrison, standing better than 6' tall and weighing 235 pounds, threw the 2½ pound shoes with the easy of flinging toothpicks but with deadly accuracy as he dominated the competition and the prizes.

Champion Breen won the Mayor Thomas D'Alesandro trophy and the AAU gold medal, then nosed out his closest competitor, Ray Griffin, for the special trophy for coming from the most distant point, totaling 740 travel miles, 40 more than Mr. Griffin.

Scores 364 Points

In his seven games, Mr. Breen scored 364 points, making 215 ringers, 65 double ringers, while throwing 336 shoes. His ringer percentage for the day was 64 percent.

While beating Bernie Schreiber, of Baltimore, in the first round, 55 to 5, the champ won the trophy for the highest ringer percentage for one game, 70 percent, by pitching 21 ringers out of 30 throws.

To the smiling southpaw, though, this was like eating pie. He holds the world marathon pitching record—2,436 ringers in ten consecutive hours of pitching set in 1940 and once pitched a perfect game of 38 straight ringers, without a miss.

Praises Hospitality

Last night, weary from handshaking, the champ complimented Baltimore's hospitality then flew back with his load of trophies to Chicago and to his "horseshoe widow" and 8-year-old daughter.

The new doubles champions from Sykesville, Leslie Holman, 39, a meat cutter and Irving Ruby, 39, a laboratory technician at Springfield

State Hospital, were playing as partners for the first time in tournament competition.

Tied for first after three rounds, they hit their peak in the fourth round, swamping the favorites, Frank and James Garrison, the Burlington Mills brothers entry, by a walloping 50 to 18.

Third place in the doubles went to the Wicomico Horseshoe Club, Team "A," from Salisbury, Md., composed of Scott Bennett and Grover F. Chatham. They came from being in the fifth and final round to whip Burlington Mills, 50 to 23.

Chauncey W. Ashley, National AAU horseshoe pitching chairman, spent a twelve-hour working day and supervised the tournament with ease and precision. As official referee, he never once had to take out his calipers for a close decision.

Mr. Ashley awarded trophies to the youngest contest, Edwin Baker, 19, an entrant in the doubles team competition and to the oldest Charles O. Jones, 61, of Richmond, Va., a veteran in national competition.

Dr. Stephenson Absent

Missing this year was Dr. Hugh Stephenson, a St. Louis surgeon, who plays not only for the fun of it, but to keep his co ordination balanced and his hand and wrist muscles in condition.

According to *Amateur Athlete*, the stats for the 1953 events were:

By Round Results of Singles Games

First Round –

Griffin 50	Ruby 51	Bennett 52	Breen 55
Spencer 1	Garrison 38	Jones 42	Schreiber 5

Second Round –

Griffin 53	Bennett 51	Ruby 54	Breen 50
Garrison 47	Schreiber 5	Spencer 16	Jones 13

Third Round –

Breen 51	Jones 51	Garrison 54	Ruby 51
Bennett 22	Schreiber 6	Spencer 9	Griffin 48

Fourth Round –

Griffin 54	Breen 50	Garrison 52	Jones 51
Bennett 49	Ruby 17	Schreiber 9	Spencer 44

Fifth Round –

Bennett 51	Griffin 53	Breen 52	Spencer 50
Ruby 22	Jones 37	Garrison 13	Schreiber 12

Sixth Round –

Griffin 50	Garrison 52	Breen 52	Jones 51
Schreiber 0	Bennett 45	Spencer 10	Ruby 48

Seventh Round –

Bennett 54	Garrison 50	Breen 52	Ruby 50
Spencer 17	Jones 23	Griffin 31	Schreiber 0

1953 National AAU Senior Singles Championship Finals

	Player	City	W	L	Pts	R	DR	SP	%
1.	Frank Breen	Elgin, IL	7	0	364	215	65	336	.639
2.	Ray Griffin	Atlanta, GA	5	2	339	180	38	374	.509
3.	James Garrison	Burlington, NC	6	3	405	268	63	570	.470
4.	Scott Bennett	Salisbury, MD	4	4	359	225	55	466	.483
5	Irving Ruby	Sykesville, MD	4	4	329	167	45	428	.390
6.	Charles O. Jones	Richmond, MD	3	4	268	147	20	430	.350
7.	Robey Spencer	Westminster, MD	1	6	154	102	21	322	.316
8.	Bernie Schreiber	Baltimore, MD	0	7	37	16	0	208	<u>.076</u>
									.418

By Round Results of Singles Games

First Round –

Sykesville 53	Burlington Mills 51	Wicomico 'A' 53
Edgewood 46	Wicomico 'B' 33	Ferndale 14

Second Round –

Wicomico 'B' 52	Burlington Mills 52	Sykesville 50
Ferndale 40	Edgewood 15	Wicomico 'A' 48

Third Round –

Wicomico 'A' 50	Burlington Mills 52	Sykesville 51
Edgewood 17	Ferndale 15	Wicomico 'B' 19

Fourth Round –

Edgewood 50	Sykesville 50	Wicomico 'A' 52
Ferndale 38	Burlington Mills 18	Wicomico 'B' 35

Fifth Round –

Sykesville 50	Wicomico 'A' 50	Wicomico 'B' 50
Ferndale 12	Burlington Mills 23	Edgewood 20

1953 National AAU Senior Doubles Championship Finals

	Team	W	L	Pts	R	DR	SP	%
1.	Sykesville Fish & Game, MD	5	0	253	124	39	290	.437
	Irving 'Jack' Ruby & Leslie Holman							
2.	Wicomico 'A', Salisbury, MD	4	1	252	131	31	318	.111
	Scott Bennett & Grover Chatman							
3.	Burlington Mills, NC	3	2	205	130	28	273	.441
	Frank Garrison & James Garrison							
4.	Wicomico 'B', MD	2	3	189	89	13	342	.274
	Eugene Oakley & Howard Smith							
5.	Edgewood Chemical, MD	1	4	148	86	9	306	.281
	James Green & Edward Gall							
6.	Ferndale Club, MD	0	5	119	61	5	290	.210
	Gilbert Hammerbacher & Edwin Baker							

During the 40 years of AAU championships, many articles were written about individual players and champions, most of which are interesting to read, but none are more comprehensive than the article published by the *Elgin Daily-Courier* about their hometown hero. The article was difficult to locate, however, because it was printed on November 10, 1953, almost a month after the tournament. It's only through the persistent efforts of the Elgin Historical Society that it's possible to include it here:

Frank Breen, Nation's Top Barnyard Golfer
Elgin's Own

If it takes perseverance to be a champion, in any sport, the big Frank "Lefty" Breen, 1953 National AAU horseshoe champion, earned the title. He attained the No. 1 position among barnyard golfers after 25 years of work.

Breen, 39, whose home is in Elgin, won the national championship at Baltimore, Md., this year by whipping Ray Griffin, of Atlanta, Ga., in the finals 50-31. There were 236 horseshoe tossers entered in the event.

The new national horseshoe champ got his start in the game when he was about 10 years old. Just a youngster in grade school, Frank used to hang around an Elgin fire barn watching the firemen pitch horseshoes.

"It was at the No. 5 fire barn," muses Breen today, "that I first pitched horseshoes. We either had to play horseshoes or we were chased home." That was 29 years ago.

Big and husky, Breen soon developed a love for the sport and within a short time he was fair competition for those who had been tossing horseshoes at a steel stake some 40 feet distant for a good number of years.

It was 25 years ago that Frank first entered competition and since that time he has kept exceptionally complete records on his wins, losses and other vital statistics.

In those 25 years, he has won 12,211 games and lost 289. He has made 512,000 ringers out of a possible 750,000 and has a ringer percentage of 68.3.

Based on the fact that it is 40 feet between stakes, Frank says he has walked 15 million feet or a distance of 2,845½ miles while in competition and as each horseshoe weighs 2½ pounds, has lifted a total of 1,875,000 pounds of steel or 937½ tons—all in actual competition.

These figures do not include 10 hours of practice each week, the year around. Then too, the average game takes one-half hour, according to Breen, and on that basis, he has spent 6,250 hours on the horseshoe courts in competition or better than 781 eight-hour days pitching horseshoes.

Frank likes his record for the past five years better than his overall total. Claims he's hitting his stride. Since 1948, he has won 2,133 games and lost seven, with 98,446 ringers out of 128,400 shoes for a ringer percentage of 76.7.

In those five years and seven losses, only two have been from the same person, Hilmer Magnuson of Rockford, Ill.

Besides his 1953 national title, Breen placed second in national competition in 1939 at Anderson, Ind., and in 1940 in Chicago. He has been the Central AAU singles champion for the past five years and Breen and Harry Durkee of Elgin shared the Central AAU doubles title for four years and with Earl App, also of Elgin, for one year (1953).

City champion for 23 consecutive years, Breen holds several world's records, those being 90 ringers out of 100 shoes, 278 points in 100 shoes, 38 straight ringers in one game, 2436 ringers in 10 consecutive hours using 4 shoes and 1,362 ringers in six hours of straight pitching with two shoes.

Breen is an inspector at the Ironer division of Speed Queen Corp. Algonquin, manufacturers of washing machines and dryers. He is a regular member of the Royal Order of Moose Lodge No. 799 of Elgin horseshoe team, a group he considers the top team in the nation, has won 69 matches and lost only five.

Frank, a 225-pound six-foot hefty, was laid up for 18 months four years ago because of successive automobile accidents, but during his recuperation laid the groundwork for what he claims are "the finest indoor horseshoe courts in the country" at the Elgin YMCA.

Today, an industrial horseshoe league is in operation, with more than 80 persons representing six industries of the Elgin area. The league will operate through the winter on the indoor YMCA courts.

The national horseshoe champ is married and he and his wife Ruth have one daughter, Patricia, who does not aspire to become a horseshoe champion, but who loves to watch her daddy collect trophies and medals.

Breen says that all his efforts in the game of horseshoe have "been just for fun." Maybe it is just for fun, but if spending three hours every Saturday afternoon teaching youngsters at the YMCA how to pitch horseshoes is any indication, Elgin might have more champions in the future.

1954

A Hall of Famer Wins

The 1954 tournament was held in Marietta, Georgia, on September 4th and 5th. It was the furthest south the tournament had traveled in the almost twenty years of National AAU horseshoe pitching. The *Marietta Daily Journal* printed a brief announcement of the 1954 event and a rather interesting history on the sport overall:

Horseshoe Pitching Champions to Get AAU Medal, Trophies

Three medals and several trophies will be presented to winners in the National AAU Senior Horseshoe Pitching Championship Tournament Saturday and Sunday at Larry Bell Park.

Some 14 participants will vie for the National AAU Senior Amateur title and gold, silver and bronze medals will be awarded to first, second and third place winners, respectively. Trophies will be given to each contestant with the highest ringer percentage for the tournament in the round robin series to determine the single and doubles champions, the oldest contestant, the youngest contestant and the player coming from the most distant point.

Qualifying competition will get underway at 10 a.m., Saturday, with each contestant pitching 100 shoes. Final qualifiers will compete in a round robin series to determine the tournament champion.

Total scores of partners in singles qualifying round will be used as the basis for doubles qualification.

Originated By Romans

Horseshoe pitching originated with camp followers of the Roman armies, who could not afford discus throwing. They tried throwing a horseshoe bent to form a circle and the game of quoits, in which the circle is tossed underhand at a mark on the ground, began. One camp follower placed a stake in the ground and tossed the shoe in its original form, thus starting the modern game.

The first set of rules applying to quoits and horseshoes was drawn up by the English in 1869 and later the two games were separated and a different set of rules was drafted for each.

It is not known exactly when horseshoe pitching became a sport in America but pitching was popular among soldiers of both armies during the Revolutionary War. The first actual horseshoe pitching club in this country was formed in Long Beach, California in 1900.

First International

The first International Horseshoe Pitching Contest opened in 1909 in Bronson, Kansas. This tournament led to others and in 1915, the National Horseshoe Pitchers Association of America was formed. The American Horseshoe Pitchers Association was organized in 1929, with headquarters in Chicago. It enlisted the aid of newspapers throughout the country to conduct tournaments.

The tournament this weekend is the first national meet to be held in Marietta.

The same paper reported the final results on September 7th:

Toole Wins Title in AAU
Horseshoe Pitching Contest

Frank Toole of Little Rock, Ark., is the new Amateur Athletic Union National Horseshoe Pitching Champion. He won out in a surprise finish Sunday at Larry Bell Park in a tourney in which more than five tons of steel was thrown through the air.

Toole defeated defending champion Frank Breen, of Elgin, Ill., with a tournament record of eight wins and one loss. Breen's record was 7-2 and 1952 champion Ray Griffin, of Atlanta, who came in third, had a 6-3 record. Griffin was also runner-up last year. Toole had not previously participated in a national contest.

The Winston-Salem team of Conrad Murphy and W. W. Thomas took the double championship in the final game against the Baltimore twosome of Jack Ruby and Leslie Holman. If Murphy and Thomas had lost that game the tournament would have ended in a three-way tie.

Second and third place teams had to be decided on the basis of points, according to AAU rulings since the Cramerton, N.C., team and the Dayton duet both ended with a 5-2 record. A brother team, James and Frank Garrison of Cramerton, was named second place winner. Third place went to Glenn Riffle and Marion Shadley, of Dayton, while the Baltimore team of Ruby and Holman came out fourth with a 4-3 record.

The tournament was conducted by the Georgia Chapter of the AAU and Al Bishop, chairman of the horseshoe pitching section in cooperation with Larry Bell Park. Chauncey Ashley, of Baltimore, the AAU horseshoe pitching chairman, assisted with the tournament.

A total of 22 players participated in the qualifying matches Saturday morning, with ten playing in the singles championship and eight teams in the doubles championship.

Trophies went to first, second, and third place winners in both singles and doubles and four individual trophies were given: L. T. Couch, 74, of Little Rock, received the award for the oldest participant and the youngest was Woodrow Kelly, 16, of Atlanta. Frank Breen won the highest ringer percentage award with about 63 percent. Earl App, also of

Elgin, was adjudged the player from the longest distance on the basis of his boarding the train before Breen.

"It was a good tournament," Bishop commented. "It will go a long way towards development of horseshoe pitching in the state of Georgia in the future."

Thanks are due to the city of Marietta for their hospitality to the players. Scores Evelyn Richards, Art and Lila Benton, Julius DeGive and Harry S. Glancy did a fine job scoring. A special note of praise goes to the efficient ground keepers and prepared who watered the pits so well. The1955 tournament will be held in Elgin, Ill., and sponsored by the Moose Lodge of that city.

The following stats are taken from the October 1954 issue of the *Amateur Athlete*:

1954 National AAU Seniors Singles Championships Finals

	Player	City	W	L	Pts	R	DR	SP	%
1.	Floyd Toole	Little Rock, AR	8	1	430	394	116	630	63.0
2.	Frank Breen	Elgin, IL	7	2	438	364	116	580	63.8
3.	Ray Griffin	Atlanta, GA	7	2	450	369	99	646	56.7
4.	Glenn Riffle	Dayton, OH	6	3	453	327	98	580	57.7
5.	Marion Shadley	Dayton, OH	5	4	410	332	95	596	55.6
6.	Woody Thomas	High Point, NC	5	4	338	309	87	572	53.4
7.	James Garrison	Cramerton, NC	3	6	339	299	71	604	49.6
8.	Frank Garrison	Cramerton, NC	2	7	338	339	78	634	53.3
9.	Conrad Murphy	Winston-Salem, NC	2	7	284	281	58	580	48.2
10.	Leslie Holman	Sykesville, MD	0	9	260	277	57	602	45.5
									54.7

1954 National AAU Seniors Doubles Championships Finals

	Player and City	W	L	Pts	R	DR	SP	%
1.	Conrad Murphy & Woody Thomas Winston-Salem, NC	6	1	334	238	59	436	54.5
2.	James and Frank Garrison Cramerton, NC	5	2	325	185	54	366	50.5
3.	Marion Shadley & Glenn Riffle Dayton, OH	4	3	338	243	52	460	52.8
4.	Irving Ruby & Leslie Holman Sykesville, MD	4	3	319	236	49	498	47.3
5.	Frank Breen & Earl App Elgin, IL	4	3	307	237	62	502	47.2
6.	Floyd Toole & L. T. Couch Little Rock, AR	2	5	246	133	30	356	37.3
7.	Ray Griffin & Boswell Atlanta, GA	2	5	156	126	20	252	50.3
8.	Chewning & Wright Atlanta, GA	1	6	115	34	7	278	12.2

Floyd Toole was 36 years old when he entered this tournament in Marietta, his first National AAU event. He won his first state championship in Arkansas the previous year and earned the state title again in 1958. He was an NHPA championship-class pitcher, qualifying 12 times for the World Tournament finals and achieving eight top-ten finishes. So was he an amateur pitcher through his final National AAU tournament in 1957? I would argue he did hold amateur status until his first NHPA World Tournament entry in 1958. Toole's pitching career had some significant highlights: in 1961, in a game with Hall of Fame pitcher Paul Focht, they set the World Tournament record for the longest game at 178 shoes; in a game against Hall of Famer Jim Solomon in 1964, Toole pitched 66 consecutive ringers; in the 1965 World Tournament, Toole pitched four consecutive games of 90 percent ringers against Glen Henton, Hugh Rogers, Marvin Craig, and Ted Allen. Floyd Toole was inducted to the NHPA Hall of Fame in 1981.

The 1954 tournament also marked the National AAU debut of Woody Thomas, who became the state champion of North Carolina in 1960.

1955

The First Title for Riffle

Well, the National AAU tournament was not held in Elgin, Illinois, as announced at the conclusion of the 1954 event and printed in the *Marietta Daily Journal* article. No explanation was provided, but it wasn't the first time for a change in venue—at least an alternative site was found and the event was conducted rather than cancelled. Little Rock, Arkansas, hosted the event, which was held on September 3rd and 4th.

And there was big news in 1955: not only was a new champion was crowned, but he won in a playoff victory over the defending champion, Floyd Toole. Glenn Riffle stepped into the winner's circle, marking the beginning of his run as one of the all-time great players of the National AAU championships. The Riffle family scrapbook includes this uncredited clipping that gives an in-progress report of the tournament:

Riffle Takes Lead in
Horseshoe Tournament Here

Glenn Riffle, of Dayton, Ohio, took a long stride toward the national horseshoe championship at MacArthur Park, yesterday, winning seven rounds in the opening session. Riffle wound up fourth in national competition last year.

Floyd Toole, North Little Rock, the defending national champion, closed the day with a 6-1 mark. Riffle also topped Toole in yesterday's qualifying, scoring 251 points and getting 79 ringers out of 100 tries. Toole came up with a total of 74 ringers.

Two rounds today will wind up the singles play. In the first round at 9 a.m., Riffle goes against Ed Webb, who failed to win a game yesterday, and at 9:45, Toole and Riffle collide. The pairings give Toole a decided edge.

The doubles [winners] will also be decided today beginning at 10:30 with six teams aiming for the title. The team of Woody Thomas, High Point, N.C. and Conrad Murphy, Winston-Salem, N.C., represents the defending doubles champions.

Thomas holds down the third spot in the round robin standings with 5-2. Marion Shadley, Dayton is fourth also at 5-2. Trailing are Ray Griffin, Atlanta, 4-3; Murphy 3-4; Kenneth Poff, Centerville, Ohio, 2-5; Frank Garrison, Cramerton, N.C., 2-5; James Garrison, Cramerton, 1-6 and Ed Webb, Little Rock, Ark., 0-7.

Non-qualifiers included: L. T. Couch, Little Rock; Lloyd Willman, Lonoke; Wm. Higginbottom, Jacksonville; Jimmy Riggs, Jacksonville; W. E. George, Little Rock; George Heising, Little Rock.

The September 5th edition of the *Arkansas Gazette* gave the final standings:

Ohioans Walk Off with Major Titles in AAU Horseshoe Play

Glenn Riffle, 35-year-old metal finisher from Dayton, Ohio, edged out Floyd Toole, defending champion from Little Rock, to capture the singles crown in the National AAU Horseshoe Pitching Championships which ended yesterday at MacArthur Park.

Marion Shadley, Dayton, Ohio, and Kenneth Poff, Centerville, Ohio, upset defending champs Woody Thomas, High Point, N.C., and Conrad Murphy, Winston-Salem, in a playoff for the doubles title. Both the singles and the doubles final matches were pushed into playoffs, which is rare in a national meet.

Shadley also won the trophy for the player finishing with the highest percentage of ringers in the tournament. His mark was .667. Last year's winner got the trophy with .633.

Going into the final round, Riffle was undefeated. Toole had lost once and toppled the leader and forced him into a two-out-of-three game series for the title. Toole dropped the first playoff game 51-28 and won the second 51-33. He was leading in the final and deciding contest after 58 shoes, 36-19, when the Dayton sharpie began virtually flawless play, scoring 31 ringers in the last 38 shoes. Riffle copped the last game 55-43.

Toole and Riffle both finished the nine match round robin each with records of eight victories and one loss.

L. T. Couch of Little Rock was the only player to retain his title—the oldest entrant. He is 75 and he won the same trophy for the event at Marietta, Ga., last year.

Riggs, a pint-sized tobacco-chewer, got the prize for the youngest participant. He is 25.

Riffle came in second for the ringer percentage trophy with 64.6 percent and Toole was third with 63.5. Thomas was given an award for traveling the greatest distance to the tournament.

Glenn Riffle was commissioned an "Arkansas Traveler" by J. C. Bacon, who represented Governor Orval Faubus. Mayor Pratt Remmel commissioned the ten qualifiers in the singles event as honorary citizens of Little Rock.

Noon luncheons were served the players on both days under the huge shade trees at the courts. The Arkansas Association, AAU, provided a barbeque lunch the first day and the wives of the pitchers from the little Rock area served a fried chicken dinner the second day. J. E. Bacon, tournament director and chairman of the state AAU horseshoe pitching committee, presented the trophies.

Scores of the Singles Round Robin games:

Round One –

Toole 52	Griffin 50	Riffle 51	Shadley 50	Murphy 55
Webb 16	Thomas 43	J. Garrison 43	F. Garrison 32	Poff 48

Round Two –

Thomas 52	Shadley 55	Riffle 52	F. Garrison 50	J. Garrison 50
Toole 26	Murphy 16	Poff 26	Griffin 33	Webb 12

Round Three –

Toole 55	Poff 51	Thomas 52	Shadley 50	Riffle 51
F. Garrison 34	J. Garrison 30	Murphy 36	Webb 7	Griffin 17

Round Four –

Toole 54	Riffle 52	Murphy 51	Thomas 53	Poff 41
J. Garrison 11	Shadley 32	Griffin 45	F. Garrison 15	Webb 4

Round Five –

Toole 50	Riffle 52	Murphy 53	Shadley 51	Griffin 52
Poff 23	Thomas 47	F. Garrison 39	J. Garrison 25	Webb 5

Round Six –

Toole 52	Riffle 51	Shadley 52	Griffin 52	Thomas 51
Murphy 18	F. Garrison 31	Poff 21	J. Garrison 28	Webb 13

Round Seven –

F. Garrison 51	Riffle 51	Griffin 52	Toole 52	Thomas 51
Webb 22	Murphy 29	Poff 21	Shadley 45	J. Garrison 42

Round Eight –

Toole 50	Riffle 51	F. Garrison 50	Murphy 52	Shadley 50
Griffin 10	Webb 7	Poff 36	J. Garrison 35	Thomas 36

Round Nine –

Toole 50	Shadley 53	Thomas F. Garrison 53		Murphy 53
Riffle 29	Griffin 31 Poff	J. Garrison 48		Webb 10

1955 National AAU Seniors Singles Championships Finals

	Player	City	W	L	Pts.	R	DR	SP	Pct.
1.	Glenn Riffle	Dayton, OH	8	1	437	327	113	508	64.6
2.	Floyd Toole	No. Little Rock	8	1	441	338	103	532	63.5
3.	Marion Shadley	Dayton, OH	7	2	438	340	117	510	66.6
4.	Woody Thomas	High Point, NC	6	3	426	347	106	592	58.6
5.	Conrad Murphy	W.-Salem, NC	5	4	363	284	82	520	54.6
6.	Ray Griffin	Atlanta, GA	4	5	348	323	98	546	59.1
7.	Frank Garrison	Cramerton, NC	4	5	350	317	83	604	52.4
8.	Kenneth Poff	Centerville, OH	2	7	307	278	68	544	51.1
9.	James Garrison	Cramerton, NC	1	8	277	249	60	518	48.0
10.	Ed Webb	Little Rock, AR	0	9	104	110	20	360	30.5
					2,913			5,232	55.67%

Singles Championship Playoff

Glenn Riffle	2	1	139	145	50	226	64.1
Floyd Toole	1	2	122	143	42	226	63.2

Scores of the Double Round Robin Games:

Round One –

Thomas & Murphy defeated Webb & Couch	51-12
Shadley & Poff defeated Riggs & Higginbottom	54-7
Garrison & Garrison defeated Toole & Heising	51-44

Round Two –

Thomas & Murphy defeated Toole & Heising	50-13
Shadley & Poff defeated Garrison & Garrison	52-30
Riggs & Higginbottom defeated Couch & Webb	51-32

Round Three –

Thomas & Murphy defeated Riggs & Higginbottom	52-16
Toole & Heising defeated Shadley & Poff	52-43
Garrison & Garrison defeated Couch & Webb	51-32

Round Four –

Thomas & Murphy defeated Garrison & Garrison	55-34
Shadley & Poff defeated Couch & Webb	53-13
Toole & Heising defeated Riggs & Higginbottom	50-11

Round Five –

Shadley & Poff defeated Thomas & Murphy	50-36
Toole & Heising defeated Couch & Webb	55-28
Garrison & Garrison defeated Riggs & Higginbottom	50-13

Championship Playoff

Shadley & Poff defeated Thomas & Murphy	50-38

1955 National AAU Seniors Doubles Championships Finals

	Players	State	W	L	Pts.	R	DR	SP	Pct.
1.	Shadley – Poff	OH	4	1	252	157	41	294	53.4
2.	Murphy – Thomas	NC	4	1	246	149	33	280	53.2
3.	Toole – Heising	AR	3	2	214	128	34	288	44.4
4.	Garrison – Garrison	NC	3	2	215	130	34	274	47.4
5.	Riggs – Higginbottom	AR	1	4	98	67	7	266	25.1
6.	Webb – Couch	AR	0	5	103	87	13	306	28.4

Doubles Championship Playoff

Shadley – Poff	1	0	50	45	14	78	57.6
Murphy – Thomas	0	1	38	41	14	78	52.5

Glenn Riffle had entered the 1954 event, so this was not his first AAU finals, but it was his first gold medal. This was the start of a great career during a time of objectively strong competition. Riffle heads the list of all-time AAU gold medal wins (seven), and is second on the list of total medals earned (12).

This may be the strongest field to play a National AAU Championship, with three players pitching over 60 percent ringers and eight players over 50 percent. In 1954, there was a marked improvement over previous years, with two pitchers over 60 percent and eight pitching better than 50 percent. But, before 1955, the strongest field was back in 1944. Five players averaged over 60 percent ringers and another five were over 50 percent. During the war years, the NHPA did not conduct a World Tournament, so that may have drawn out a few more of the top players to the AAU. That explanation is challenged, however, when you notice that that eleven of the final 16 players in 1944 were from Michigan, site of the tournament.

The strongest ever groups of competitors are yet to come. In 1961, for example, the finals had a smaller class of just eight players, but the entire group averaged over 60 percent ringers.

1956

One More for Breen

In 1956, the National AAU Championships returned to Ohio for the first time since 1946. The tournament was held on the home courts of defending champion Glenn Riffle on September 1st and 2nd. No doubt Riffle's anxiety had been building for weeks, as well as the anticipation of all the Ohio spectators rooting for him. But the veteran Frank Breen came out on top and regained his title.

The *Dayton Journal* announced the tournament on August 31st:

National AAU Horseshoe Meet
Here this Weekend

National championship sporting competition is to take place here Saturday and Sunday when the Amateur Athletic Union will crown its horseshoe pitching kings in both singles and double.

The tournament will be at Frigidaire Recreation Park with qualifying singles at noon Saturday launching it. Qualifiers will move into a championship round robin in mid-afternoon.

The doubles will be held Sunday. In each event the defending champs will be hometown entries. Glenn Riffle in singles and Marion Shadley and Kenny Poff in doubles. Two other singles kings will be among Riffle's rivals: Floyd Toole, Little Rock, Ark., and Frank Breen, Elgin, Ill.

The same paper gave a halfway-point update that cheers on the local competitors:

Three Local Men Closing
in on Horseshoe Champ

Three Dayton men were following close on the heels of undefeated former champion, Frank Breen of Elgin, Ill., after yesterday's first-day matches in the National AAU horseshoe tournaments at the Frigidaire Recreation Park.

After six out of nine contests, Glenn Riffle, the Daytonian who is the defending champion, had lost only once for a tie with ex-champ Floyd Toole of Little Rock, Ark.

Charlie Sipple, with a 4-2 record, was in third place and Marion Shadley, 3-3, was fourth.

The remaining three singles contests are slated for this morning, while seven teams will vie in the doubles in the afternoon.

The *Dayton Daily News* also took a local slant on their review of the final results:

Poff, Shadley Keep National
AAU Horseshoe Championship

Frank Poff of Dayton and Marion Shadley, a Dayton worker who lives in Willingham, Sunday retained their national horseshoe pitching doubles championship.

After winning five of six games in the original seven-team round robin at Frigidaire Recreation Park, they took Frank Breen and Earl App of Elgin, Ill. and Floyd Toole of little Rock, Ark. And Jimmy Riggs of Jacksonville, Ark., in the additional round robin playoff necessitated deadlock.

They beat the Illinois team 50-47 and Arkansas 50-21. The Illinois team finished second.

Breen won the national singles title for the second time by beating Toole, another ex-champ, in a playoff 50-35, 47-50, 51-38. Breen a 42-year-old driving license inspector, who's been pitching 30 years, was runner up in 1939, 1941 and 1954 and won the national title in 1953.

Toole was the 1954 champ. Sunday he finished second for the second straight year, one place up on the defending champion, Dayton's Glenn Riffle. Breen and Toole each won eight of nine matches. Riffle seven of nine.

Of the other Dayton entrants, Charlie Sipple was 5-4 for a fourth place tie, Shadley 4-5 for a sixth place tie and Herman Hartman 1-8 for ninth in the field of 10.

The October 1956 issue of *Amateur Athlete* included a summary of the event:

Breen Regains AAU Horseshoe Title

by Norman F. Saettel
Executive Secretary, Dayton District Committee

Frank Breen, representing the Elgin, Illinois, Moose Lodge, regained the National AAU horseshoe pitching championship by pitching a sensational 67.0 ringer percentage and beating Floyd Toole, the 1954 champion, two games to one in a playoff. Each had finished the regulation round robin with 8-1 records.

Glenn Riffle, defending champion, finished third with two losses, but came back in his final game to beat Breen and force the playoff between Toole and Breen.

Breen set a new qualifying score in the Illinois Association meet in August with a sensational 281 and 90.0 ringer percentage. This record will be presented to the National Convention in October for recognition.

Hot Doubles Competition

The doubles play was even closer than the singles. Three teams, Dayton (Marion Shadley and Kenny Poff), the defending champions; the Illinois team (Frank Breen and Earl App) and the Arkansas team (Floyd Toole and Jimmy Riggs) ended in a three-way tie for first place.

In the playoff, Illinois disposed of Arkansas in the first game and held an early lead of 42-21 over Dayton. Dayton came back on to take the game and then easily disposed of Arkansas to regain the doubles title won in 1955 in Little Rock.

New Scoreboard Aids

The matches were played on the courts of the Frigidaire Recreation Park and were acclaimed by the participants as the finest they have ever seen. Joe Dimatteo, Ohio AAU horseshoe pitching chairman, directed the meet. Mrs. Emma Focht, record clerk, introduced for the first time the rotating scoreboards she and her husband have developed for horseshoes. They are of tremendous spectator interest and keep everyone informed of the progress on each court continuously.

Oldest player again was L. T. Couch, 76, of Little Rock. Jimmy Riggs, also of Little Rock, was the youngest at 26. Trophies were awarded as well as medals as prescribed by National AAU rules. Dayton Chamber of Commerce awarded certifications of appreciation to each of the ten qualifiers.

A side note about Emma Focht: A more appropriate title for her would have been tournament statistician, as she was far more than a records clerk or scorekeeper. She never pitched a horseshoe in competition, but made a career of serving the Ohio Association for over twenty years, and the NHPA for nearly as long, as a statistician. Emma Focht is a member of the Ohio Buckeye Horseshoe Pitchers Hall of Fame and was inducted to the NHPA Hall of Fame in 1983. Her husband Paul, who was involved in designing the scoreboards, is also in both halls of fame. Paul Focht was also a pitcher. He won the World Championship in 1962 and was a three-time state champion of Ohio.

The *Elgin Daily Courier* covered Breen's win. They certainly gave their hometown hero more print than the Ohio papers and included more detail:

Frank Breen Wins National
AAU Horseshoe Crown

Frank "Lefty" Breen, captain of the Elgin Moose 1955 National AAU championship team, Sunday won his second AAU singles title by defeating Floyd Toole in a best two-out-of-three playoff series before more than 1,000 cheering spectators.

Breen and Toole had tied with eight victories and one defeat in the regular round robin and the Elgin southpaw then took the playoff set, 50-35, 47-50, 50-38 to wrap up the championship. Glenn Riffle, who handed Breen his only loss 43-50, finished in third place with a 7-2 record.

Whips Opposition

En route to the championship, Breen defeated Garrison 50-36; Hartman 50-8; Murphy 50-28; Shadley 50-47; Riggs 50-8; Sipple 50-42.

In the doubles, Breen and Earl App had to settle for second place as they tied then lost the deciding game of the three-way playoff series to Shadley and Kenneth Poff 47-50, a margin of only one ringer.

Those two pairs, along with the Toole-Riggs combination had won five games and lost one in the regular round robin play. Breen and App scored a decisive 50-26 victory over the Little rock team in the first playoff game but then bowed to the Dayton champs.

Win Five Straight

The Elgin pair reached the finals the hard way as they lost their first round robin game to Shadley and Poff 26-50. They then bounced back to win their next five matches to reach the playoff.

1956 National AAU Seniors Singles Championships Finals

Player	City	Qual	W	L	Pts.	R	DR	SP	Pct.
Frank Breen	Elgin, Ill.	224	8	1	450	374	120	558	67.0
Floyd Toole	Little Rock	221	8	1	449	373	116	570	65.4
Glenn Riffle	Dayton	DC	7	5	426	379	117	582	65.1
Charles Sipple	Dayton	223	5	4	427	400	119	652	61.3
Woody Thomas	High Point	212	5	4	349	297	79	548	54.1
Marion Shadley	Dayton	217	4	5	395	367	108	608	60.3
Conrad Murphy	W.-Salem	221	4	5	358	298	81	560	53.2
Frank Garrison	Cramerton	205	3	6	347	309	85	588	52.5
Herman Hartman	Dayton	196	1	8	236	224	55	646	48.2
Jimmy Riggs	Little Rock	203	0	9	166	167	30	446	37.4

Playoff Game –

		W	L	Pts.	R	DR	SP	Pct.
Frank Breen		2	1	151	173	59	252	68.7
Floyd Toole		1	2	126	165	54	252	65.5

1956 National AAU Seniors Doubles Championships Finals

Teams	W	L	Pts.	R	DR	SP	Pct
Dayton No. 1 (M. Shadley-K. Poff)	5	1		186		354	52.5
Illinois (F. Breen-E. App)	5	1		189		346	54.6
Arkansas No. 1 (F. Toole-J. Riggs)	5	1		209		366	57.1
Dayton No. 2	3	3		182		360	50.5
North Carolina No. 1	2	4		139		316	43.9
North Carolina No. 2	1	5		168		370	45.4
Arkansas No. 2	0	6		97		316	30.6

Playoff Games

	W	L	Pts.	R	DR	SP	Pct
Dayton No. 1	2	1	100	62	18	114	54.4
Illinois	1	1	99	94	27	168	55.9
Arkansas No. 1	0	2	61	75	22	154	48.7

The players on the bottom four teams were not named in any of the newspaper articles or even in *Amateur Athlete*, which had the most comprehensive finals stats. Based on other years, here is an educated guess of who those players were:

Dayton No. 2 – Glenn Riffle & Charles Sipple
North Caroline No. 1 – Conrad Murphy & Woody Thomas
North Carolina No. 2 – James Garrison & Frank Garrison
Arkansas No. 2 – L. T. Couch & Bill Higginbottom

1957

Back to Maryland, Where Toole Reigns

In 1957 the championships were held again in Maryland, this time Salisbury, from August 31st through September 2nd. The August 31st edition of the *Salisbury Times* announced the 1957 National AAU event, followed by a feature story on defending champion Frank Breen:

\Roster Shows Champs
Breen, Riffle and Toole

The complete roster of entries—singles and doubles—for the Amateur Athletic Union National horseshoe tournament here this weekend was announced today by Lorne Rickert, superintendent of the Wicomico Recreation Commission.

Most of the attention will be focused on Frank Breen, of Elgin, Illinois, present national titleholder; Glenn Riffle of Dayton, Ohio, the 1955 winner; and Floyd Toole of Little Rock, Arkansas, the 1954 national champion.

Breen and Toole finished last year's tourney tied, with Breen winning two of three playoff games.

Twenty-one other contestants, representing six states, will be tossing 100 shoes in today's qualifying rounds on the Picnic Island Courts in City Park. The best 16 pitchers will play round robin matches tomorrow and eleven doubles teams will compete on Monday. Here are the entries:

Singles –

Frank Breen, Earl App, Arthur Weir, from Elgin, Ill.; Glenn Riffle and Charles Sipple, Dayton, Ohio; William P. Sammons, Seaford, Del.; Frank Garrison, John Corns, Sid Welch, Chester Utt, James Scotten and Bernie A Morris, North Carolina Association, Durham; Woody Thomas, High Point, N.C.; Conrad Murphy, Randall R. Jones, Winston-Salem, N.C.; Al Hoover, Asheboro, N.C.; Edwin Stancik, Durham, N.C.; C. Darrell Eller, Thomasville, N.C.; F. C. Toole and Bill Higginbottom No. Little Rock, Ark.; Henry Donalds, Salisbury; Thornton M. Kohler, Jack Ruby and Leslie Holman, Sykesville.

Doubles Teams –

Elgin Moose Lodge, Elgin, Ill. – Frank Breen and Earl App; Dayton, Ohio – Glenn Riffle and Charles Sipple; Sykesville Horseshoe Club – Jack Ruby and Leslie Holman; No. Little Rock (Ark.) – F. C. Toole and Bill Higginbottom; Salisbury – Henry Donalds and Thornton M. Kohler; High Point (N.C.) – Woody Thomas and Al Hoover; Winston-Salem (N.C.) – Conrad Murphy and Randall R. Jones; North Carolina (AAU) – Frank Garrison and John Corns, Sid Welch and Chester Utt, Bennie E. Morris and Edwin Stancik, C. D. Eller and James Scotten.

Breen Is Veteran
Horseshoe Pitcher

Jolly, congenial, agreeable and soft-spoken. That just about describes Frank Breen, the big fellow from Elgin, Ill. He's in town to defend the national amateur horseshoe pitching this weekend at City Park.

Breen, 43, arrived Thursday night, motoring 934 miles from Elgin, a town of 47,000, located 38 miles west of Chicago. "Yes, I got here a day or two earlier so I could get acquainted with the courts here," he declared. "You have a red clay here, which is a little different than our blue clay in the west."

Breen is not a tender foot in this sport as he has been tossing horseshoes for the past 35 years. "Yes, I started at the corner fire house when a youngster." He holds six world records including a marathon mark of 2,435 ringers in 10 hours; most consecutive ringers, 38; 91 ringers of 100 shoes pitched; 49 ringers of 50 shoes; 281 points in a 100-shoe match and 143 points in a 50-shoe match.

Breen employed as a drivers license inspector for the state of Illinois, has been the state AAU champion the last nine years and has shared the state doubles title with Earl App, also of Elgin, the past five seasons. App is also here competing in the tournament.

"I guess I've walked from coast to coast twice pitching shoes," he said. "I've competed in 40 of the 48 states. Breen took a liking to Salisbury without too much introduction after finding the local Moose Lodge on Snow Hill Road. He has been a member of this organization for many years. "Yes, I felt at home when I met some of your Moose boys. I'm going back again too," he declared with a grin.

Breen, App and Art Wier, another fellow townsman, representing the Elgin Moose team and they are so identified on their shirts. "Our team has won 98 of the last 100 matches," Breen explained. "We'll play any team in the nation on a home and home basis. It makes no difference where."

The champion isn't a one-sport man. "I like to bowl and also follow football and baseball closely. I like the Milwaukee Braves and Chicago White Sox. We were sort of hoping these two clubs would meet in the World Series, but those darn New York Yankees took care of the White Sox this week."

The *Salisbury Times* also carried the results of the singles championship:

Arkansas Horseshoe Pitcher Wins
Floyd Toole Repeats Win Made in 1954

Floyd Toole won the singles championship of the National Amateur Athletic Union horseshoe pitching tournament here yesterday. This is a repeat performance for the 39-year-old railway engineer as he won national honors in 1954 at Marietta, Ga.

The doubles play was still in progress at a late hour last night under the lights on Picnic Island in City Park.

Following a heavy morning downpour, the courts were readied into playable condition by the Wicomico Horseshoe Club membership. At

11 a.m. the pits were a goo of red clay and a continuation of the tournament at that time appeared to be unfavorable. Each of the pits was shoveled over and burned off with gasoline and surprisingly dried off in a hurry. The round robin of 16 qualifiers were pitching away by 1 p.m.

Toole defeated another former titlist, Glenn Riffle of Dayton, Ohio, in a playoff with straight wins; 50-4 and 50-28.

Floyd Toole, two-time National Amateur Champion

Frank Breen of Elgin, Ill., the defending titlist, finished third with a 13-2 won and lost mark. He created the playoff stalemate by trimming Riffle, 50-14. Riffle had won all of his first 14 games and was undefeated going into the final round. Breen seemed difficult to unseat after clicking off 12 straight wins before dropping decisions to Charles Sipple and Toole before taking the measure of Riffle. Toole posted six in a row, dropping one to Riffle, then nabbed the last eight.

Several hundred spectators watched these ringer experts perform during the five-hour grind. The marksmanship of these craftsmen became monotonous at times as they rang up ringer after ringer.

A noteworthy feature of this classic was the sportsmanship exhibited by all contestants. Compliments were exchanged frequently between players and Toole was roundly congratulated at the finish by most of the 15 other entries.

We all share one another's wins," declared Breen. "This is all for fun, you know. There's a fellowship enjoyed in horseshoe pitching that doesn't exist, I believe in any other sport. We look forward each summer to this occasion when we renew acquaintances. Most of us have been doing this for years and years."

An *Amateur Athlete* summary compiled by C. H. "Doc" Ashley, vice chairman of the National AAU Horseshoe Pitching Committee, provided the complete stats for the final standings:

1957 National AAU Seniors Singles Championships Finals

	Player	City	W	L	Pts	R	DR	SP	Pct
1.	Floyd Toole	Little Rock	14	1	750	509	157	808	63.4
2.	Glenn Riffle	Dayton, Ohio	14	1	738	501	160	770	66.5
3.	Frank Breen	Elgin, Ill.	13	2	725	489	157	782	62.9
4.	Charles Sipple	Dayton, Ohio	12	3	723	438	121	828	53.6
5.	Frank Garrison	Cramerton, NC	10	5	689	432	111	812	54.3
6.	Bill Higginbottom	Little Rock	10	5	607	414	86	920	45.5
7.	Art Wier	Elgin, Ill.	8	7	621	440	109	914	53.2
8.	Earl App	Elgin, Ill.	7	8	585	410	77	950	43.1
9.	Woody Thomas	High Point, NC	6	9	546	360	74	856	42.0
10.	Edwin Stancik	Durham, NC	6	9	448	279	67	584	47.7
11.	Darrell Eller	Thomasville	6	9	617	372	87	802	46.3
12.	Jack Ruby	Sykesville, MD	4	11	420	328	60	780	42.0
13.	Leslie Holman	Sykesville, MD	4	11	464	306	61	780	39.2
14.	Randall R. Jones	W-Salem, NC	4	11	498	277	55	740	37.4
15.	Al Hoover	Thomasville	2	13	423	267	32	662	40.3
16.	Conrad Murphy	High Point, NC	0	15	229	194	37	546	34.2

Playoff for the championship, best two out of three games:

Floyd Toole defeated Glenn Riffle 50-4, 50-28.

For the third year in a row, the singles championship was decided in a playoff. In each case, the same three players were involved—either by winning a decisive game to cause the playoff or being one of the playoff contestants: Glenn Riffle, Floyd Toole, and Frank Breen. They were three of the National AAU's all-time star pitchers.

The September 3rd *Salisbury Times* announced the 1957 doubles champions:

Riffle, Sipple Win Horseshoe Doubles Crown

Glenn Riffle and Charles Sipple of Dayton, Ohio, won the doubles championship of the National Amateur Athletic Union horseshoe pitching tournament Sunday on the Picnic Island in City Park. They pitched 61.2 percent ringer average.

Doubles play followed the singles bracket of the tourney and finished up under the arc lights at 10:15 p.m.

This is the third straight year that a Dayton entry has won the doubles title and with a different team. Marion Shadley and Kenny Poff teamed up last year in the 1956 tourney in Dayton.

The North Little Rock array consisting of Floyd Toole and Bill Higginbottom were awarded runner-up honors although it had the same 5-2 won and lost mark as the Elgin Moose entry. The Arkansas aggregation was given the edge due to its better ringer average—56.1 to 44.7. Frank Breen and Earl App represented the Elgin Moose organization.

1957 National AAU Seniors Doubles Championships Finals

Team & Players	W	L	Pts	R	DR	SP	Pct
1. Dayton, Ohio (Glenn Riffle & Charles Sipple)	7	0	363	232	73	382	61.2
2 No. Little Rock (Floyd Toole & Higginbottom)	5	2	333	233	56	430	56.1
3. Elgin Moose (Frank Breen & Earl App)	5	2	308	204	52	448	44.7
4. High Point, NC (Woody Thomas & C. Murphy)	4	3	293	194	43	452	42.9
5. Winston-Salem, NC (Frank Garrison & R.R. Jones)	3	4	297	207	43	462	44.6
6. Thomasville, NC (Darrell Eller & Al Hoover)	3	4	288	179	40	456	39.2
7. Sykesville, MD (Jack Ruby & Leslie Holman)	1	6	231	151	28	408	36.2
8. Salisbury, MD (Scott Bennett & Howard Smith)	0	7	222	155	29	414	39.0

1958

Riffle Continues Dominance

The 1958 National AAU event, held on August 30th and 31st, was at a new site—or rather, a new site for the senior event. Back in 1940 and 1941, Winston-Salem hosted the junior championships. Horseshoe pitching has been active and strong in North Carolina for a long time. An uncredited clipping from the Riffle family scrapbook provided this tournament preview:

U. S. Horseshoe Pitching
Meet Opens Here Today

Horseshoe pitchers from North Carolina, Arkansas, Georgia, Illinois, Ohio, New Jersey and Virginia began tuning up for the National AAU tournament today and Sunday with practice rounds yesterday at Miller Park Horseshoe Courts.

The number of entries for the tournament, according to tourney director Joe White, has reached 45, more than double the previous high of 22 participants.

Entries will be accepted until registration at 8 a.m. today. Qualifying begins immediately afterwards continuing through 11 a.m.. Round robin singles competition begins at 1 p.m.

[According to one of the competitors, Frank Breen,] "This looks like the toughest field I've ever been in. From the entry list I noticed Ray Griffin (1952 champion from Atlanta, Ga.), Glenn Riffle (1955 champion from Dayton, Ohio) and names of several other real good boys."

"There are also some real good pitchers from Carolina. That King (Walter of Asheboro) fellow is good. So are James Garrison, Conrad Murphy and a lot of other Carolinians.

"Earl App and I were real impressed with the horseshoe courts. They are as good as any I have ever pitched on. The clay and stakes are in perfect shape. Somebody deserves a lot of credit for laying out such a [great] course."

Local entries include Conrad Murphy, Wes Blakely, Richard Carter, Joe Collette, John Corns Jr., James Hester, R. R. Hooker, George Hrenko, Randall Jones, James Maners, Howard Rayfield, Arlie Worrell and Raymond Wall.

Among the favorites are Frank Breen, Earl App, Elgin, Ill.; Griffin; Glenn Riffle, Charles Sipple, Dayton, Ohio; James Garrison, Cramerton; James Scotten, Woody Thomas, High Point; Walter King; Sol Berman, Elizabeth, N.J.; Linwood Dove, Lynchburg, Va., and L. T. Couch, Little Rock, Ark.

A barbeque will be held for contestants and scorers at 6 p.m. with matches resuming at 7 p.m. until midnight. Singles will continue Sunday morning if necessary. Doubles competition is scheduled for 1 p.m. Sunday following a barbeque chicken dinner.

Among the contestants getting in practice licks at Miller Park yesterday were Frank Breen, two-time national singles champion (1953 and 1956) and Earl App. Breen and App have won the Illinois AAU doubles championship for the past 7 years and were runner-up to Riffle and Sipple in the national tourney last year.

Breen, a southpaw, has won the Illinois state title 10 years in succession and never finished lower than third in 12 years of nation amateur competition. Breen also has to his credit a perfect game, 38 ringers in 38 pitches. He holds the amateur world's marathon record of 2,436 ringers in 10 hours of unbroken pitching; an average of better than 4 ringers a minute. He has pitched 91 ringers in 100 pitches and scored 278 points with 100 shoes.

The scrapbook also includes a midtournament update:

Riffle, Last Year's Runner-Up, Leads in AAU Horseshoe Pitching Tourney

Horseshoe pitching partners, Glenn Riffle and Charles Sipple, were first and second, respectively, in the National AAU singles tournament when first day firing ceased at 9 p.m. last night at Miller Park.

Riffle, runner-up in last year's tourney, leads the field with a 10-0 record. Sipple is close behind with a 9-1 mark. They have not played each other yet.

Singles competition resumes today at 9 a.m. with five matches remaining in the round robin tournament of 16 participants.

Doubles playoffs, limited to 12 entries, follow at 1 p.m. Riffle and Sipple are defending doubles champions.

A record field of 43 qualified. The top 16 qualifiers were placed in the championship flight and eight in the Class B flight. Sipple, a southpaw, posted the highest qualifying score, 242. Ed Stancik of Durham won the Class B title with a 7-0 record.

Surprise of the tournament is Darrell Eller of Thomasville who finished the first day with an 8-2 record tied for third place with Frank Breen.

One of the tensest matches of the day came at closing time when Eller and Sipple engaged in a 98-pitch duel. Sipple came from behind a 39-47 deficit to win 54-47.

Sipple's only loss was to Conrad Murphy. Murphy is deadlocked with Walter King, Carolina's AAU champ, for fifth place with 7-3 records. Frank Garrison of Cramerton is seventh with a 6-4 mark.

The pace-setting Riffle has matches remaining with Sipple, Breen, Murphy, James Terry of Rust Hall and Sid Welch of Winston-Salem. Riffle's ringer percentage of 82, 46 ringers in 56 pitches, was tops for a match. Eller has position on the rest of the leaders. He has already faced Riffle (losing 48-52) and Sipple.

Breen made the finest comeback of the day. The former two-time champion (1953 and 1956) dropped two of his first three games, then bounced back with seven straight triumphs.

Riffle and Breen praised the Miller Park Horseshoe Courts as among the best they've ever played on. Both also cited the tournament field as the toughest in recent years.

"Why, it was tough just to qualify in this tournament," said Breen. "You can't let up on any of these boys at any time. I had Murphy down by nearly 30 points and he pulled within 10 before I went out.

"I believe there are more good horseshoe pitchers in this tournament than any I have ever competed in. We ought to have a lot of fun out here tomorrow."

1958 National AAU Senior Horseshoe Pitching Championship

Championship Flight Qualifying

	Ringers	Score
Charles Sipple, Dayton, Ohio	73	242
Glenn Riffle, Dayton, Ohio	72	239
Walter King, Asheboro, NC	64	235
Woody Thomas, High Point, NC	63	231
Frank Garrison, Cramerton, NC	64	220
Frank Breen, Elgin, Illinois	62	218
Darrell Eller, Thomasville, NC	61	210
Conrad Murphy, Winston-Salem	54	209
R. R. Hooker, Winston-Salem, NC	59	207
Lowell Hurley, Trinity, NC	58	206
James Terry, Rural Hall, NC	57	206
Sid Welch, Winston-Salem, NC	55	204
G. B. Guynn, High Point, NC	58	202
John Corns Jr., Winston-Salem, NC	54	193
Earl App, Elgin, Illinois	51	188
Warren Stewart, Burlington, NC	52	188

Class 'B' Flight

James Scotten, High Point, NC	50	188
Al Hoover, Asheboro, NC	48	188
Ed Stancik, Durham, NC	49	185
Homer Hammonds, Asheboro, NC	51	185
J. E. Austin, Graham, NC	51	184
Gilbert Moore, Burlington, NC	52	183
Glynden Moore, Burlington, NC	49	183
James Garrison, Cramerton, NC	50	181

	R	Pts
Robert L. Toney, Lynchburg, VA	49	180
Randall Jones, Winston-Salem, NC	47	177
Roy Houser, High Point, NC	51	175
Melvin Howard, Jamestown, NC	45	174
Arlie Worrell, Winston-Salem, NC	41	171
Howard Hayfield, Winston-Salem	46	169
Joe Coble, Mebane, NC	47	168
George Hrenko, Winston-Salem	47	167
Ray Griffin, Atlanta, GA	46	166
Howard Hester, Winston-Salem	41	162
C. G. Simpson, Elon Col., NC	37	162
Linwood Dove, Lynchburg, VA	44	161
Allen Simpson, Elon, Col., NC	41	160
Joe Collette, Winston-Salem, NC	34	148
Robert Harris, Durham, NC	37	144
Raymond Wall, Winston-Salem	36	142
W. B. Stinson, Durham, NC	29	130
L.C. Couch, Little Rock, AR	32	122
James Maners, Winston-Salem, NC	23	117

Doubles Entries and Qualifying Scores

Sipple & Riffle 481	Murphy & Thomas 430	Hooker & Terry 413
Hoover & King 411	Breen & App 405	Garrison & Garrison 401
Scotten & Eller 398	Hauser & Hurler 381	Howard & Guynn 376
Stewart & Austin 372	Jones & Stancik 362	Worell & Hammonds 356

This clipping was found in the Riffle family album:

Glenn Riffle Wins Horseshoe Title
Teams With Sipple to Cop Double Crown

Glenn Riffle won an unprecedented 15 consecutive matches to capture the National AAU horseshoe singles championship and then teamed up with Charlie Sipple to cop the doubles title yesterday at Miller Park.

It was the second national crown for Riffle who won in 1955 and was runner-up last year. The 40-year-old Ohioan averaged 67.8 percent ringers for the 15 matches and scored 673 points.

Riffle and Sipple won their second national doubles titles with eight straight triumphs to close out the two-day tournament. The duo posted a ringer percentage of 64.7.

Runner-up in the singles was Darrell Eller, who tacked five victories onto his first day total of 8-2 for a 13-2 record. Eller, the tournament surprise, lost only to Riffle and Sipple.

Walter King, Carolina AAU champion, was third with a 12-3 record. Frank Breen and Sipple posted 11-4 records, but Sipple was awarded fourth place with a higher ringer percentage of 62.2 to Breen's 61.9.

Breen and Earl App edged out Roy Hauser and Lowell Hurley for second place in the doubles. Both teams posted 6-2 records, but Breen and App had the edge in ringer percentage.

Ed Stancik won the Class B singles championship over seven other contestants with a 7-0 record. Glyden Moore was second at a 6-1 mark and Al Hoover, third with a record of 5-2.

A record number of 43 qualified for the tournament Saturday morning. Sixteen were accepted in the championship flight and eight in the class B division. The previous high number of qualifiers was 22.

An estimated crowd of over 800 watched yesterday's finals.

1958 National AAU Senior Singles Championships

	Player	City	W	L	Pts	R	DR	SP	%
1.	Glenn Riffle,	Dayton, Ohio	15	0	673	525	181	774	67.8
2.	Darrell Eller,	High Point, NC	13	2	664	492	160	772	63.8
3.	Walter King,	Asheboro, NC	12	3	662	481	142	830	57.9
4.	Charles Sipple,	Dayton, Ohio	11	4	661	569	175	914	62.2
5.	Fran Breen,	Elgin, Illinois	11	4	720	549	166	886	61.9
6.	Lowell Hurley,	Trinity, NC	9	6	649	569	175	944	60.5
7.	Frank Garrison,	Cramerton, NC	9	6	625	510	140	926	55.1
8.	Conrad Murphy,	Winston-Salem	9	6	580	440	123	872	50.4
9.	Woody Thomas,	High Point, NC	7	8	511	430	107	830	51.9
10.	Earl App,	Elgin, Illinois	6	9	487	387	98	766	50.5
11.	G. B. Guynn,	High Point, NC	5	10	543	473	125	948	50.0
12.	Jim Terry,	Rural Hall, NC	4	11	388	344	96	688	50.0
13.	R. R. Hooker,	Winston-Salem	4	11	532	443	106	928	47.7
14.	Warren Stewart,	Burlington, NC	3	12	533	434	113	904	50.2
15.	John Corns,	Winston-Salem	1	14	380	361	83	794	45.5
16.	Sid Welch,	Winston-Salem	1	14	254	236	51	544	43.4

1958 National AAU Senior Doubles Championships

Player	City	W	L	Pts	R	DR	SP	%
1. Glenn Riffle, Dayton, Charles Sipple	Ohio	8	0	412	317	106	490	64.7
2. Frank Breen, Earl App	Elgin, Illinois	6	2	399	271	69	518	52.5
3. Roy Hauser, Lowell Hurley	High Point, NC	6	2	353	221	19	442	50.0
4. Al Hoover, Walter King	Asheboro, NC	3	5	311	262	67	498	52.5

Awards

Highest Ringer Percentage – Glenn Riffle Youngest Contestant – Howard Rayfield Oldest Contestant – L. C. Couch Traveling the Most Distance – L. C. Couch

None of the resource documents provide the full field of the doubles teams. *Amateur Athlete* magazine printed the most complete statistical report of the final standings, but named only the top four teams. Initially, it seemed possible that there were just four teams playing a double round robin. In that case, though, each team would have played six games, which doesn't match the reports. The games do not add up properly (there should always be the same number of wins and losses) which leads to the conclusion that there were eight teams in the class. Based on the reported qualifying scores, the unnamed teams in the finals were: Conrad Murphy and Woody Thomas; R. R. Hooker and James Terry; Frank Garrison and James Garrison; James Scotten and Darrell Eller.

1959

Finally to Elgin

Many of the newspaper articles covering the 1958 event reported that the next year's national championship would be held in Elgin, Illinois. And they were—on September 3rd and 4th, 1959, the National AAU Championships were held in Elgin, the home of past champion Frank Breen.

The *Elgin Daily Courier* provided some coverage of the event, but no final statistics, and *Amateur Athlete* magazine carried no coverage at all. Here is what we have, starting with a pretournament announcement:

National AAU Horseshoe Tourney at Wing Park

Riffle and Sipple will be in Elgin over the weekend. The pair, Glenn Riffle and Charles Sipple of Dayton, Ohio, are the defending doubles champions as the National AAU Horseshoe Pitching Tournament is contested on the Wing Park courts Saturday and Sunday. Riffle is also the defending singles titlist in a field generally believed to be one of the strongest ever to compete in the national meet.

Singles qualification will start at 9 a.m. Saturday with the 20 highest scores meeting in a round robin final at 1 p.m. Doubles competition will follow the singles but probably will not get underway until Sunday morning.

Liddle Seeded

William Liddle of Crystal Lake is seeded number seven in the singles matches in which Riffle and Walter King, champion pitcher from the Carolinas, are rated favorites.

William Danhauer of Chicago is an outside threat in the singles as is unseeded Roger Ehlers of St. Charles. Ehlers will team up with Frank Breen of Elgin Moose Lodge 799 in the doubles matches. Along with the team of Tom Limbaugh and Liddle, the Breen-Ehlers team could make trouble for the defending champs.

Tossing in the meet for Elgin, in addition to Ehlers and Breen will be Art Wier, Clint Sjurset, Hugo Honert and George Bradley.

Crystal Lake Tossers

From Crystal Lake will come Bing Benson, Scotty Hansen, Bill Baldwin, Hank Zollick, Tom Kollinger, Vic Freudenberg, Bud Limbaugh and Tom Limbaugh. Other tossers area tossers entered are James Feeley, Jack Stout, John Pavelenko of Chicago and Abraham L. Austin of Hinsdale.

Woody Thomas and Conrad Murphy of the Carolinas, who won the doubles meet at Little Rock, in 1954, also will compete.

This short uncredited clipping is from the Riffle family scrapbook:

Four Daytonians
'Shoe' In for AAU Finals

Three Dayton pitchers head into tomorrow's final phase of singles play in the National AAU Horseshoe tournament. A forth joins them in the final doubles phase.

Glenn Riffle, Charles Sipple and Paul Helton are the singles trio and Mickey Broughton completes the Ohio team's foursome. All four are members of the East Dayton Horseshoe club.

Horseshoe pitching champions—Charles Sipple, left, and Glenn Riffle, right, National A.A.U. horse shoe pitching doubles champions, flank Norman Saettel, National A.A.U. chairman of the sport. Riffle also won the singles title and high ringer percentage trophy. (Photo by Arlie L. Worrell).

Riffle and Sipple each sport 5-0 records and Helton and Broughton are 4-1, but Helton won a spot for tomorrow by winning on ringer percentage.

The three other singles survivors are James Feeley of Chicago, Darrell Eller of Thomasville, N.C., and Melvin Howard of Jamestown, N.C., all with 5-0 records.

The following article from the Riffle family scrapbook describes an incredible and rare ending to the doubles competition:

Horseshoe Doubles
Ends in a 3-Way Tie

After seven hours of playoff failed to produce a doubles champion, officials of the National AAU Horseshoe Pitching Championships at Wing Park declared a three-way tie for first place Sunday.

Frank Breen and Roger Ehlers of the Elgin Moose Horseshoe Club, defending titlist Glenn Riffle and Charles Sipple, and Darrell Eller and Melvin Howard of Jamestown, N.C., were declared winners in an unprecedented move ending the two-day matches at 11 p.m. Sunday The regular round robin matches had ended at 4 p.m. Sunday with the overtime extending the meet. Officials of the meet will award three doubles trophies.

Breen and Ehlers moved to the finals of the meet by taking five matches, including one from Vic Freudenburg and Bud Limbaugh of Crystal Lake, 50-44.

It was the first national tournament for Ehlers, who is from St. Charles. He out-pitched Riffle, national singles champion, in every match contested in the doubles. Riffle took the singles event with little difficulty for the second straight time. Eller placed second with Paul Helton third. Breen did not enter the singles event this year.

Earl App served as head scorekeeper for the national meeting with Warren Lippold of Crystal Lake acting as judge.

1959 National AAU Senior Singles Championships

	Player	City	W	L
1.	Glenn Riffle	Dayton, Ohio	9	0
2.	Darrell Eller	Jamestown, NC		
3.	Paul Helton	Dayton, Ohio		
	Mickey Broughton	Dayton, Ohio		
	James Feeley	Chicago, Illinios		
	Melvin Howard	Jamestown, NC		
	Charlie Sipple	Dayton, Ohio		

1959 National AAU Senior Doubles Championships

	Player City	W	L
1.	Glenn Riffle-Charlie Sipple Dayton, Ohio	5	2
1.	Frank Breen-Roger Ehlers Elgin, Ill.	5	2
1.	Darrell Eller- Melvin Howard Jamestown, N.C.	5	2
	Vic Fredenburg-Bud Limbaugh Crystal Lake, Ill.		

While the three-way tie for first in doubles is remarkable, the big question of the 1959 event is: Why didn't Frank Breen enter the singles competition? Certainly, to win the national title in his hometown would have been a career highlight. Perhaps he was exercising his sportsmanship and playing the role of a host while letting visiting players have a shot at the title. We may never know for sure, but because he entered the doubles portion of the tournament, an injury is an unlikely explanation.

This was the second straight title for Glenn Riffle. He was not the first player to win two in a row—Hubert Trinkle and Dale Carson did so in previous years and later Walter King achieved consecutive wins. Not only was this a consecutive title for Riffle, it was his third overall National AAU singles championship, a feat realized by only one other player, John Lindmeier.

Now about that three-way tie for the doubles championship. A tie for first place is common, and even a three-way occurs occasionally. In those cases, a playoff usually decides the matter—but in 1959 they played for seven hours without breaking the tie, so the officials let the championship be shared by three teams. Several options were available to the officials to break the deadlock. First would be to determine who beat whom (of those who tied, who beat who in their direct games). But with three teams in the playoff, that might have been part of the dilemma—especially if further playoff round robins were held among them. The next, and best, option would have been to rank the three teams based on total points or total team ringers and hold a stepladder playoff. The playoff would have been concluded in two games and a clear-cut champion team determined. In any event, they could have determined which team had the most ringers or points scored (including playoff games) and let those totals break the tie. With a national championship at stake, the proper thing would have been to resolve the event with one champion team.

1959 was Frank Breen's final National AAU event. He was a star of the sport and the all-time leader in total AAU medals won.

He earned just three gold medals, but combined with his five silver and five bronze medals, and he leads the National AAU all-time medal count with 13 medals, one more than Glenn Riffle.

Frank Breen on home practice courts.

Frank Breen with trophy and family.

AAU National Amateur Horseshoe-Pitching Championships

1960

A Record-Setting Day For Riffle in Hometown

In Dayton, Ohio, on September 3rd and 4th, 1960, the circumstances were ripe for a new record: Glenn Riffle, a three-time champion, sought an unheard of third-straight title—and the in front of his hometown crowd. The Riffle family scrapbook provides a number of unmarked clippings that tell the story. First, an update following the first day's action:

Riffle Nears Title Repeat

It'll be youth against years of experience today in the singles of the National Horseshoe Pitching Championship at Delco Moraine grounds. Glenn Riffle, 41-year-old from Dayton, the defending champion in both singles and doubles, faces a 24-year-old television technician from Elgin, Illinois, Roger Ehlers, as his chief rival toward a repeat. Both men scored seven victories without losing a game yesterday in the preliminaries. They paced four other finalists who beat out a starting field of 24 crack pitchers.

Riffle shot 68.3 percent ringers, tops among the six. The assembler at Frigidaire was better than five percent more accurate than Darrell Eller, Durham, N.C., who hit 62.4 percent while losing just one game.

Qualifiers yesterday where divided into three sections of eight pitchers each. Two men in each section went to the finals. Other qualifiers with 6-1 records; are Walter King, Winston-Salem, N.C.; Charles Sipple, Dayton, 47-year-old employee of NCR; and Mel Howard, High Point, N.C.,

6-1. Ehlers had a 61.4 percentage on ringers while Sipple had a 61.8, as did King. Howard had 57.9.

Round robin play begins at 9 a.m. for the singles championship. Eight teams will square off in the doubles starting at 1 p.m. Riffle and Sipple are defending doubles champions.

Riffle Continues Horseshoe Hold

Glenn Riffle hadn't lost a game in two years of pitching horseshoe in the National AAU tournament and this year was no exception. Riffle took his third straight National AAU singles title yesterday by sweeping all 6 of his games at Delco-Moraine grounds.

Raising his ringer percentage for the two-day meet to 68.9, Riffle eased past Walter King after trailing by as much as 49-32, to win the title.

Second place went to Roger Ehlers, who defeated Charles Sipple in a playoff. Sipple was third.

Ehlers, who had opened the singles meet Saturday by matching Riffle with seven victories without a setback, got some revenge in the doubles. Ehlers combined with Jack Stout to dethrone Sipple and Riffle in the doubles throwing. Stout and Ehlers, undefeated, had a ringer percentage of 61.5 after trimming the Dayton twosome, 50-31.

Mel Howard and Darrell Eller were third in doubles, after playing off with the Dayton duo.

Conrad Murphy took a high qualifying medal with 245. North Carolina's four-player aggregate score of 925 won the team title.

The coverage provided by the *Amateur Athlete* gave a bit more information:

Riffle Retains Horseshoe Title
But Young Illinois Team Captures
National Double Crown in Major Upset

by Norman F. Saettel

Chairman, National Horseshoe Pitching Committee

Glenn Riffle of the East Dayton Horseshoe Club, cool and confident in the 90 degree-plus temperature at the Delco Moraine Recreation Park, won his third successive AAU Horseshoe Pitching Championship by closing out 12 consecutive games without a loss September 3-4.

Riffle ran his consecutive winning streak to 37 games covering three years, and tied the record set by Frank Breen in 1941, by amassing a 68.9 ringer percentage in the meet.

The team of Roger Ehlers and Jack Stout pulled a real upset in dethroning the defending doubles champions, Riffle and Sipple, in the doubles competition. The young Illinois team (both are 24 years old) set a new record for a game ringer percentage of 64.5, in disposing of the former champions decisively, 50-31.

The competition in the preliminary rounds was particularly keen, as all six finalists pitched over 60 percent ringers. In fact Jack Stout, the Illinois champion, tossed 61.9 percent and failed to make the final in his bracket. Five years ago, 60 percent would have been good enough for one of the championship medals.

Riffle pitched superbly in the singles final. After being down 32-49 in his game with Walter King, Riffle put on the pressure by pitching 90 percent ringers and eased past King 50-49. Roger Ehlers took the second[-place] medal and Charles Sipple won the bronze medal.

The Carolinas team of Mel Howard and Darrell Eller placed third in the doubles. The team trophy was won for the first time by the Carolinas Association and was awarded to team captain Randall Jones. The Carolinas team amassed a total of 925 points.

The meet was sponsored by the Dayton District of the AAU in conjunction with two of its member clubs and the Delco Moraine Division, General Motors Corporation. Joseph Dimatteo of Dayton served as meet director.

The Carolina Association expressed a desire to return the National Championships in 1961 to Winston-Salem under the sponsorship of the Winston-Salem Recreation and the Carolinas Horseshoe Club.

The final standings and statistics are incomplete, despite the *Amateur Athlete* summary. The complete standings never appeared in the magazine or the newspaper articles. The stats provided below are incomplete, but at least indicate the participants. The games-won totals shown include the semifinal games pitched by the player, which is appropriate because the final class was determined through a qualifying process. The qualifiers then moved into a semifinal and then finals structure.

1960 National AAU Senior Doubles Championships

1. Roger Ehlers, St. Charles, IL, and Jack Stout, Melrose Park, IL
2. Glenn Riffle and Charles Sipple, Dayton, OH
3. Melvin Howard, High Point, NC, and Darrell Eller, Durham, NC

1960 National AAU Senior Singles Championships

	Player	City	W	L	%
1.	Glenn Riffle	Dayton, OH	12	0	68.9
2.	Roger Ehlers	St. Charles, IL	11	1	
3.	Charlie Sipple	Dayton, OH	6	6	
4.	Walter King	Winston-Salem, NC	6	6	
5.	Melvin Howard	Jamestown, NC			
6.	Darrell Eller	Jamestown, NC			
	Conrad Murphy	Winston-Salem, NC			
	Tom Jones	Winston-Salem, NC			
	Randall R. Jones	Winston-Salem, NC			
	Woody Thomas	High Point, NC			
	Ed Stancik	Durham, NC			
	Mickey Broughton	Dayton, OH			
	Paul Helton	Dayton, OH			

The 1960 event marked Glenn Riffle's final National AAU championship, though he did compete in 1961, when he placed third. So, after all his heroics, was Riffle still an amateur at this point? Ohio was a highly competitive horseshoe pitching area, and Riffle was the state champion twice—but not until 1965 and then 1975. Riffle had a tremendous NHPA career after his AAU participation. He entered his first World Tournament in 1962 and from 1964 to 1978, he qualified 10 times for the men's championship class finals. Throughout his NHPA career he won 176 games, and he still ranks fortieth on the all-time wins list. In the 1964 NHPA World Tournament, Riffle won 15 games while averaging 75.54 percent. In that tournament, a record thirteen players averaged over 80 percent ringers—and Riffle placed fifteenth in the 36-player championship class. Riffle is not in the NHPA Hall of Fame, but he has been nominated and is on the ballot. So—taking his later NHPA achievements into consideration, I would say that, yes, Glenn Riffle was an amateur during his AAU career.

1961

A New Star Arrives

The 1961 National AAU Tournament returned to Winston-Salem, North Carolina, and all the attention was on a man named Riffle. Would he accomplish the unprecedented feat of winning a fourth consecutive title? The *Winston-Salem Journal* covered the two-day event, which began on September 2nd:

Riffle Seeks 4th Title in Horseshoe Meet Here

Glenn Riffle of the East Dayton (Ohio) Horseshoe Club will seek his fourth straight National AAU Horseshoe singles championship when the National Tournament opens at 10 a.m. today.

Qualifying began yesterday and will resume this morning and continue until 10 a.m., when the championship pitching will start. The thirty-two top qualifiers will place in the championship bracket with the next 16 going in the Class B flight. Singles will begin today and the doubles competition, along with any remaining final singles matches will be pitched Sunday.

More than 50 of the nation's outstanding horseshoe pitchers are expected here for the two-day tournament. Pitchers from Georgia, North and South Carolina, Virginia, New Jersey, Ohio and Illinois have indicated that they will compete.

The national doubles champions, Roger Ehlers and Jack Stout, along with Riffle arrived yesterday.

The national tournament was held here three years ago. Then it was shifted to Elgin, Illinois, and last year it was held in Dayton, Ohio.

Riffle has a world record in his grasp, when the matches begin here Saturday. He equaled the accepted mark of capturing 37 straight games in the last three championship tournaments. In winning the title last year, Riffle had an amazing 68.9 "ringer" percentage as all six finalists, for the first time, bettered the 60 percent figure in competition.

The September 3rd *Winston-Salem Journal* contained this feature article on the defending doubles champions from Illinois:

Country Boys From Illinois
By Frank Spencer

A couple of young men from the Chicago area, who in their spare time are National AAU horseshoe doubles champions, rested at a table in Miller Park yesterday and talked about horseshoe pitching and their involvement in the sport.

Rogers Ehlers of St. Charles and Jack Stout from Melrose will defend their doubles title today in the National AAU tournament. The twosome that forms the AAU defending titlist are not natives of Illinois and have been pitching together for only three years. Yet, they set two national records last year.

Stout is from Berwick, Pa., and Ehlers found his way into the Chicago suburb from Fort Atkinson, Wis. So, after all, they are country boys in what is known as the barnyard sport.

"I don't know but I guess we are horseshoe crazy," said Stout, "to pile in an automobile and drive more than 700 miles to pitch in a tournament. But it's fun and you can't take that away from us. Then," he added with a grin, "it also gives us a chance to get away from our wives." He was joking of course.

Both husky men, they divide their recreation between horseshoes and bowling. "Roger is a 185 average bowler—I'm just a 181 bowler," said Stout.

"We've pitched in a lot of horseshoe tournaments but these pits here in Winston-Salem are the best in the country. Only one, at Muncie, Ind., can be compared with them. The only difference is that the ones in Muncie are cement down the lanes and permit pitching just after a hard rain. We might be in trouble here if it rained hard for some time.

Rain, No Deterrent in Muncie

"We participated in a tournament at Muncie recently (Stout finished fifth and Ehlers seventh in a singles event) and it rained hard several times but just after the rain, they swept off the walkways and we went right along," Stout said.

The pits here have grass lanes but the pits are constructed of ground shale, which the city recreation department gets from Pine Hall Brick. The pits are watered several times each day during the tournament, which makes the shale sticky and prevents skidding of the shoes and dust.

Stout and Ehlers say that pitching doubles is more difficult than singles. "You've got to make each pitch count in doubles," pointed out Stout. "In singles, you pitch with a stride and keep going but there is a rest between pitching turns that prevents this type of flow. Yes, we believe that it's a bit more difficult to pitch in doubles."

The two National AAU records set by Stout and Ehlers were posted last year. They have the high singles game average of 81.2 percent and high tournament average of 65.7.

They get together every two months and practice doubles. Last winter they got in more practice by working on the indoor courts at Garfield Park, Ill. Stout's first major tournament was at these courts three years ago.

250–300 Shoes Pitched Daily

The two men have similar occupations, Stout is a sheet metal layout man and Ehlers is a toolmaker.

"The secret to horseshoe pitching is practice," said Stout. "I pitch between 250 and 330 shoes every day to stay in practice. Ehlers also gets in his daily work."

Stout gives a veteran Illinois pitcher, Ralph Dykes, credit for making him into a fine horseshoe pitcher. Dykes is president of the Illinois

Horseshoe Pitcher's Association. "I was using a three-quarter turn when Dykes began to work with me," said Stout. "He changed me into a one-and-a-quarter pitcher and that did the job. Both Ehlers and I used the one-and-a-quarter pitch now."

They say it's real fun and from a championship standpoint, it was lucky that Chicago brought the two together to form the defending National AAU title team in doubles.

They conceded that doubles was less complicated than it appears. "In most cases you just grab a partner and go to work," said Ehlers. "I guess we are lucky in that we get the chance to work together more than many of the teams in this tournament."

They also said that the trip from Chicago to Winston-Salem made it all worthwhile. Horseshoe pitching in tournaments is kind of a "See America First," for those who follow the tournaments. "We like to pitch in as many as we can," said Stout. "It's fun."

Let's take a moment to discuss what they meant by a three-quarter turn and one-and-a-quarter turn? A turn shoe is held on its side and is fairly level out of the release and remains level in flight as it approaches the stake. The alternative is pitching a flip-flop shoe, which results from pitching a shoe held up on the toe, or curved part, of the shoe. A right-handed pitcher will hold the shoe on the left side (or blade) of the shoe and when released the shoe will turn one and a quarter turns to be open when approaching the stake and thus a ringer. The pitcher will hold the right side of the shoe to pitch a one-and-three-quarter-turn shoe—and the opposite holds true for left-handed pitchers. Over ninety percent of all championship-class men pitchers pitch a turn shoe, whether a one-and-a-quarter, one-and-three-quarter, or three-quarter turn. The majority of women players, however, pitch a flip shoe.

The local paper published a midtournament update:

Ohio Duo
Sets Horseshoe Pace

Glenn Riffle, champion the past three years, and Paul Helton, a fellow townsman, led eight horseshoe pitchers into the championship finals after qualifying and first-round elimination in the National AAU tournament yesterday at Miller Park. Both finished with 7-0 records. Riffle set an AAU record in straight victories when he added seven to his record of 37 posted over the past three years. The preliminaries yesterday gave him a string of 44 straight games.

Eight pitchers qualified for today's finals in each of the championship, consolation and Class B flights, cutting a record AAU National tournament field from 53 to 24. Play will begin at 9 a.m. today at Miller Park. Doubles are set just after the competition of the singles.

Four North Carolinians made the championship flight. Darrell Eller, Walter King, James Scotten and Glynden Moore will compete against the four out-of-state stars. The defending doubles champions, Roger Ehlers and Jack Stout, also joined the two Ohio stars in the finals.

While Riffle and Helton were undefeated, the high percentage for ringers in the first round was made by Moore, who posted 311 ringers in 450 pitches (69.1). Second high in percentage was King with 420-285 for 67.8. Riffle, who won all his games, had 430 pitches, 287 ringers for a 66.8 percentage.

The qualifiers and scores (high 32 made up the championship class and next 16 class B):

Championship Bracket

Player – City	Pts.	Player – City	Pts.
Walter King, Asheboro NC	250	Glyden Moore, Burlington, NC	233
Buck Lanning, Lexington, NC	231	Glenn Riffle, Dayton, OH	231
Paul Helton, Dayton, OH	230	Woody Thomas, High Point, NC	230
Dr. Sol. Berman, New Jersey	229	Darrell Eller, Thomasville, NC	229
Fred Childress, Lynchburg	229	Royal Williams, Lynchburg, VA	226
Robert Toney, Lynchburg, VA	226	Melvin Howard, Archdale, NC	222
Conrad Murphy, W-Salem	219	Roger Ehlers, St. Charles, IL	218
Howard Hester, W-Salem	213	Ed Stancik, Durham, NC	212
Rodney Luck, Thomasville	212	James Scotten, High Point, NC	211
Henry Freeman, Detroit, MI	207	Al Hoover, Asheboro, NC	202
Jack Stout, Elgin, IL	200	Marion Broughton, Dayton, OH	200
Meril Anleitner, Detroit, MI	199	John Corns, Winston-Salem	198
Gilbert Moore, Burlington	198	Howard Lunsford, Winston-Salem	198
Mel Montgomery, OH	197	Harvey Hooker, Westfield, NC	195
Ellis Greer, Lynchburg, VA	193	A. D. Burnett, Lynchburg, VA	193
Sam Pyrtie, Westfield, NC	185		

Class B

Player – City	Pts.	Player – City	Pts.
James Phillips, Atlanta, GA	180	W. B. Stinson Jr., Durham, NC	179
Paul Woody, Lynchburg, VA	177	James Terry, Rural Hall, NC	177
Ray Hooker Winston-Salem	177	Pete Seagraves, Greensboro, NC	176
Glenn Maoe, Winston-Salem	176	James Bullion, Forest, VA	172
Donald Longtin, High Point	170	Tommy Jones, Winston-Salem	167
Garvey Billings, Greensboro	165	Charles Flippin, Greensboro, NC	164
Marvin May, Lynchburg, VA	161	Thorne Barker, Austell, GA	150
Arlie Worrell, Winston-Salem	147	Frank Pickett, Durham, NC	146

Those who failed to qualify

Player – City	Pts.	Player – City	Pts.
C. C. Robinson, Austell, GA	145	James Mathis, Winston-Salem	141
Clarence Dowdy, Lynchburg	141	Randall Jones, Winston-Salem	99
Dick Seagraves, Greensboro	85		

In the qualifying earlier in the day each pitcher tossed 100 shoes. The preliminary round was seven games to 50 points. Each ringer counts three points and those shoes within six inches of the stake, one point.

The pitchers and families were entertained at a fried chicken dinner at Miller Park last night after competition of the preliminary games.

Players qualifying for the finals out of preliminary rounds:

Championship Class

Player	W	L	R	SP	Pct.
Riffle	7	0	287	430	66.8
Eller	6	1	273	414	65.9
King	6	1	285	420	67.8
Scotten	6	1	290	482	60.2
Ehlers	6	1	287	450	63.8
Helton	7	0	267	432	61.8
Stout	6	1	288	472	61.0

Consolation Flight

Player	W	L	R	SP	Pct.
Stancik	4	3	206	400	51.5
Corns	4	3	204	378	53.9
Berman	5	2	255	384	66.4
Hester	5	2	277	466	59.5
Thomas	5	2	312	458	68.1
Toney	4	3	236	382	61.8
Lanning	4	3	290	500	58.0
Hoover	4	3	257	478	53.8

Class B

Player	W	L	R	SP	Pct.
Terry	6	1	250	472	52.9
Pickett	5	2	190	472	40.3
Hooker	4	3	215	446	48.2
May	4	3	193	416	46.4
Stinson	5	2	195	396	49.2
Seagraves	5	2	183	396	46.2
Billings	4	3	164	448	36.6
Woody	4	3	203	496	40.9

And then, short and sweet, there is a new champion:

Illinois Pitchers Win
AAU Horseshoe Titles

Roger Ehlers captured the National AAU horseshoe pitching singles championship yesterday and then teamed with Jack Stout to retain the doubles title in the annual meet at Miller Park. Ehlers and Stout were forced into a pitch-off with Darrell Eller and Melvin Howard before retaining the doubles crown.

Ehlers lost only one game, to Walter King, 54-34, in winning the singles. King went on to defeat the defending champion, Glenn Riffle in a playoff to take second place and drop Riffle to third in the final standings.

Riffle, who went into the finals with a string of 40 straight victories in three years of championship competition, had his string blasted in the first game of the championship bracket. Paul Helton defeated Riffle 54-44. Ehlers then dropped Riffle in the second game of the series, 52-38.

King, Carolinas AAU champion, took second place and also won the qualifying trophy with 74 ringers for 250 points. It looked for a while as if North Carolina would take the doubles crown as Darrell Eller and Melvin Howard defeated Ehlers and Stout in round robin for the four teams that qualified for the finals. Luck went against Eller and Howard as they dropped John Corns and Howard Lunsford on a big upset. That loss forced the playoff which Ehlers and Stout won.

Summaries of the finals:

1961 National AAU Singles Championship

		W	L	Pct.
1.	Roger Ehlers	6	1	65.9
2.	Walter King	6	2	69.5
3.	Glenn Riffle	5	3	66.0
4.	Paul Helton	4	3	59.9
5.	Jack Stout	3	4	60.6
6.	Glynden Moore	2	5	63.0
7.	Darrell Eller	2	5	61.8
8.	James Scotten	1	6	61.4

Consolation

		W	L	Pct.
1.	Buck Lanning	6	2	59.6
2.	Ed Stancik	5	3	54.6
3.	Dr. Sol Berman	4	3	64.1
4.	Robert Toney	4	3	50.0
5.	Woody Thomas	3	4	63.0
6.	Howard Hester	3	4	57.6
7.	John Corns	3	4	57.3
8.	Harvey Hooker	1	6	57.9

Class B

		W	l	Pct.
1.	James Terry	7	0	51.1
2.	Ray Hooker	6	1	46.8
3.	W. B. Stinson Jr.	6	2	47.1
4.	Pete Seagraves	4	3	47.3
5.	Marvin May	3	4	42.9
6.	Paul Woody	2	5	37.8
7.	Frank Pickett	1	6	38.6
8.	Garvey Billings	0	7	38.3

1961 National AAU Doubles Championship

		W	l
1.	Ehlers – Stout	3	1
2.	Eller – Howard	2	2
3.	Lunsford – Corns	2	2
4.	Thomas – Murphy	1	3

Roger Ehler, 1961 National Champion

1961 boasted another highly competitive singles final class, one of the more competitive groups of the AAU games. Essentially, the entire class averaged 60 percent ringers or better.

This was Rogers Ehlers only singles competition gold medal. He earned four golds altogether since he was half of a championship doubles team three consecutive years—1959, 1960, and 1961. Ehlers was 25 years old in 1961 and, he is alive and well today, still living in Illinois.

He remains active an active sportsman and is still achieving national championships. In 2011, fifty years after winning the National AAU horseshoe pitching title, Roger was the National Senior Bowling Champion for his age group (70–74). He scored that triumph in Las Vegas after qualifying by winning a regional tournament. In May 2012, Ehlers pitched for an Illinois team in the Team World competition, held in Beloit, Wisconsin. He entered with a ringer average of 48.2 percent.

1962

Go West, Young Amateurs

The August 3rd edition of the *Independent Record* of Helena, Montana, announced the upcoming National AAU tournament, which was being held west of the Mississippi for the first and only time. While the event had some interesting aspects, it may not have contributed to the AAU's mission to continue its horseshoe-pitching program. Nearly all the competitors hailed from Montana—just two players were from out of state, both from Indiana. The western site failed to draw players from the western states, a similar situation as in the 1949 tournament in Baltimore, which was also almost exclusively composed of local players.

Plans Progress for 1962
National Horseshoe Meet

Plans are going ahead rapidly for the 1962 National AAU Horseshoe Pitching Championships which will be hosted September 1–3 by the city of Helena. The big September event will mark the first time the national tournament has been held in Montana.

The tournament will open at Bausch Park across from Memorial Park on Saturday, Sept. 1, with qualification rounds. The qualifying rounds are scheduled from 9 a.m. to 10 p.m. on opening day. On the following two days the regular competition in both singles and doubles will be held with play scheduled to begin at 9 a.m. and close at 9 p.m.

Entry blanks have already been sent out to horseshoe clubs through-out the United States and a huge field is expected to compete for the national titles. The big horseshoe tournament is open to any AAU regis-tered amateur horseshoe pitcher in the U.S. A pitcher who has competed for cash prize contest is not eligible. All pitchers entered in the tourney must be registered with the AAU and if the contestant is not from Helena he must carry a travel permit from the AAU. If a contestant does not pro-duce a travel permit he will not be permitted to participate.

Method of Competition

Each contestant in the singles will pitch 100 shoes using ringers and shoes within six inches of the stake to count qualifying points. The quali-fying scores will be used solely to place players in flights for competition. No player will be excluded from the tourney. In each class, round robin play will be used to determine the champion. The top class, Class A, will be composed of eight to 16 players, depending on the number of entries in the tournament. All other classes will be composed of eight players.

In the event of a tie for an award position in any class, each player will pitch 100 shoes using the count-all method to break the tie.

In the doubles event, the combined total of the partners qualifying scores for the singles will be used for the doubles qualifying. Doubles partners must be from the same association.

The entries for the national event will close on August 31, at 4:30 p.m. No entries to the meet will be accepted unless accompanied by the entry fee of $4.00 for each double team and $2.00 for singles. The spon-soring groups reserve the right to refuse any entry.

The singles and doubles champions and runners-up will each receive a trophy as will the highest qualifier. National AAU medals of gold, silver and bronze will be awarded to the first, second and third place winners.

The tournament will officially open on Sept. 1 and contestants not able to report at that time are asked to notify the chairman of the entry committee. Contestants will be allowed to use their own shoes in the national event if the shoes meet all specifications of measurement as set by the guidelines of the governing body.

Any Helena resident wishing to watch or participate in this big meet are urged to make their plans now.

The champion's hometown paper had the best summary of the media coverage. The final standings that follow have been enhanced with information from *Amateur Athlete* and the win/loss records shown for the players in the men's singles final, except for Jensen, are from the final day only:

Ira Jensen Wins National Horseshoe Honors in Helena

Culbertson area resident, Ira Jensen, took top honors in the National AAU Horseshoe Tournament in Helena over the Labor Day weekend. He won 13 out of 14 singles games to cop the National AAU horseshoe championship, competing against 32 other players.

The competition was open to interested non-professional members of horseshoe clubs in the Unites States. Of the 32 players who responded to the invitations, 30 were from Montana, the other two, Bob Rambo and Ronald Colvin, being from Indiana, Jensen said.

A modest man, Jensen admits to having played horseshoe for the past 25 years. Unofficially, his tournament score was the highest ringer percentage in singles play. In the 1962 season play as a member of the Culbertson Horseshoe Club, Jensen has yet to lose a game, with 27 wins to his credit.

Teaming up with Phil Prescott, Poplar, Jensen placed second in the double competition. Five sets of doubles were played. Also, competing in the tournament was Jake Thomsen, Culbertson.

Second in the singles was Art Olson of Helena. Bob Rambo, who drove 1,950 from his home in Jeffersonville, Ind., for the tourney, took third. Winners for the Class A consolation flight were Walt McChesney of Sidney and John McKinnon of Helena.

Ace Cantrell of Sand Coulee and Darryl Lee of Helena finished first and second in the Class B flight.

Ed Holmberg of Big Timber and Olson won the doubles championship. Second were Jensen and Phil Prescott, and the third place team was Chuck Douglas, Helena and Walt McChesney Jr., Sidney. The top 3 teams ended in a tie for first place after the regulation play, which was a 7-game round robin. The team of Jensen & Prescott beat McChesney & Douglas in the first playoff game and then lost to Olsen & Holmberg in the final game for the championship.

High man in the qualifying rounds was W. D. Hubbard of Baker with 226 points of a possible 300.

Holmberg had the longest string of ringers with eight. Rambo had the most ringers in a single game with 51 and the highest number of ringers for the two-day tournament, 407.

1962 National AAU Singles Championship

	Player	City	W	L	%
1	Ira Jensen	Culbertson, MT	13	1	52.4
2.	Art Olson*	Helena, MT	5	2	41.2
3.	Bob Rambo*	Jefferson, IN	5	2	44.1
4.	Ronald Colvin	Indiana	4	3	49.2
5.	Phil Prescott	Montana	3	4	45.0
6.	Ed Holmberg	Big Timber, MT	2	5	44.0
7.	Norm Scheckloth	Montana	2	5	33.4
	W. D. Hubbard	Baker, MT			

*100 shoes were throw to break the tie for second place.

1962 National AAU Doubles Championship

	Players	W	L	%
1.	Ed Holmberg & Art Olson	7	1	49.7
2.	Ira Jensen & Phil Prescott	7	2	52.1
3.	Chuck Douglas & Walt McChesney Jr.	6	2	44.4
4.	John McKinnon & Norm Schneckloth	4	3	37.4
5.	Ronald Colvin & Robert Rambo	3	4	43.3

1963

Back to Salisbury and a New Champion

The September 1st *Salisbury Times* printed an announcement of the 1963 national event, which was planned for August 31st through September 2nd:

National Horseshoe Tournament Here This Weekend
Horseshoe Pitching Begins at Park Tomorrow;
Champ May Not Appear

Tons of steel will be dropped on Picnic Island in City Park starting tomorrow during the annual National AAU Horseshoe Pitching Championship tournament. Pitching begins at 10 a.m. and will continue until Monday afternoon after singles and doubles champions are decided.

It's still an uncertainty whether the singles champion, Harold Reno of Dayton, Ohio, will be available. If not, a new titlist will be crowned.

At the moment, six states have representatives bidding for top honors. Salisburians bidding for honors include Henry Donalds, 1963 South Atlantic AAU champion; Lawrence Windsor; Paige Kelly; Parker Sturgis; Alan Tull and Lloyd Anderson. Another popular Eastern Shore entry is William Sammons of Seaford, 1962 South Atlantic AAU singles titlist.

The sport of horseshoe pitching goes back to the soon after the shoeing of horses was started by the ancient armies of Greece, Rome and other nations some centuries after the dawn of the Christian Era.

Other Maryland pitchers include William Baugher and Richard Baugher of the Cecil County Horseshoe Club and Emmanuel Harmon and Gilbert Hammerbacher of Baltimore's Ferndale Club.

Among the standouts out of state contestants are: Robert Rambeau, Kentucky champ, third place finisher in the National tourney last year. He has an 80 percent ringer average. Also from Kentucky will be Ronald Colvin, who ranked fifth in the 1962 National event.

Also to be observed is Dr. Sol Berman, New Jersey champion, averaging 72 percent and William Kolb, runner-up this year for state honors. Another New Jersey entry is Paul Paglise, ranking eight in the state.

The Ohio champ in readiness is Leroy Hill, winner of the state AAU tourney three of the last five years.

North Carolina's eight entries are led by Melvin Howard of High Point, winner of the Tar Heel State championship the past five years; Woody Thomas; Glynden Moore, Walter King, Darrell Eller, Conrad Murphy, Ed Stancik and Randall Jones.

The Wicomico Recreational Commission is host of this event in cooperation with the city, the Wicomico Horseshoe Club and the South Atlantic Amateur Athletic Union.

The Delaware Poultry Industry Inc., is holding a barbeque for the players and their families at 6 p.m. tomorrow on Picnic Island.

There is no way to determine what the newspaper writer was trying to explain in the paragraph about Harold Reno as a defending champion who may not be in attendance and, "If not, a new titlist will be crowned." Harold Reno is one of the greatest horseshoe pitchers of all time. He was the World Champion in 1961 and 1964 and an 11-time Ohio state champion. It's difficult to imagine that he would have considered entering the National AAU tournament. In fact, I could find no record that he ever entered an AAU competition. The most likely explanation is that the writer made a research or note-taking error.

On first glance, the article seemed to imply that the eastern states took offense when the 1962 AAU event was held in Montana so they held some sort of mini-national somewhere in the East. But that theory falls short since the article does identify Bob Rambo as the third-place player in the 1962 National

AAU event, which is accurate (other than the misspelling of Rambo's name). However, Rambo was never a Kentucky state champion—both he and Colvin were from Indiana, and Rambo was never a state champion there either.

Melvin Howard was not North Carolina state champion for five straight years. He won that honor in 1962, 1963, and 1964. Walter King was the North Carolina champion 1959 and 1971, Glynden Moore in 1961 and 1977, and Darrell Eller in 1965.

The *Salisbury Times* offered a final account of the event:

North Carolinian
Wins Shoe Match

Walter King of Asheboro, N.C., won the National AAU Senior Singles Horseshoe Championship yesterday at Picnic Island in City Park. He won 15 games and lost none while pitching 533 ringers out of a total of 780 attempts, giving him an overall ringer percentage of 68.3. His highest single game percentage was 85.3—29 ringers out of 34 shoes pitched—when competing against Glynden Moore of Burlington, N.C.

Eighteen entries representing six states, participated in this three-day event, which was well attended by a cross-section of representatives from the Eastern Shores.

King and Moore won the doubles championship, going unbeaten in 35 games with a 55.7 ringer percentage. North Carolina dominated the picture. Conrad Murphy of Winston-Salem finished second followed by Ed Stancik of Durham and Darrell Eller of Thomasville.

Finishing fifth was William Kolb of Belleville, N.J., who was the top qualifier with a 222 score and a 63 ringer percentage.

Other places in doubles play were taken by the Tar Heel contestants. Stancik and Murphy placed second while Eller and Don Longtin of High Point, finished third.

Unable to compete because of a cut hand was Henry Donalds of Salisbury, who recently won the singles championship of the South Atlantic Association.

The champion's hometown paper, the *Courier-Tribune*, carried this feature article:

King Takes National AAU Horseshoe Laurels

Asheboro has a national horseshoe champion. Walter King climaxed a victory in the men's singles play in the U.S. National AAU Horseshoe Tournament at Salisbury, Md., by teaming up with another North Carolinian to take the men's doubles honors too.

Play opened Friday, August 31st and continued through Monday, September 2nd. The top twenty players entered in the national contest were selected to play a round robin, King coming out on top and bringing home two trophies, two medals and a certificate testifying to his skill on the horseshoe courts.

King Was Quick To Share His Honors with His State

"Six North Carolina men took all top honors," he told a *Courier-Tribune* reporter. "This is the first time for the National Championship to ever be in North Carolina and also the first time for one state to take all top honors."

King teamed up with Glynden Moore of Burlington to capture the doubles crown after taking the singles honor. Other men from North Carolina were Conrad Murphy of Winston-Salem, who placed second in both singles and doubles after teaming up with Ed Stancik of Durham. Stancik also placed third in the singles. Darrell Eller of Thomasville teamed with Don Longtin of High Point to capture third place in the doubles competition.

King himself seemed a bit surprised at his clean sweep, "I practiced less this past year and I did better than ever," he mused.

He said he intended to enter the Hill City Open Invitational at Lynchburg, Va., on September 15–16, as well as being eligible to seek the World's Championship in horseshoe tossing in August of next year. This gives him a year to practice, the Asheboro champion observed. He also noted that an Olympics team was in the making next year.

Sports Illustrated magazine is expected to carry a full report this month on the horseshoe tournament, he said, as a photographer was at the scene for four days. NBC's "Wide World of Sports" was supposed to broadcast the proceedings in Maryland but reportedly lacked sufficient mobile units.

King gave credit to several local firms for making his trip possible as sponsors: Garner-Morgan Hardware, Central Bakery, Stedman Manufacturing Company, all in Asheboro and Founder's Furniture in Pleasant Garden, his employer.

The Asheboro horseshoe champ has another goal too, creating several local teams to make use of the horseshoe courts in Memorial Park. The park has five courts now with lights for night play and with the addition of five more—something King hopes for in the future—the State Tournament could be held here.

King was once instrumental in organizing local teams of players, but organized activity has lapsed recently. But if he had his way, several more potential champs will be hurling the irons at distant stakes in future years.

1963 National AAU Singles Championship

1. Walter King	Asheboro	15-0	68.3%
2. Conrad Murphy	Winston-Salem		
3. Ed Stancik	Durham		
4. Darrell Eller	Thomasville		
5. William Kolb	Belleville, NJ		
6. Glynden, Moore	Burlington		

1963 National AAU Doubles Championship

1. King & Moore	55.7%
2. Murphy & Stancik	
3. Eller & Longtin	

As the newspaper account indicates, *Sports Illustrated* was at the event covered it with an article in their September 16, 1963 issue. The article was not intended to advance the sport of horseshoe pitching, or even contribute to the popularity of the event. Regardless, it presents an interesting folksy view from the sidelines. Here, in part, is that article, by John O'Reilly:

HIGH OLD FLING AT THE NATIONAL RINGER DERBY

At first, the crowd was lost to Miss Crustacean, but some high-pressure pitching and an assist from Miss Delmarva Chicken Runner-up helped North Carolina carry the day—not to mention the grandstand

It was summer's last holiday weekend and the whole thing had the peaceful, bucolic air of an old-time American picnic. The occasion was the AAU's National Horseshoe Pitching Championships. The setting in Salisbury, Md. was a shady grove of maple trees, by a purling stream where ducks paddled placidly against the current, small boys still-fished for sunnies and watermelons were stacked in a high pile. It was as wholesome and serene as you please, but there was one small thing wrong with the picture—on the first day, with the exception of one old man on a bicycle, nobody showed up to watch. This initial lack of interest was so obvious to the competitors that one of them eyed the elderly cyclist and muttered sarcastically, "Here comes our spectator."

There was, however, one good reason why spectators were scarce. The rival town of Crisfield, Md., only 33 miles from Salisbury, was holding its annual hard-shell-crab race and as a bonus attraction, they were crowning Miss Crustacean of 1963, a hazel-eyed beauty named Christine Massey. To top it off, the outgoing Miss America, with only one week left in her reign, was dropping by to give the proceedings an extra touch of class. What were the horseshoe people to do?

Moving quickly, the sponsoring Wicomico County Recreation Commission announced it would give away barbecued chicken by the plateful (chickens outnumber people in Salisbury by some 150 million to 1). Then the commission put on display its own hazel-eyed beauty queen. According to the ribbon across her front she was Miss Runner-up of 1963 and according to her own admission she was a runner-up for Miss Delmarva Peninsula Chicken Festival. "I'm here today as a chicken representative and I don't know exactly what my duties are," said Miss Runner-up.

It was obvious that whatever her duties she was fulfilling them handsomely: 135 people came to the pitching grounds to look her over, to sample the chicken and at least, to watch the horseshoe tournament. (As for Crisfield, it was having its own troubles. Governor J. Millard Tawes's entry won the hard-shell-crab race. To avoid any suggestion that they ran a tainted crab race, the embarrassed officials disqualified the first finisher and awarded the victory to the second-place crab.)

Meanwhile, back in Salisbury, with the six-row metal grandstand packed with chicken-fed spectators, the horseshoe pitching contest was about to get underway. For a moment the horseshoe officials were as close to embarrassment as those at the crab race: one of the stobs (the AAU rule book calls them stakes, but everybody knows they are stobs) on Court 4 was a full inch under the regulation height of 12 inches. The matches were momentarily delayed while a stob-puller was brought in, the stob pulled out and a one-inch plug inserted in the bottom of the stob hole. Ready once more, the 19 players from five states dug in for the qualification round, grumbling as they did so about the quality of the red clay for the pits imported from Baltimore just for the championship. But then, horseshoe players are always critical of the clay. It is either too sticky or not sticky enough, too hard or too soft. Dr. Sol Berman from New Jersey, who is such a horseshoe perfectionist that he uses shoes custom-made of a copper alloy, said you get the best clay by going to a brickyard and getting soft bricks discarded as imperfect. "You have to get there before they bake the bricks, of course," Dr. Berman said in amplification.

As the eight-man round-robin finals progressed, spectators forgot about Miss Chicken Festival Runner-up and leaned forward in their seats to watch the players. They leaned out so far, in fact, that several people in the front row came close to getting the 2½-pound iron horseshoe wrapped around their necks. To avert such a grim possibility, play was suspended while spectators and players lifted the entire grandstand and carried it back eight feet. Mayor Frank R. Morris of Salisbury, who had come out to lend the dignity of his office to the occasion, was right in there hefting with the rest of them.

Out of the pits it became apparent that the championships were going to have an all-North Carolina finish. Walter King of Asheboro, tossing ringers with nonchalant skill, had moved well out in front; and the only man with even a remote chance to beat him was Conrad Murphy of Winston-Salem. At 51, Murphy has a top weight of 143 but had trained down to 136 (including the wad of tobacco that resides in his right cheek) for the nationals.

Near the end the round robin, Murphy had to face his friend King, who was still undefeated. As the two men fought it out, no words were heard except the scores being called and the insights of Ramrod Jones, who observed, "There's pressure on every shoe." The pressure undid Murphy who failed to get a ringer on his last toss. But he shook King's hand and smiled briefly at the end. The next day King teamed up with Glynden Moore of Burlington, N.C., to win the doubles from Murphy and Ed Stancik of Durham, N.C. It was a clean sweep for North Carolina and somebody said, a matter of historical interest, since a sweep by one state has never happened before at the AAU nationals.

That last statement is not quite accurate. In several previous instances, the singles and doubles champions were all from the same state. However, in 1941 the top three singles and top three doubles teams were all from Illinois. At the 1944 national championships, Michigan took the top two singles and top two doubles places. Although this may not be fair to count, in 1949 all eight singles participants and all three doubles teams were from Maryland. Now that is a sweep! Perhaps it's unfair to be critical of the writer's accuracy on horseshoe-pitching history. It's doubtful much documentation of previous events was available to him. Regardless, though, the North Carolina pitchers' achievement was remarkable—and they repeated the accomplishment in 1966.

The 1965 coverage indicates that an unnamed Montana youth won the National AAU junior championship. Perhaps the 1965 winner was also the junior champion in 1963. There's little evidence of junior involvement in this era, and no evidence of junior champions. This short article from a Miles City newspaper, which opens the door to a possible national junior champion, explains the situation rather well:

Big Timber Athlete Wins
Horseshoe Pitching Contest

Ronnie Mosness, pitching for the Big Timber Jaycees, won the Northwestern United States Regional Junior AAU Horseshoe Pitching Championships Saturday here in Miles City.

The event was conducted in connection with Montana's Sports Spree. If there are no other regional tourneys conducted in the United States this year, there is a good chance that Mosness will be officially declared the National Junior Champ for 1963. Regional tournaments have not been scheduled until this year.

Silver medal winner in the 16-boy tourney was Herb Sand of Glasgow. Terry Mosness brother of the champ, finished third and Joe Longmire, representing the Helena, Montana, Last Change Ringer Flingers, was fourth and Class B Champion. Behind him in Class B were: Rene Navarro, Percy Comes Last and Thomas Fagan.

Class C winners were the champion, Larry Good, Glenn Azure, Patrick Doherty, all of Miles City, and the Class D victors were Bob Hutchinson, the champion, followed by Ron Johnson and Harvey Riggs, of Miles City.

The championships were sponsored by the Miles City Kiwanians and were under the direction of Committee Chairman Pete Langdorf.

The AAU's *Amateur Athlete* magazine did not list Mosness as a national junior champion in 1963, nor did suggest there were other regional tournaments that year. You can be the judge on this issue, but given the lack of corroboration, I have chosen not to list Ron Mosness as the national junior champion.

1964

New Site, Same Champ

In 1964 the National AAU Championships were held for the first time in Middlesex, New Jersey, on September 5th, 6th, and 7th. A couple of the now elderly promoters who helped plan and conduct the event provided this clipping that tells about the victor. Vince Yannetti, an NHPA Hall of Fame member, and Bill McIntyre—both longtime promoters and horseshoe-pitching historians in New Jersey have each kept scrapbooks on pitching events for decades, including the three National AAU Championships held in Middlesex.

Here is an unaccredited clipping from their scrapbooks:

Walter King Still Ruler of AAU 'Shoe Pitchers

Nothing could be finer than to come here from North Carolina and take top honors in the National AAU horseshoe championship tournament.

This was the way that Walter King felt yesterday after retaining his singles title and then teaming up with Darrell Eller, another Tarheel State competitor, to capture the doubles crown.

The 44-year-old, tall, lean King, who lives in the nice-sounding community of Pleasant Gardens, N.C., displayed his usual top-notch effortless form but was forced into a championship playoff when Eller ended his string of 14 victories Sunday night.

Labor Day Labors

Eller, 50, of Thomasville, N.C., had been upset by Walter Haring of Middletown earlier. But he beat King in the last match 52-17, to give each man a 14-1 record and necessitate a Labor Day morning playoff.

King downed Eller, 51-14 in the first game of the best of three title series. The second game was nip-and-tuck until King wrapped it up with a pair of ringers for a 53-46 triumph and a second straight diadem. King had a ringer percentage of 68.5 for the playoff tilts as opposed to Eller's 56.8.

King and Eller then teamed up in the afternoon to turn back another pair of North Carolinians, Conrad Murphy of Winston Salem and Woody Thomas of High Point, in a playoff set that went the full three games. King and Eller won the first game, 50-35, lost the second, 54-49 and won the deciding third game, 51-27. Each team had posted an 8-1 log in the regular competition. King was a co-holder of the doubles crown last year with a fellow Tarheel, Glynden Moore.

D. R. Eberhardt of Middlesex defeated Elmer Hendren of Bexley, Ohio, 51-38 to win the class B title and Jim Nardiello, of Roselle Park was unbeaten in seven games to lead Class C.

34 Qualifiers

Thirty-four of the 36 entrants qualified Saturday. The top 16, led by Eller's 231 points, were bracketed in the "A" group; the next 10 competed in the "B" division and the final eight were placed in the "C" class.

King, who only took up the sport seven years ago, also has a second, third, and fourth place finish in the championship class singles to go along with his back-to-back national championships.

Dr. Sol Berman of Elizabeth finished sixth behind King in the top singles flight. Berman was the lone Union County representative in Class A. Charlie Worsham of Fanwood, George Blake of Rahway and Joe Malinowsky of Linden, placed third, fourth and fifth, respectively, in the "B" bracket. Otto Szurely of Elizabeth was second to Nardiello in the "C" final. Jim Donovan of Clark and Len LaDanco of Westfield were fifth and sixth.

The marathon tournament, which opened Saturday morning, concluded at 7 p.m. yesterday with the King-Eller triumph in the doubles.

1964 National AAU Senior Singles Championships

	Player	Town	W	L	%
1.	Walter King	Pleasant Garden, NC	16	1	71.6
2.	Darrell Eller	Thomasville, NC	14	3	66.1
3.	Roger Ehlers	St. Charles, IL	11	4	65.7
4.	Woody Thomas	High Point, NC	11	4	61.3
5.	William Kolb	Belleville, NJ	10	5	65.8
6.	Jack Stout	Melrose, IL	10	5	63.1
7.	Asa Brown	Butler, NJ	10	5	63.1
8.	Dr. Sol Berman	Elizabeth, NJ	8	7	62.5
9.	Conrad Murphy	Winston-Salem, NC	7	8	57.4
10.	John Giddes	Martinsville, NJ	7	8	52.3
11.	Walter Haring	Middletown, NJ	5	10	49.5
12.	Leroy Hill	Broadway, OH	4	11	51.9
13.	Lee Davis	Ridgewood, NJ	4	11	51.9
14.	Joseph McCrink	West Orange, NJ	3	12	51.1
15.	Neil DeNuzzio	Staten Island, NY	2	13	40.4
16.	A. J. Dykstra	Englewood, NJ	0	15	43.4

King defeated Eller, 51-14, 53-46 in the title playoff.

Class B Finals

	Player	Town	W	L	%
1.	D. R. Eberhardt	Middlesex, NJ	8	2	34.4
2.	Elmer Henderson	Bexley, OH	7	3	38.9
3.	Walt Broch	Iselin, NJ	6	3	33.2
4.	Charles Worsham	Fanwood, NJ	5	4	40.0
5.	George Blake	Rahway, NJ	5	4	33.9
6.	Joseph Malinowsky	Linden, NJ	4	5	34.0
7.	William Fournier	Hasbrouck, NJ	4	5	32.6
8.	Henry Hodiman	East Paterson, NJ	4	5	28.9
9.	Donald Vogel	Short Hills, NJ	2	7	31.1
10.	Phillip Zozzaro	Paterson, NJ	1	8	25.2

Eberhardt defeated Henderson, 51-38 in title playoff game.

Class C Finals

	Player	Town	W	L	%
1.	James Nardiello	Roselle Park, NJ	7	0	34.5
2.	Otto Szurley	Elizabeth, NJ	5	2	28.2
3.	George Swaiko	Annapolis, MD	4	3	32.8
4.	Thomas Czado	Middlesex, NJ	4	3	30.0
5.	James Donovan	Clark, NJ	4	3	29.0
6.	Leonard LaDanco	Westfield, NJ	3	4	18.7
7.	Hal Hanania	Middlesex, NJ	1	6	20.2
8.	Garrett Connolly	Summit, NJ	0	7	Withdrew

1964 National AAU Senior Doubles Championships

	Player	W	L	%
1.	Walter King & Darrell Eller	10	2	60.8
2.	Conrad Murphy & Woody Thomas	10	2	54.0
3.	Asa Brown & Joseph McCrink	7	2	57.2
4.	Jack Stout & Roger Ehlers	6	3	56.0
5.	Dr. Sol Berman & William Kolb	6	3	51.8
6.	Walter Haring & Lee Davis	4	5	47.1
7.	Charles Worsham & Joseph Malinowsky	3	6	34.1
8.	Ron Vogel & John Giddes	2	7	36.0
9.	George Blake & Otto Szurley	1	8	31.1
10.	James Donovan & James Nardiello	0	9	30.0

This tournament marked Walter King's final National AAU gold medal, though he did enter the 1966 event where he earned his final medal, a silver. Walter King was one of only six players to earn four gold medals in his AAU career.

During the research process, the fine fellows who managed the New Jersey event not only provided extremely helpful information about the tournament—they also reproduced an actual original program from the 1964 National Tournament.That program is reproduced over the next few pages.

1964 National A. A. U.
Horseshoe Pitching Championship

AMATEUR ATHLETIC UNION
OF THE UNITED STATES

Sponsored by the

N. J. STATE HORSESHOE PITCHING ASSN.

WARINANCO PARK
ELIZABETH, NEW JERSEY

SEPTEMBER 5, 6, 7, 1964

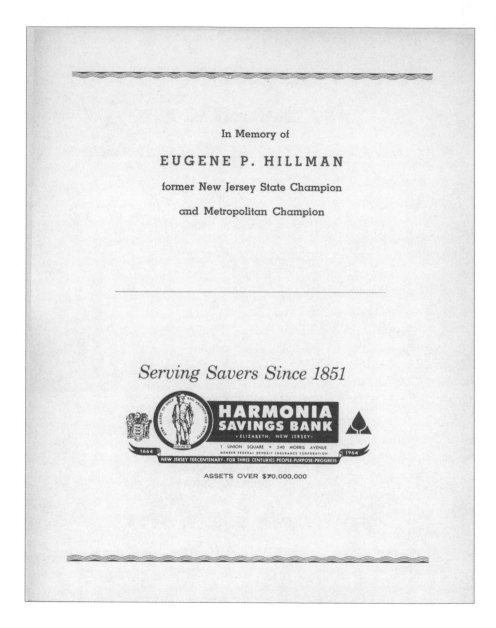

In Memory of

EUGENE P. HILLMAN

former New Jersey State Champion

and Metropolitan Champion

Serving Savers Since 1851

HARMONIA SAVINGS BANK
· ELIZABETH, NEW JERSEY ·

1 UNION SQUARE • 540 MORRIS AVENUE
MEMBER FEDERAL DEPOSIT INSURANCE CORPORATION

1664 · 1964
NEW JERSEY TERCENTENARY · FOR THREE CENTURIES PEOPLE · PURPOSE · PROGRESS

ASSETS OVER $70,000,000

THE 1963 NATIONAL A.A.U. CHAMPION

WALTER KING, Pleasant Garden, N. C.

SANCTIONED BY
THE NEW JERSEY
AMATEUR
ATHLETIC UNION

SPONSORED BY
THE N. J. HORSESHOE
PITCHERS ASSOCIATION

Walter King of Asheboro, N. C. is the defending Champion. He teamed with Glynden Moore of Burlington, N. C. to win the doubles Championship.

His overall ringer average in the singles was 68.3%. He had a high game of 85.3%.

King will be back to defend his Title. His entry blank has already been received.

Roger Ehler 1961 Singles Champion from St. Charles, Ill. and Jack Stout of Melrose, Ill. his doubles partner when they won the 1960 and 1961 Doubles Championship have filed their entry.

CONRAD MURPHY

Runner-up in 1963 in both Singles and doubles. National Doubles Champion in 1954.

NATIONAL A.A.U. HORSESHOE PITCHING CHAMPIONS
and Sponsors

1963   Recreation Dept., City of Salisbury, Maryland.
Singles—Warren King, Carolinas Association.
Doubles—King and Glynden Moore, Carolinas Association.

1962   Montana Sports Spree, c/o David Rivenes, 203 N. Custer, Miles City, Montana.
Singles—Ira Jensen, Culbertson, Montana.
Doubles—Art Olsen, Helena, Montana and Ed Holmberg, Big Timber, Montana.

1961   Recreation Dept. Winston-Salem, North Carolina.
Singles—Roger Ehlers, St. Charles, Illinois.
Doubles—Ehlers and Jack Stout, Melrose Park, Illinois.

1960   Dayton, Ohio Recreation Department
Singles—Glenn Riffle, Dayton, Ohio.
Doubles—Jack Stout, Melrose Park, Ill. and Roger Ehlers, St. Charles, Illinois.

NEW JERSEY'S TOP PITCHERS

SOL BERMAN, M.D., three time 1962-63-64 N. J. A.A.U. Champ. Nine times New Jersey Doubles Champ.

BILL KOLB, Ten times N. J. State Champion. Twice State Doubles Champion. Finished 4th 1963 National A.A.U.

LEE DAVIS, State Champion and State Doubles Champion several years ago.

THE NEW JERSEY A.A.U.

PRESTON FAIRLAMB, President, New Jersey A.A.U.
GEORGE R. HOAGLAND, Secretary-Treasurer, New Jersey A.A.U.

The current National Championships are sanctioned by the New Jersey Association of the Amateur Athletic Union.

The Association conducts championships in all 16 A.A.U. events throughout the year for its more than 5,000 registered athletes. Its success in this effort has been particularly outstanding in track and field and in swimming. Among its Olympians of the past have been track stars Andy Stanfield, Milt Campbell, Eulace Peacock, Bill Albans, Elias Gilbert and Bill Alley and Olympic swimming record holder Carin Cone.

The working relationship between the New Jersey Association of the A.A.U. and the New Jersey Jaycees has been particularly close and rewarding. For the past eight years these two organizations have worked together in conducting the state-wide Junior Olympics track and field championships for thousands of the state's youngsters.

The Association, organized in Newark, N. J., in 1930, covers that portion of New Jersey north of and including Mercer and Monmouth Counties except for that part of Hudson County east of the Hackensack River.

President of the New Jersey Association is Preston Fairlamb of Fayson Lakes, Butler, and secretary-treasurer is George Hoagland of Rahway. Other officers are: Thomas F. Dalton, 1st Vice President; William Wiklund, 2nd Vice President; Robert Roden 3rd vice president; Lou Choquette, 4th vice president, and Joseph sharpless, 5th vice president.

Other AAU officials from the Garden State include: Albert R. Post, Bloomfield, chairman of the Records Committee for Men's Track and Field and vice chairman of the Men's Track and Field Committee; Robert Alexander, of Wayne, state registration chairman; James Nicholas, of Chatham, state member of the Track and Field Committee; and Mrs. Catherine D. Meyer, Glen Rock; Dr. Richard Willing, Pompton Lakes; Mrs. Dolores Seaman, Newark; N. Matthew Nilssen, Oradell, and George T. Cron, Elizabeth.

OUR HOST

Union County Park Commission – Warinanco Park

Warinanco Park has been the site of many National Championships. This is the first time that a National Horseshoe Pitching Championship has been held here.

NATIONAL A.A.U. PENTHALON CHAMPIONSHIPS
Warinanco Park

Year	Winner		Total Points
1943	Eulace Peacock,	USCG Manhattan Beach, New York	3225
1944	Eulace Peacock,	USCG Manhattan Beach, New York	2852
1945	Eulace Peacock,	USCG Manhattan Beach, New York	3148
1946	Charles E. Beaudry,	Marquette Club, Milwaukee, Wisconsin	2885
1947	John Voight,	Baltimore OTFC, Baltimore, Maryland	2972
1950	Wilbur Ross,	Baldwin Wallace College, Borea, Ohio	3277

NATIONAL A.A.U. DECATHLON CHAMPIONSHIPS

1944	Irving Mondschein	Brooklyn Army Base Terminal, New York	5743

WORLD HORSESHOE PITCHING CHAMPIONS

FRANK JACKSON, Many times 1909-1926   LATE GUY ZIMMERMAN, 1954
TED ALLEN, 1933-34-35-40-46-53-55-56-57-59   DON TITCOMB, 1960
FERNANDO ISIAS, 1941-47-48-49-50-51-52-58   HAROLD RENO, 1961
PAUL FOCHT, 1962

NEW JERSEY A.A.U.
HORSESHOE PITCHING CHAMPIONS
Senior

1964	Sol Berman, M.D., Elizabeth	1962	Sol Berman, M.D., Elizabeth
1963	Sol Berman, M.D., Elizabeth	1961	William Kolb, Belleville

Junior

1964	Walter Haring, Middleville	1962	Joseph McCrink, East Orange
1963	Joseph McCrink, East Orange	1961	William Kolb, Belleville

WORLD HORSESHOE PITCHING CHAMPIONS
Men's Division

NOTE: Official tournaments were held only in the years listed. Both winter and summer tournaments were held as indicated during some of the early years. No official ringer percentages were kept prior to 1923. The total number of ringers thrown by the champion is listed here for those years. All records are from the official files of the N.H.P.A.

Year		Champion, Home Town	Ring., Pct.	Played at
1909		Frank Jackson, Kellerton, Ia.	....	Bronson, Kan.
1915		Frank Jackson, Kellerton, Ia.	97 R	Kansas City, Kan.
1919		Fred Brust, Columbus, Ohio	367 R	St. Petersburg, Fla.
1920	W	George May, Akron, Ohio	430 R	St. Petersburg, Fla.
1920	S	Frank Jackson, Kellerton, Ia.	850 R	Akron, O.
1921	W	Charles Babbit, Lancaster, O.	439 R	St. Petersburg, Fla.
1921	S	Frank Jackson, Kellerton, Ia.	391 R	Minneapolis, Minn.
1922	W	Charlie Davis, Columbus, O.	448 R	St. Petersburg, Fla.
1922	S	Frank Lundin, New London, Ia.	424 R	Des Moines, Ia.
1923	W	Harold Falor, Akron, O.	55.3	St. Petersburg, Fla.
1923	S	George May, Akron, O.	60.0	Cleveland, O.
1924	W	Charlie Davis, Columbus, O.	57.9	Lake Worth, Fla.
1924	S	Putt Mossman, Eldora, Ia.	62.5	Minneapolis, Minn.
1925		Putt Mossman, Eldora, Ia.	67.6	Lake Worth, Fla.
1926		Frank Jackson, Kellerton, Ia.	61.4	St. Petersburg, Fla.
1927	W	Charlie Davis, Columbus, O.		
1927	S	Charlie Davis, Columbus, O.	64.8	Duluth, Minn.
1928		Charlie Davis, Columbus, O.	70.2	St. Petersburg, Fla.
1929		Blair Nunnamaker, Cleveland, O.	69.5	St. Petersburg, Fla.
1933		Ted Allen, Boulder, Colo.	73.5	Chicago, Ill.
1935		Ted Allen, Boulder, Colo.	75.5	Moline, Ill.
1940		Ted Allen, Boulder, Coo.	82.4	Des Moines, Ia.
1941		Fernando Isias, Los Angeles, Calif.	82.9	Des Moines, Ia.
1946		Ted Allen, Boulder, Colo.	83.9	Des Moines, Ia.
1947		Fernando Isias, Los Angeles, Calif.	83.2	Murray, Utah
1948		Fernando Isias, Los Angeles, Calif.	84.2	Milwaukee, Wis.
1949		Fernando Isias, Los Angeles, Calif.	83.3	Murray, Utah
1950		Fernando Isias, Los Angeles, Calif.	83.5	Murray, Utah
1951		Fernando Isias, Los Angeles, Calif.	85.7	Murray, Utah
1952		Fernando Isias, Los Angeles, Calif.	83.5	Murray, Utah
1953		Ted Allen, Boulder, Colo.	83.2	Murray, Utah
1954		Guy Zimmerman, Danville, Calif.	84.8	Murray, Utah
1956		Ted Allen, Boulder, Colo.	86.5	Murray, Utah
1956		Ted Allen, Boulder, Colo.	83.4	Murray, Utah
1957		Ted Allen, Boulder, Colo.	85.1	Murray, Utah
1958		Fernando Isias, Los Angeles, Calif.	84.3	Murray, Utah
1959		Ted Allen, Boulder, Colo.	84.4	Murray, Utah
1960		Don Titcomb, Los Gatos, Calif.	84.9	Muncie, Ind.
1961		Harold Reno, Sabina, Ohio	83.8	Muncie, Ind.
1962		Paul Focht, Dayton, Ohio	81.8	Greenville, Ohio
1963		John Monasmith, Yakima, Wash.	82.3	South Gate, Calif.
1964		Harold Reno, Sabina, Ohio	84.1	Greenville, Ohio

Carl Steinfeldt, Rochester, N. Y. was second 30-5 ringer percentage 83.3. Two games back. Glenn Henton, Iowa, 3rd, Elmer Hohl, Canada fourth, both 29.6. Curt Day, Indiana was fifth, 28-7 highest ringer percentage 84.4.

FORMER NATIONAL A.A.U. SINGLES CHAMPIONS

Glenn Riffle 1959 and 1960, Floyd Toole, Arkansas 1954 and 1957 and Arny Lindquist of W. Va. reached the finals of the 1964 World's Championship.

The Late Guy Zimmerman

One of the greatest horseshoe pitchers of all times. He won the World's Championship at Murray, Utah, in 1954 with an average of 84.2.

Guy pitched the only perfect game in a World Contest. Milwaukee, 1948—44 shoes pitched —44 ringers.

Instead of the regular 36 man round-robin this was a specially arranged tournament by agreement in advance. The 36 men were divided into 6-6 man round-robins. The two low men of each group were eliminated the first day. The 24 remaining were divided into three 8 man round-robins. At the end of this play the top two of each group engaged in a 6 man round-robin, with the top two of the six scheduled to play best 3 out of 5 for the championship. The two emerging from this play-off were Mr. Zimmerman and Mr. Isais. Guy took 3 straight games. Summary of the 3 shown below:

SUMMARY OF ALL 3 GAMES

	ZIMMERMAN		ISIAS
FIRST GAME			
Points	51	Points	36
Shoes P.	132	Shoes P.	132
Ringers	117	Ringers	113
Percent	88.6	Percent	85.6
SECOND GAME			
Points	52	Points	39
Shoes P.	128	Shoes P.	128
Ringers	114	Ringers	110
Percent	89.1	Percent	85.9
THIRD GAME			
Points	50	Points	40
Shoes P.	142	Shoes P.	142
Ringers	122	Ringers	118
Percent	85.9	Percent	83.1

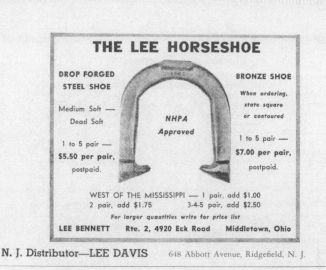
Fernando Isais

FORMER WORLD'S CHAMPION

Fernando was born in Mexico in 1915. His wife named Hope Isais. They have a married daughter and a Grandson born in April, 1963. So Fernando and Hope are now Grand parents.

Fernando owns and operates a bar and restaurant on Santa Barbara Avenue which is directly across the street from the Sports Arena.

Tennis was one of Fernando's favorite games and he used to compete with Pancho Gonzales, whom he defeated at times. At one time Fernando operated a tennis shop.

Fernando won the World's Horseshoe Championship 8 times: 1941, 1947 through 1952 and in 1958. He was State of California Champion 8 times: 1931, 1932, 1933, 1937, 1940, 1941, and 1953. In the 1952 State Tournament he pitched a perfect game of 30 ringers. He averaged well over 80% each time he won the World's title. He maintained this caliber of pitching in the 5 meets since World War II in which he was champion. In 1951 he averaged 85.7% which was his best. In 1947 and 1949 he lacked one ringer of perfect games.

In 1954, Fernando and the late Guy Zimmerman met in a best out of five in the finals for World Championship. Guy won the wirst three games straight although Fernando averaged 85.3%. The three games required 402 shoes.

In 1956 Fernando met Ted Allen in a 168 shoe game winning it with 148 ringers, 65 doubles, and 51 four deads. In 14 World Tourney games with T. Allen, Fernando won 9 times although Ted won the Championship two of the times he lost to Fernando.

Fernando is a happy, warm, friendly fellow. He has great determination and confidence though, and is all business when the bell rings. If the people of Southern California are lucky, they will see this great champion in action this year. Ice runs in his veins when the pressure is on. He plays for the streak—20 and 30 straight ringers. Fernando practices by himself. He uses only two shoes. He practices until he "has it". When he "has it" you've "had it".

From a friend with many pleasant memories

Arthur P. Scolari

NEW JERSEY TERCENTENARY

1664-1964

What We're Celebrating

The New Jersey Tercentenary Celebration marks the 300th anniversary of the state's birth. King Charles II of England, in March, 1664, granted a region between the Hudson and Delaware Rivers to James, the Duke of York. A month later York conveyed the land to Lord Berkeley and Sir George Carteret and named the area New Jersey.

The area had been explored and settled years before, of course. John Cabot sighted these shores in 1498 and Giovanni de Verrazano, the Florentine explorer, sailed along the coast in 1524. Swedish and Dutch settlers both came before Charles's grant and Peter Stuyvesant had founded Bergen, now Jersey City, as the area's first permanent town in 1660.

The official symbol of the celebration was suggested by the tercentenary slogan, "People — Purpose — Progress". The two sections of the symbol's base represent people and purpose. From this foundation comes the form of a tree or leaf representing progress. The three sections form a triangle, pointing to the future. Blue and buff, the state colors, are used.

First Capital of New Jersey
ELIZABETH
Man's Vision Justified

three centuries of progress

1664-1964

ELIZABETH TERCENTENARY COMMITTEE

13 WOLF PRESS, 308 Clinton Street, Linden, N. J.

1965

Only a Junior Champ Crowned

No National AAU senior horseshoe championship was held in 1965. The senior event was scheduled to begin on September 6th, in Jamestown, North Dakota, but was canceled due to weather.

The junior championship that year was planned as part of a huge AAU Sports Spree over the Fourth of July weekend in Miles City, Montana. To demonstrate the scope of the Spree, the entire calendar of events is reproduced below. No other junior horseshoe-pitching championship was ever held as part of such a large event.

Official Sport Spree Schedule

Friday, July 2

8:00 a.m.	Junior Golf at Town and Country Club
1:00 p.m.	Swimming and Diving Championships at City Pool
7:00 p.m.	Physical Fitness Competition at City Park
7:30 p.m.	Baton Twirling Championships

Saturday July 3

9:00 a.m.	Water Polo, City Pool
9:00 a.m.	National Junior Horseshoe Pitching Championships. Pitchers will start qualifying for class seeding at 9:00 a.m. at State Industrial School.

10:00 a.m.	Weightlifting Championships—123, 132, 148 and 165 lb. classes, Old Tennis Courts
10:00 a.m.	Junior Tennis Championships, New Tennis Courts
1:00 p.m.	Sport Spree Gymnastics, City Park
1:00 p.m.	Junior Olympics Judo Championships, Washington School Gym.
2:00 p.m.	Weightlifting Championships—181, 198 and Heavy-weight classes, Old Tennis Courts
3:00 p.m.	Montana Marathon Race, Plaza Shopping Center. Race will go east on old Highway 10, on Interstate to Fort Keogh exit, then into city for finish at Courthouse.
5:50 p.m.	Race Walking—1 mile, race starts at Leon Park on Highway and finishes at the Crossroads.
6:00 p.m.	Junior Bowling at Recreation Lanes
7:00 p.m.	A.B.I. Cycling, 10-mile race starts at Plaza, east to Baker interchange, then west to Fort Keogh with finish at City Park.

Sunday, July 4

9:00 a.m.	National Junior Horseshoe Championships comple-tion at State School
9:00 a.m.	Junior Tennis Championships continued at New Ten-nis Courts
1:00 p.m.	Region 6-mile race. Starts at Plaza, finishes at City Park, same course as the Marathon.

The newspaper coverage of the AAU Sports Spree was brief and limited. Considering a National AAU event was being held in their midst, it's difficult to understand why the media chose not to print feature articles or descriptions of the action, but did provide the final standings. Perhaps, in their view, dedicating that much print was big coverage. Here is the summary of the junior horseshoe-pitching winners:

National AAU Junior Horseshoe Pitching: 1. Ron Mosness, Big Timber, 5-0 (ringer average 38 percent). 2. Randy Ford, Helena, 4-1 3. Terry Mosness 3-2; Class B – 1. Jack Blake, Missoula 2. Roy Ducharme, Polson; Class C – 1. Rick Elass, Clarkston, Wash. 2. Gary Hale, Big Timber; Class D – 1. Richard Burland, Polson 2. Ron Paulson, Great Falls.

The 1965 National AAU junior champion, Ron L. Mosness, currently resides in Helena, Montana. He recalls the event, some 55 years later, but any memorabilia or newspaper clippings about the event have been lost or misplaced over the years. He recalls that his trip to the Spree was sponsored by a local business. Their support enabled him to enter the event, make the trip to Miles City, and stay in a motel for the weekend. He added that the classes were made up of six players, so his record was 5-0 since he said he didn't loss a game.

1966

Hometown Heroes

Before proceeding with a discussion of 1966 event, let's look back at the January 1966 issue of the NHPA publication *The Horseshoe Pitcher's News Digest*, which contained an article describing a meeting between the NHPA and the AAU. The account of the meeting is worthy of remark since there has been no evidence over the past few decades that the two organizations communicated or had any interest in the each other's events. The NHPA's publications, for example, have little or no coverage of scheduled AAU events—either announcing them to the NHPA membership or posting the results. The article conveys some pretty big hopes and plans:

NHPA and AAU Officials Hold Meeting
Discuss Future Relationships

The nebulous relationship between the AAU and the NHPA may soon change to a more concrete understanding, which will result in benefits to the game of horseshoes as a result of a recent meeting in Chicago between NHPA Secretary Bob Pence and AAU Vice President David Riveness of Montana.

Whereas the NHPA is the only national organization devoted solely to horseshoe pitching and makes no distinction between amateurs and professionals, the AAU is the governing body of amateur sports of all types and is also in charge of the Olympic program in this country. The AAU's main concern is with swimming, track and field and other Olympic sports, where it does an exceptionally good job, but it is also interested in other amateur sports including horseshoes.

The AAU does have an amateur horseshoe pitching program and conducts a number of tournaments each year including a National Amateur Championship. In those areas where it is active, the AAU is a real asset to the game.

At this point in time, practically all entrants in AAU tournaments are also NHPA members. This is particularly true in New Jersey, North Carolina and Virginia and to some extent, Montana. In these areas, AAU officials and NHPA clubs generally work together. NHPA members who head the horseshoe committee of the various AAU geographic divisions include Dr. Sol Berman and Paul Puglisle of New Jersey, Randall Jones and Joe White of North Carolina, John Snyder of California, Clarence Giles of Utah and Cecil Monday of Virginia.

The meeting in Chicago between Mr. Riveness and Mr. Pence brought out a number of areas where the two groups can join forces. Increasing horseshoe participation by youngsters in the junior age bracket is one area. The NHPA has the know-how and the contacts in the game of horseshoes while the AAU has the outside contacts with Park and Recreation departments, schools etc. there is a possibility that horseshoe pitching can gain a place on the Junior Olympics program under the sponsorship of the Quaker Oats Co.

Another possibility is the joint sponsorship of a comprehensive horseshoe handbook, which would find its way into the hands of athletic and recreation directors in the armed services, schools, parks and industry.

A working agreement between the AAU and the NHPA could possibly result in horseshoes gaining a place on the Olympic Games program the next time the event is held in the United States.

The host country of the Olympic Games may if it chooses add one new sport to the program in the form of a game native to that country. Japan added Judo in the 1964 games under this provision.

Mr. Riveness feels that horseshoes is a possible choice the next time the games come to the U.S. Towards this end, the NHPA is working with the Canadian players and clubs in an effort to have horseshoe placed on the program of the 1967 Pan American Games to be held in Winnipeg, Canada. These games will be a prelude to the 1968 Olympics.

Despite the lofty goals of the meeting, there is absolutely no available evidence that any efforts toward the items discussed were ever pursued beyond its conclusion.

In 1966, on September 3rd and 4th, the National AAU Championships returned to Winston-Salem for a third time (from the September 1966 *Amateur Athlete*):

Horseshoe Tourney at Winston-Salem

Twelve clay pits built to championship specifications and lights for night play will glamorize Mille Park in Winston-Salem, N.C., September 3–4, for the National AAU Senior Horseshoe Tournament.

The competition, directed by Joe White, chairman of the AAU Horseshoe Pitching Committee, is being held in conjunction with the 200th anniversary of Winston-Salem.

The *Winston-Salem Journal and Sentinel* printed this tournament announcement:

Horseshoes Crown
Up For Grabs Here

A field of about 50 of the national's top horseshoe pitchers is expected to take part in the National AAU horseshoe championships at Miller Park today and Sunday.

Tournament officials said that complete field will not be known until the pitchers arrive and register.

Entries have been received from many pitchers, including stars from Ohio, Delaware and Virginia.

Qualifying began last night and will continue until noon today when pitching in the various classes for the championship will begin. Both singles and doubles will be pitched.

Two women pitchers have entered the national event, Cindy Dean of McGaheysville, Va., who won Class I in the Southeastern Tournament last weekend and Sandy De Santo of Cleveland, Ohio, have entered.

Should rain delay the event today and Sunday, it will be pitched Monday. Should the entire program be hampered by weather it will be pitched next weekend, Sept. 10–11.

The tournament last year was scheduled at Jamestown, N.D., but was cancelled because of bad weather.

North Carolinians have been highly successful in past National AAU championships.

Walter King of Asheboro won the singles and teamed with Darrell Eller of Thomasville to win the doubles at Elizabeth, N.J., in 1964. Conrad Murphy of Winston-Salem was runner-up in both singles and doubles in 1963 when Tar Heels also swept the field. King won the singles and with Glyden Moore of Burlington took the doubles at Salisbury, Md., that year.

A Southern fried chicken dinner will be served contestants and their families at the Miller Park pits on Queen Street this afternoon.

The National AAU tournament is being sponsored by the Winston-Salem Horseshoe Pitcher's and the City Recreation Department. Joe White, city recreation director, is chairman of the National AAU Horseshoe Pitching Committee.

Harold Reno of Sabina, Ohio, won the Southeastern Classic here last weekend. Reno is not expected to take part in the AAU event; he will be defending his Ohio state championship.

The midtournament standings were provided in the September 4th edition of the *Journal*:

Two Men Tie in Horseshoes

Defending champion, Walt King of Asheboro, remained in a tie with Darrell Eller of Thomasville at the mid-point of the National AAU horseshoe tournament at Miller Park yesterday. Both had 7-0 records.

Gurney York of Harmony was third at 6-1. James Scotten of High Point, fourth at 5-1 and Conrad Murphy of Winston-Salem was tied with John Leach of Columbus, Ohio, for fifth at 4-2.

In the women's division, Sandy De Santo of Cleveland, Ohio, tied Francis Kacala of East Cleveland, Ohio, 3-1. Mrs. De Santo defeated Mrs. Kacala, 25-16 in the playoff. Dorothy Jones of Winston-Salem was third at 0-4.

Class B did not pitch.

King who won the tournament in 1963 and 1964, was voted top athlete in North and South Carolina last year.

The doubles championship was also decided yesterday. Defending champions Walt King and Darrell Eller tied Gurney York and James Scotten. Both teams had 5-2 records.

In the playoff, Eller and King edged York and Scotten 50-49. The victors had 49 ringers out of 80 tosses while York and Scotten earned 46 ringers out of 80 tries.

In the Class B doubles class, there was a three-way tie. Nelson Ashburn and Fletcher Dunlap, Randall Jones and James Martin, and Garvey Billings and Ray Samples all had 5-2 marks. Ashburn and Dunlap won the title in a playoff.

Qualifying Scores

	Pts.	R		Pts	R
1. Walter King, Asheboro,	DC		2. Woody Thomas, High Point	254	77
3. Gurney York, Harmony	252	76	4. John Corns, Winston-Salem	250	77
5. Martin Poppe, Long Island	247	75	6. John Leech, Columbus, O	247	77
7. Conrad Murphy, Winston-S	246	75	8. Carl Young, Columbus, O	236	72
9. Darrell Eller, Thomasville	236	70	10. Jack Giddes, Martinsville	236	69
11. Glynden Moore, E. College	236	68	12. Bill Kolb, Belleview, NJ	233	70
13.Sol Berman, Elizabeth, NJ	229	65	14. Howard Hester, W-Salem	216	63
15. James Sotten, High Point	215	61	16. Joe Hefner, Claremont	213	60

			Pts	R
Class B High Qualifier:	Walter Hering	Middeville, NJ	205	54
Class C:	Don Longtin,	High Point	190	51
Class D	Joe Cable,	Menace	166	35
Women's Class	Dorothy Jones,	Winston-S.	95	9

The article that was to cover the final day of action could only offer an incomplete report because rain caused delays and the paper had to go to press:

King Trails York in Horseshoes

Defending champion Walt King was trailing by two games when the National AAU horseshoe tournament neared its conclusion at the Miller Park courts late last night.

King, with a 9-2 record, was playing Gurney York, who was leading the tournament with an 11-1 mark. Darrell Eller was in second place with a 10-2 slate. The only other competitor in the running was James Scotten at 8-3.

Burrell Brobeck led the Class B standings with a 5-0. Fletcher Dunlap was a close second at 5-1. Two others were 3 games behind at 3-2.

The tournament was scheduled to end at 8 p.m. yesterday. However, afternoon showers halted action around 4:40 p.m. It resumed again at 8.

One of the most difficult situations in horseshoe pitching is playing in rainy weather. The players are pitching into pits filled with blue clay, which is kept moist for pliability—but when it becomes too wet and muddy, the clay gets slick and the players' shoes lose traction, which makes it difficult to pitch.

The men's championship class final standings below are reprinted from *Amateur Athlete*:

1966 National AAU Senior Doubles Championships

	W	L	
1. Walter King – Darrell Eller	6	2	Playoff Game
2. Gurney York – James Scotten	5	3	King – Eller 50
3. Carl Young – John Leech	4	3	York – Scotten 49
4. Jack Giddes – Bill Kolb	4	3	
5. Corns – Hester	3	4	
6. Walter Haring – Sol Berman	3	4	
7. Joe Hefner – Don Longtin	2	5	
8. Conrad Murphy – Woody Thomas	1	6	

Class B Doubles

1. Asburn – Dunlap	6-2	2. Jones – Martin	6-3	3. Billing – Samples	5-3
4. Cable – Austin	4-3	5. Wingate – Hill	4-3	6. Temalston – Terry	2-5
7. Hampton – Hine	2-5	8. Stinson – Sammons	1-6		

3-way playoff: Jones – Martin defeated Billings – Samples 52-44; Ashburn – Dunlap defeated Jones – Martin 52-16.

Women's Division

	W	L	Playoff Game
1. Sandy De Santo	4	1	De Santo 25
2. Francis Kacala	3	2	Kacala 16
3. Dorothy Jones	0	4	

Men's Class B

	W L
1. Burrell Brobeck	5-0
2. Fletcher Dunlap	4-1

Men's Class C

	W L
1. James Terry	3-1
2. W. B. Stinson	3-1
3. Ray Samples	3-1
4. Don Longtin	1-3
5. Dester Austin	0-4

Men's Class D

1. James Martin	5-0
2. Joe Cable	4-1
3. Willard Sammons	3-2
4. J. D. Mathis	3-2
5. Randall Jones	1-4
6. Harry Barr	0-5

1966 National AAU Senior Singles Championships

		W	L	SP	R	%
1.	Gurney York, Harmony, N.C.	14	1	1104	737	66.8
2.	Walter King, Asheboro, N.C.	12	3	910	657	72.2
3.	Darrell Eller, Thomasville, N.C.	11	4	950	640	67.4
4.	Jim Scotten, High Point, N.C.	11	4	1010	639	63.3
5.	John Leach, Columbia, Ohio	10	5	798	502	62.9
6.	Dr. Sol Berman, Elizabeth, N.J.	9	6	874	553	60.8
7.	Carl Young, Columbus, Ohio	8	7	1010	645	63.8
8.	John Corns, Winston-Salem, NC	7	8	872	508	58.2
9.	Woody Thomas, High Point, NC	7	8	997	622	62.5
10.	Martin Poppe, West Hempstead	7	8	644	393	61.0
11.	Conrad Murphy, Winston-Salem	6	9	856	460	53.7
12.	Jack Giddes, Martinsville, N.J.	6	9	884	529	59.8
13.	Bill Kolb, Belleview, N.J.	5	10	912	549	60.2
14.	Howard Hester, Winston-Salem	5	10	734	434	59.1
15.	Glynden Moore, Elon College	3	12	760	447	58.8
16.	Joe Hefner, Claremont, N.C.	0	15	314	120	38.2

The 1966 tournament featured a very talented and competitive championship class. Pointing out that the player in fifteenth place posted a performance of nearly 60 percent ringers offers some perspective on how competitive this group was.

1967

A Series of Questions

1967 leaves us with a lot of questions that my research so far could not answer. First, this announcement appeared in *The Horseshoe Pitcher's News Digest* in March 1967:

Kansas City Club Announces Tournament Dates

The Heart of America Horseshoe Club of Kansas City, Missouri, announces that It will again host the National AAU Junior Tournament. Date of the meet has been set for Saturday, May 20, at Northeast Athletic Field, in Kansas City. Starting time will be 10:00 a.m. Location of courts is at St. John and Belmont streets, just east of the Montgomery Ward store.

Winner in the 1966 Tournament of Champions was Floyd Toole of Little Rock, Arkansas. Harry Strohm of Kansas City, Missouri, will be the defending champion in the second annual AAU Juniors National Tournament.

Another great tournament will be the annual Tournament of Champions scheduled for Saturday and Sunday, June 3 and 4. The listing of entries will be the deciding factor in starting the meet. With the assumption that there will be enough players entered, there will be at least 5 classes with 12 to 16 men in Class A. The other four classes will have 8 men each. Mr. Harry Strohm, who is in charge of both meets, would like to have qualifying scores sent to him by May 20 along with an entry fee of $3.00. His address is: Mr. Harry Strohm, 419 South White Street, Kansas City, Missouri 64123. On the Juniors AAU meet, there is no age limit.

The article provides a considerable amount of information, but only leads to unanswered questions. I could find no newspaper articles or final results summaries, which is unusual since dates were provided. The inability to locate documentation doesn't necessarily mean a National AAU junior event wasn't held. It could simply reveal that the event results weren't reported to the media.

Beyond press coverage, my research included contacting the children of Harry Strohm, but their family albums and scrapbooks did not contain any articles pertaining to the 1966 or 1967 events.

Weather is always a likely suspect in forcing the cancellation or postponement of a pitching event. Nonetheless, the 1968 information indicated a National AAU junior champion was named in 1967, so if junior events were held in 1966 and 1967, the summary of results can't be reported at this time. (There is no evidence of senior events.)

1968

New Yorkers Reign in New Jersey

Before launching into a report of the 1968 National AAU Senior National Championship, more non-reporting of a national junior event is necessary. The following article appeared in the NHPA's March 1968 edition of *The Horseshoe Pitcher's News Digest*:

National AAU Juniors Tourney at Kansas City, Missouri

The National AAU Juniors meet will again be held in Kansas City, Mo., on Saturday, May 25, 1968, starting at approximately 10 a.m. If entries warrant, [the playing] will extend into Sunday. Would like to have at least 48 pitchers this year as we hope to make a successful bid for the Seniors next year. The Junior event is being sponsored by the Recreational Department of Kansas City, Mo. There will be four trophies for the eight-man classes and three trophies for the six-man classes. We have two AAU Junior champions, Harry J. Strohm, 1966 winner, and Ray Calvin, 1967 winner, living in this area. Winners of all classes will be eligible to qualify for the Senior event, which is being held in New Jersey this year. Anyone interested in entering this event, please contact Harry J. Strohm, 419 S. White, Kansas City, Missouri 64423, by sending in your combined 1967 percentage average.

As was the case in 1967, my research didn't uncover the results of a 1968 National AAU junior event. It's unfortunate that I can't report tournament accounts and results for this year and the two previous years. Particularly since there have been only two national junior champions listed since 1942, and literally no information about the specific events. In all those years, there's little doubt that junior events were held and national junior champions crowned, but my research has found no traces except in 1952 and 1965. Now there is evidence of the events—even locations and dates—but the results remain lost.

The 1968 National AAU's senior championships fared better, though. The event was held in July in Middlesex, New Jersey. The leaders of the sport in New Jersey, who were hosting the national event for a second time, were a very proficient group. They placed a number of event announcements in the NHPA's July 1968 edition of *The Horseshoe Pitcher's News Digest*:

National AAU Meet To Have Ladies Division

In addition to the National AAU men's tournament being held July 26-28 in Middlesex, New Jersey, there will be a ladies division added for singles competition. All women players are urged to enter. Entry blanks may be secured from Hal Hanania, 448 Ruyan Ave, Middlesex, New Jersey 08846.

1968 National AAU Tournament Housing Reservations

Those wishing to make reservations for rooms during the National AAU Tournament July 27 and 28 may do so by contacting Vincent J. Yannetti, 322 Longwood Avenue, Bound Brook, New Jersey, 08805. Motels and trailer camps are available.

World Champion in Exhibition at National AAU Meet

The New Jersey State Horseshoe Pitchers Association is conducting the National AAU Tournament at Middlesex, New Jersey, July 26–28, just prior to the World Horseshoe Pitching Championships at Keene, New Hampshire. It is only a short drive from Middlesex to Keene and many of the pitchers are expected to stop off for a tune-up session.

As an added attraction, the New Jersey Association will have Danny Kuchcinski, World Champion, put on two exhibitions. One will be at the tournament, the other at Dr. Sol Berman's Teenage Night Club in nearby Elizabeth, New Jersey, on Sunday afternoon, July 28 and in the evening at 8 p.m. at the club (Vertigo Teenage Nite Club).

The Middlesex Horseshoe Pitching Club has built 24 new courts complete with lights and hopes to complete the fence and added bleachers by tournament time.

A brochure has been prepared and some will be available at the Keene meet. It is the hope of the club that the 1970 World Tournament will be staged in Middlesex.

Why not stop off on the way to the World Tournament and enjoy the surroundings and hospitality of this fine up-and-coming club. It is only a few miles off of the course.

The *Middlesex Mirror* announced the national event:

Horseshoe Meet To Start Friday

Friday, July 26 is the day! The day when horseshoe pitchers from around the country will converge on Middlesex to take part in the National AAU Horseshoe Pitching Championships.

The tournament will be played on the Mountain View Park Courts beginning Friday, when qualifying rounds will be held. The pitchers will then square off for real on Saturday, pitching until 10 p.m. The tourney will be completed beginning at 10 a.m. Sunday.

Several state champions have given notice that they will compete in the three-day event. John Rademacher, state champion of Florida and Virginia's best, Bob Dean, are making long trips to take part.

The New Jersey State Horseshoe Pitcher's Association is handling all expenses. There will be no admission charge.

And then the report of the final standings by the *Middlesex Chronicle*:

Gancos' 'Sneak' to Victory in National AAU Horseshoe

Lou Gancos has been sneaking up on a first place finish at the Mountain View Horseshoe Courts for the past month and when he finally got it, it was a dandy.

Gancos, a 49 year old housing inspector for the city of New York, nosed out John Rademacher of Plant City, Fla. To win the National Senior Men's AAU Horseshoe Pitching Championship last weekend.

The past month has seen three major tournaments come to the attractive new 24-court facility. Gancos was third in the Mid-Atlantic States Championship and second in the New Jersey Open prior to nailing down the most important of all, the national championship.

Gancos compiled a 4-1 match game mark and a 71.6 ringer percentage. Rademacher threw 72.6 percent ringers, but dropped two matches while winning three to slip to the runner-up spot.

Third went to another pitcher who had made a long journey to get to the tourney, Robert Dean of McGaheysville, Va. Dean was also 3-2 in match play, but had a 68.6 ringer percentage.

Jack Giddes of Martinsville was the top local finisher. Jack, the 1967 state champ, threw 61.2 percent ringers while compiling a 3-2 mark. He is a member of the Middlesex Horseshoe Pitching Club, which hosted the tournament. The event was sponsored by the New Jersey State Horseshoe Pitcher's Association.

Dr. Sol Berman of Elizabeth, a former state titleholder posted a 2-3 record in the matches and a 65.7 ringer percentage in finishing fifth. Gene Rademacher, John's son, rounded out the top six. He dropped all five of his matches while slipping to a 49.6 ringer percentage.

A special feature of the tournament was the senior women's event. Mrs. Ruth Hangen of Buffalo, N.Y., easily out-classed the field, winning her three matches and putting up an excellent 67.9 ringer percentage. She finished third in the World's Championship last year and is entered in this year's world event this week in Keene, N.H.

Second in the women's division went to the Virginia state champ, Mrs. Cindy Dean of McGaheysville. Another Virginian, Mrs. Elizabeth Michael of West Augusta, was the third with a 1-2 match game mark and a 19.5 ringer percentage. Mrs. Dean tossed a very credible 55.1 percent ringers. Mrs. Ellen Anderson of Fawn Grove, Pa., was fourth, dropping all three matches with an 11.4 percentage.

Giddes teamed with another veteran, former state champ William Kolb of Belleville, to win the men's doubles with a 3-0 mark. Gancos and Charles Wilson of Peekskill, N.Y., were second at 2-1, while the Deans were third at 1-3 and the Rademachers fourth at 0-3.

Robert Bishe of Cranford swept through all opposition posting a 7-0 mark en route to the Class B singles title. John Loughery of Bronx, N.Y. won a playoff from Bound Brook's Vince Yannetti for the second spot after both had finished with 5-2 match game records. Middlesex pitchers occupied the next three positions, all with 3-4 records. Dale Eberhart was fourth, Lee Marshall fifth and Ron Vogel sixth.

Lougherty teamed with Bill Rogers of Mt. Vernon, N.Y., to win the class B doubles, beating out Vogel and Marshall on ringer percentage. Both tandems posted 4-1 records in match play. John Baugher and Gilbert Fridlinger of New Oxford, Pa., came in third at 3-2, beating out Yannetti and Eberhart.

Ben Michael of West Augusta, Va., ran away with the Class C title, putting up a 7-0 mark. His nearest opponent was Parker Sturgess, who won a playoff with Alton Adkins. Both are from Salisbury, Md. They, like Henry Mullen of Plainfield, posted 4-3 marks. Mullen came in fourth and Richard Peterson of Kenilworth was fifth.

Mullen teamed up with Leo Miller of South Plainfield to bring the Class C doubles crown to the Middlesex club. They compiled a 3-0 mark. Lawrence Windsor and Gary Chatham of Salisbury, Md., were second.

The Middlesex Club took the unusual step of expanding the number of classes, especially in the doubles competition. In past years, the tournament director would have thrown all the doubles teams into one class and let them duke it out. More recent years show an interest in expanding the number of classes, which certainly leads to more medal winners. It's likely the organizer's were hoping to lure in more participants, but three classes in doubles and five classes in singles is unheard of. A high number of players signing up would account for the additional classes. If Class A was limited to just six individuals, the expansion was a generous gesture to the other players.

1968 National AAU Women's Singles Championships

Class A	Player	City	W	L	%
1.	Ruth Hangen	Buffalo, N.Y.	3	0	67.6
2.	Cindy Dean	McGaheysville, Va.	2	1	55.1
3.	Elizabeth Michael	West Augusta, Va.	1	2	19.5
4.	Ellen Anderson	Fawn Grove, Pa.	0	3	11.4

1968 National AAU Senior Men's Singles Championships

Class A	Player	City	W	L	%
1.	Louis Gancos	Brooklyn N.Y.	4	1	71..6
2.	John Rademacher	Plant City, Fla.	3	2	72.6
3.	Robert Dean	McGaheysville, Md.	3	2	66.6
4.	Jack Giddes	Martinsville, N.J.	3	2	61.2
5.	Sol Berman	Elizabeth, N.J.	2	3	65.7
6.	Gene Rademacher	Plant City, Fla.	0	5	49.6

Class B	Player	City	W	L	%
1.	Robert Bishe	Cranford, N.J.	7	0	50.1
2.	John Loughery	Bronx, N.Y.	6	2	49.1
3.	Vincent Yannetti	Bound Brook, N.J.	5	3	48.6
4.	Dale Eberhart	Middlesex, N.J.	3	4	
5.	Lee Marshall	Middlesex, N.J.	3	4	
6.	Ron Vogel	Middlesex, N.J.	3	4	
7.	Robert Anderson	Fawn Grove, Pa.	2	5	
8.	Wilbert Hyland	Corning, N.Y.	0	7	

Class C	Player	City	W	L	%
1.	Ben Michaels	West Augusta, Va.	7	0	45.8
2.	Parker Sturgis	Salisbury, Md.	5	3	39.0
3.	Alton Adkins	Salisbury, Md.	4	4	40.0
4.	Henry Mullen	S. Plainfield, N.J.	4	3	
5.	Richard Peterson	Kenilworth, N.J.	3	4	
6.	Henry Hoodiman	E. Peterson, N.J.	3	4	
7.	James Donavan	Clark, N.J.	2	5	
8.	Thomas Young	Elizabeth, N.J.	1	6	

Class D	Player	City	W	L	%
1.	William Herrmann	Clark, N.J.	7	0	41.7
2.	Hal Hanania	Middlesex, N.J.	5	2	29.2
3.	Leo Miller	S. Plainfield, N.J.	4	3	31.1
4	George Van Dorn	Roselle, N.J.	4	3	
5.	Phil Zozzaro	Little Falls, N.J.	3	5	
6.	Joseph Pavis	Middlesex, N.J.	2	5	
7.	Wm. MacIntyre	Middlesex, N.J.	2	5	
8.	Alfred Price	Cranford, N.J.	1	6	

Class E	Player	City	W	L	%
1.	John Karczewski	Cliffwood, N.J.	5	0	23.4
2.	Alex Pluhar	Middlesex, N.J.	3	2	20.5
3.	Harry Schmidt	Fairlawn, N.J.	3	2	20.7
4.	Joseph Hanania	Middlesex, N.J.	3	2	
5.	Ralph Coleman	Middlesex, N.J.	1	4	
6.	Anthony Derwitz	Middlesex, N.J.	0	5	

1968 National AAU Senior Doubles Championships

Class A	Player	W	L
1.	William Kolb – Jack Giddes	3	0
2.	Louis Gancos – Charles Wilson	2	1
3.	Robert Dean – Cindy Dean	1	2
4.	John Rademacher – Gene Rademacher	0	3

Class B	Player	W	L
1.	William Rogers – John Loughery	4	1
2.	Ron Vogel – Lee Marshall	4	1
3.	John Baugher – Gilbert Fridlinger	3	2
4.	Vincent Yannetti – Dale Eberhart	2	3
5.	Alton Adkins – Parker Sturgis	2	3
6.	Willard Sammons – Robert Anderson	0	5

Class C	Player	W	L
1.	Henry Mullen – Leo Miller	3	0
2.	Lawrence Windsor – Gary Chatham	2	1
3.	George VanDorn – George Fleck	1	2
4.	Phil Zozzaro – Henry Hoodiman	0	3

Danny Kuchcinski won his first world championship in 1967 at the young age of 18. Some of the newspaper accounts for this 1968 AAU event mention that Kuchcinski was the youngest world champion ever, which is inaccurate. (Harold Falor won the world horseshoe pitching title in 1923 when he was just 15 years old.) Kuchcinski went on to win two more world titles, in 1969 and 1970. He joined Putt Mossman as the only player to win two world championships prior to the age of 20. Then he exceeded that feat with a third title before age 21, a record that still stands.

The 1968 newspapers also covered Kuchcinski's appearances, including photos of some of his amazing trick shots. Several of his tricks were similar to other pitchers' exhibition tricks in previous years, but one certainly was different. Two 50-gallon barrels were placed in front of the pit he was pitching toward, and a board was set across the two barrels. A man stood on that board with his feet spread far apart and another man, Vince Yannetti in 1968, stood in the pit with his feet on each side of the stake. Kuchcinski pitched the shoe, which went through the first man's legs, landing for a perfect ringer between Yannetti's feet. As they say, don't try this at home.

Kuchcinski's career was not just doing the trick shots. In competition he could get down to business. For his 1967 National AAU title he averaged an 84.37 ringer percentage—and then 84.75 percent in 1968 and 84.89 percent in 1970. In World Tournament competition, he once hit 66 consecutive ringers, pitching 97.1 percent for the game. (As a side note: the world record for consecutive ringers in a game is 72, a feat accomplished by the great Ted Allen.)

Kuchcinski retired from competitive horseshoe pitching at an early age and the went on to spend a few years taking his program of tricks around the nation—including appearances on *The Tonight Show* with Johnny Carson, *What's My Line?*, *The Mike Douglas Show*, and many other national programs.

The question of amateur status has cropped up several times in this book. Why not take a look at the 1968 women's champion with that question in mind? After all, Ruth Hangen was one of the all-time great women pitchers, a five-time world champion and a member of the NHPA Hall of Fame. Her world titles were won in 1970, 1971, 1972, 1973, and 1976. So she was still an amateur of sorts in 1968.

The Middlesex Club, the local hosts of the 1968 National AAU tournament, was made up of a group of tremendous promoters of the game. The 1971 World Tournament came to their home courts thanks to their efforts. A few individuals who were involved in this tournament are still living in New Jersey and were instrumental in providing the information on 1968 AAU event:

Hal Hanania was elected NHPA's vice president in 1968. He was presented the NHPA's 1971 Stokes Memorial Award for his efforts to promote, foster, and build the sport, and was induced into New Jersey's horseshoe-pitching hall of fame.

Bill MacIntyre, a five-time New Jersey state champion, served as president of the New Jersey State Horseshoe Pitchers Association and was inducted into the state association's hall of fame.

Vince Yannetti served for many years as an officer in the New Jersey State Horseshoe Pitchers Association. He was a recipient of the NHPA's Stokes Award in 1985. He was inducted into the state association's hall of fame, and the NHPA's Hall of Fame in 1995.

Though he passed away in 2003, it would not be fitting to speak of prominent members of the Middlesex Club without mention of Sol Berman. He was a participant in the 1968 National AAU tournament and was half of the winning National AAU doubles team in 1976. He was a nine-time New Jersey state champion, served as the state association's president, received the NHPA's Stokes Memorial Award in 1982, and holds places in multiple halls of fame—in New Jersey, Florida, and the NPHA

Bill MacIntyre provided a program book from the 1968 event, which is an incredible artifacts of the AAU era. That program is reproduced over the next few pages.

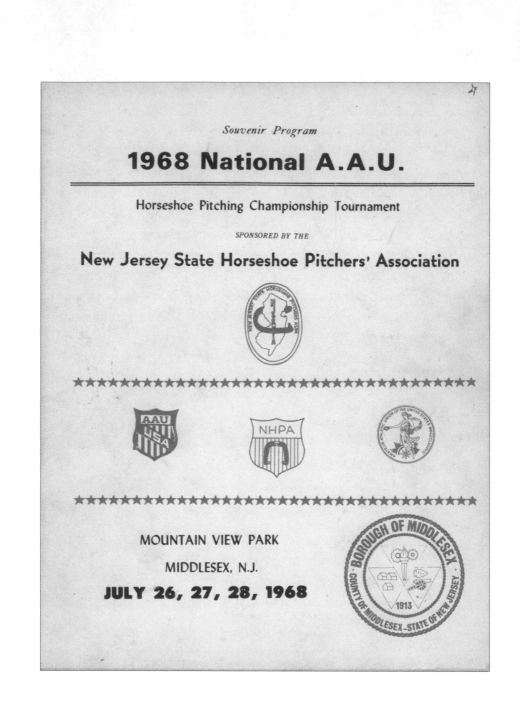

Souvenir Program

1968 National A.A.U.

Horseshoe Pitching Championship Tournament

SPONSORED BY THE

New Jersey State Horseshoe Pitchers' Association

★★

★★

MOUNTAIN VIEW PARK

MIDDLESEX, N.J.

JULY 26, 27, 28, 1968

Mayor Charles S. Judson

On behalf of the governing body and the people of Middlesex Borough, may I extend to you a warm and cordial welcome to our municipality.

We are honored to have been chosen by the A.A.U. for the site of their National Horseshoe Championship Tournament and hope that you and your families enjoy your stay with us as you avail yourselves of the facilities in our new Mountain View Park.

CHARLES S. JUDSON,
Mayor
Borough of Middlesex

MIDDLESEX
HORSESHOE PITCHERS
CLUB HISTORY

Clubs are formed for lots of reasons, some of them social, some sport, some even financial. The Middlesex Horseshoe Club was formed because of time.

For a local cop, time takes the form of an eight-hour shift, which would be normal except that every few days the shift changes, rotates. While it is the fairest way to run a police department, a rotating shift causes problems. It costs a rookie a lot of sleep until he gets used to it, and after he does it costs him a lot of time away from his family or friends, who think conventionally in terms of sunrise and sunset.

As a sergeant, Hal Hanania has had thirteen years on the local force to get used to the idea of changing his life every week. In the last four years, though, at least one thing has gotten better: He finds it easier to get up a game of horseshoes. And so do a lot of other guys.

Back in 1963 (which seems like a long time ago) Hal had a pretty rough time digging up competition. He spent lots of hours riding around town looking for stakes stiking out of the ground — a sure clue that a horseshoe pitcher was nearby. Whenever he found them, he would introduce himself to the owner of the house and, more often than not, would be pitching a game with a new partner before too long.

During these rounds, Hal asked players if they would be interested in starting a club. With enough encouraging responses, he talked with Lee Davis of Ridgefield, then eastern representative of the National Horseshoe Pitchers Association and himself a former state champion. Davis came to Middlesex on October 22, 1963. He gave a talk, put on an exhibition of trick pitching, and before the evening was over the Middlesex Horseshoe Club was more than a gleam in Hal Hanania's eye.

One night in January, 1964, the group met in Hal's cellar and elected him president, a post he held for two years Then the real work began.

The club, which had 49 charter members from within a 10-mile radius of Middlesex, built six horseshoe courts on a local recreation field (digging up clay, appropriately enough, from a marsh at the end of the borough's Clay Avenue). That first year they met once a week in league competition, and installed lights so the games could continue far into the night.

Several club members joined the state association to play in its tournaments, and an occasional state competition was held in Middlesex. But by 1965 the six courts became so well-liked that more state tournaments were scheduled. Three more courts were added that year, but they, too proved insufficient, and in 1967 three portable courts were added, making a total of 12.

With such rapid growth, a club might be content to rest on its laurels for awhile. But this year it's a whole new ballgame all over again — 24 brand-new courts in Middlesex' brand-new Mountain View Park. The new courts equal the largest layout in the world.

The new courts, built entirely by the club, have brought this year's National AAU Championship Tournament to Middlesex. The club, not unreasonably, hopes to bring the World Tournament here in the future.

Club members have kept pace with the growth of local facilities. The state championship has been held by a club member for the past several years. The present champ, Jack Giddes of Martinsville, improved his game so quickly that he traveled to Keene, N.H., to play in the world tournament, becoming the first N.J. player to face world competition.

The club is interested in the formation of other clubs in the area with an eye toward future inter-club competition. Membership is open to all players, experienced or not, within reasonable traveling distance of Middlesex. Tom Czado of Middlesex is president.

5

1967 N.J. State Champ

Jack Giddes of Martinsville, N.J., a charter member of the Middlesex Horseshoe Pitchers' Club won the N.J. State Championship after competing in organized competition for only four years.

In 1965 and in 1966 Jack gained the runner-up position. In 1965 Jack also qualified for, and played in, the Championship Division of the World Tournament.

Giddes has a unique style - one of the most "relaxed" players in the state, he uses a two step delivery pitching the one-and-three-quarter turn shoe.

HORSESHOE SPORTSMANSHIP

Good sportmanship and courteous conduct on the courts is an important factor and in fact is written into the rules .

A player must not make any distracting noise or movement while his opponent is in the act of pitching. This includes filing or "clinking" his shoes together, talking or standing in front of the stake.

The rules state that a player must stand on the opposite side of the pitcher's box and to the rear of the stake while his opponent is pitching.

The player who pitches first in a frame cannot walk to the other end while his opponent is pitching.

Players may pitch from which ever side of the pitcher's box they choose, and there is nothing in the rules to prevent both players from using the same side as only one can pitch at a time.

When a scorekeeper is being used, the player who scores in the frame should call the score to the scorekeeper, but before he does the two players should agree on the score.

Never pick up or move the shoes until agreement has been reached.

Do not step over the foul line when delivering your shoes until after the shoe has left your hand.

6

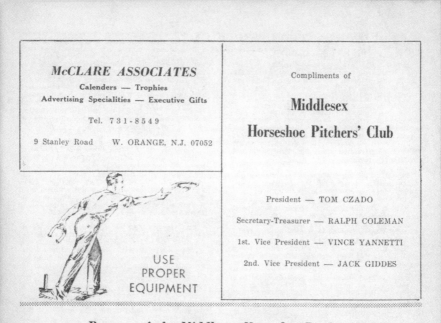
Patrons of the Middlesex Horseshoe Pitchers' Club

Hank Mullen	Ted Risberg	Vince Yannetti
Hal Hanania	Alex Pluhar	Dale Eberhart
Tom Czado	Leo Miller	Ben Thevenet
Ron Vogel	Ralph Coleman	Jack Giddes

Patrons of the Middlesex Volunteer Rescue Squad

Phil Ackermann, President	Bob Canavan, Secretary	Tom Pollard
Harry Whalen, Captain	Charles Semmer, Treasurer	John Tomassetti
Frank Conrad, Ass't. Captain	Don Ellery, Corres. Secretary	Ray Martin
Ray Wheelan, 1st Lieut.	Frank Guibleo	Frank Perez
Andy Wnek, 2nd Lieut.	Leonard Winters	Herb Bennett
Lou Gearino, Sergeant	William J. Bald	Sylvester Conrad
John Degutis, Corporal	Chick Stazo	Gavan Flanagan
	Ray Rood	Paul Kulpak

7

Patrons of the Middlesex Volunteer Fire Department

Darrell R. Dent, Chief	Michael P. Duffy	Robert E. Blair
John H. Ross, Ass't. Chief	Kenneth Van Nostrand	Marty Matuskiewicz
Joseph Lecesse, Ass't. Chief	Eddie Vanderhoof	Bill Freeman
George H. Schaub	Henry Shipley	Paul Van Avery
Robert E. Flynn	Elmer Smith	James G. Henry
George Stazo	Richard Sharkey	Frank A. Taylor
Richard C. Maehr	Robert Kellerman	Ralph W. Nye
John J. Cotter	Robert Poltorak	Howard Frederickson
Richard A. Davis	John Poltorak Sr.	Victor Palazzi
Ernie Derby	Charles Kriney	Bill Bayous

Patrons of the Middlesex Special Police Association

John H. Griffith, President	Joseph E. Tomaszewski	Milt Garretson
John P. Haller, Vice Pres.	John M. Young Sr.	John Van Ness
William J. Shanahan	Harry Peterson	John Pacewicz
Edward Brosky	George Ray	Edmund G. Hallinan
Albert Kelly	Edward Seder	Joseph F. Ambrose
Matthew E. Seiler	Donald J. Cook	Dominic Argensy
Frank L. Panella	Richard J. Mac Grath	Joseph Lothringer
Alan W. Chase	Eugene E. Crossman	Paul Eytel
Fred Worowski	John E. Heard	Ned Howard
John H. Keiser	Frank E. Bitting	Tom Trautwein
Phillip J. Myers	Bernie Becchine	Steve Meyer
		Frank Palazzi

Patrons of the Middlesex Police Department

Chief Andrew C. Simpf	Sgt. Joseph A. Pirone	Ptlmn. Robert A. Palazzi
Capt. S. E. Kulpak	Police Commissioner John Sylvia	Ptlmn. John F. Giuliano
Lt. Robert H. Agans	Judge Ronald V. Rockoff	Ptlmn. Earl S. Thompson
Lt. William Potynsky	Court Clerk Louie Staffelli	Ptlmn. William Townes
Lt. Donald H. Lang	Ptlmn. Donald J. Wells	Ptlmn. Gerald W. Cummins
Sgt. Anthony DiBartolomeo	Ptlmn. Edward J. King	Ptlmn. Jerome Nowak
Sgt. Edward W. Meyer	Ptlmn. Joseph E. Erb	Ptlmn. Martin J. Merbler Jr.
Sgt. Hal Hanania	Ptlmn. Sylvester Conrad	Ptlmn. Virgil Haney
		Ptlmn. James J. Donohue

11

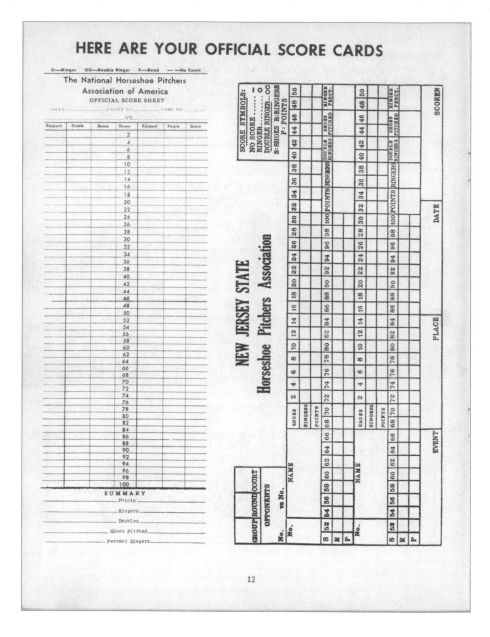

HERE ARE YOUR OFFICIAL SCORE CARDS

World Horseshoe Pitching Records

Established in the annual World Tournament

MEN'S DIVISION

Complete Tournament:

Ringer Pct., 31 Games	87.5	Casey Jones, Waukesha, Wis.	1948
Ringer Pct., 35 Games	86.5	Ted Allen, Boulder, Colo.	1955
Ringer Pct., 17 Games	86.6	Curt Day, Frankfort, Ind.	1966
Total ringers	2903	Ralph Maddox, Poca, W. Va.	1964
Double ringers	1173	Ralph Maddox, Poca, W. Va.	1964
Shoes pitched	3476	Ralph Maddox, Poca, W. Va.	1964

Single Game — Individual

Ringer Pct., winner	100	Guy Zimmerman, Danville, Calif.	1948
Ringer Pct., loser	89.7	Ray Martin, Philo, Ill.	1965
Total ringers, winner	175	Glen Henton, Maquoketa, Iowa	1965
Total ringers, loser	174	Ray Martin, Philo, Ill.	1965
Double ringers, winner	80	Glen Henton, Maquoketa, Iowa	1965
Double ringers, loser	77	Ray Martin, Philo, Ill.	1965
Consecutive ringers	72	Ted Allen, Boulder, Colo.	1951
Shoes, shortest game, winner	22	Roland Kraft, Lecompton, Kan.	1941

Single Game — Both players

Longest game, shoes pitched	194	Glen Henton & Ray Martin	1965
Ringer Pct.	91.2	Paul Focht, Dayton, Ohio &	
		Marvin Craig, Parker, Ind.	1965
Total ringers	349	Glen Henton & Ray Martin	1965
Double ringers	157	Glen Henton & Ray Martin	1965
Cancelled ringers	316	Glen Henton & Ray Martin	1965
"Four Deads"	63	Glen Henton & Ray Martin	1965
Consecutive "Four Deads"	15	Elmer Hohl, Ontario, Canada &	
(all 4 shoes on stake)		Carl Steinfeldt, Rochester, N.Y.	1964

Qualifying — 200 Shoes (Possible 600 points)

Total points	571	Harold Reno, Sabina, Ohio	1966
Total ringers	187	Ted Allen, Boulder, Colo.	1955
Double ringers	87	Harold Reno, Sabina, Ohio	1966
Ringers, 100 shoes pitched	96	Don Titcomb, Los Gatos, Calif.	1958

WOMEN'S DIVISION

Complete Tournament — 7 Games

Ringer Pct.	81.3	Caroline Schultz, Harvey, Ill.	1934
		Sue Gillespie, Portland, Ind.	1964
Total ringers	344	Sue Gillespie, Portland, Ind.	1964
Shoes pitched	502	Anna Lindquist, Morgantown, W. Va.	1964

Single Game — Individual

Ringer Pct., winner	93.3	Sue Gillespie, Portland, Ind.	1964
Ringer Pct., loser	73.9	Lorraine Thomas, Lockport, N.Y.	1965
Total ringers, winner	76	Sue Gillespie, Portland, Ind.	1965
Total ringer, loser	71	Lorraine Thomas, Lockport, N.Y.	1965
Double ringers, winner	31	Sue Gillespie, Portland, Ind.	1965
Double ringers, loser	23	Lorraine Thomas, Lockport, N.Y.	1965
Consecutive ringers	30	Sue Gillespie, Portland, Ind.	1964

15

(Continued on page 23)

WORLD HORSESHOE PITCHING CHAMPIONS

Men's Division

NOTE: Official tournaments were held only in the years listed. Both winter and summer tournaments were held as indicated during some of the early years. No official ringer percentages were kept prior to 1923. The total number of ringers thrown by the champion is listed here for those years. All records are from the offcial files of the N.H.P.A.

Year	Champion, Home Town	Ring. Pct.		Played At
1909	Frank Jackson, Kellerton, Ia.			Bronson, Kan.
1915	Frank Jackson, Kellerton, Ia.	97	R	Kansas City, Kan.
1919	Fred Brust, Columbus, O.	367	R	St. Petersburg, Fla.
1920 W	George May, Akron, O	430	R	St. Petersburg, Fla.
1920 S	Frank Jackson, Kellerton, Ia.	850	R	Akron, O.
1921 W	Charles Bobbitt, Lancaster, O.	439	R	St. Petersburg, Fla.
1921 S	Frank Jackson, Kellerton, Ia.	391	R	Minneapolis, Minn.
1922 W	Charlie Davis, Columbus, O.	448	R	St. Petersburg, Fla.
1922 S	Frank Lundin, New London, Ia.	424	R	Des Moines, Ia.
1923 W	Harold Falor, Akron, O.	55.3		St. Petersburg, Fla.
1923 S	George May, Akron, O.	60.0		Cleveland, O.
1924 W	Charlie Davis, Columbus, O.	57.9		Lake Worth, Fla.
1924 S	Putt Mossman, Eldora, Ia.	62.5		Minneapolis, Minn.
1925	Putt Mossman, Eldora, Ia.	67.6		Lake Worth, Fla.
1926	Frank Jackson, Kellerton, Ia.	61.4		St. Petersburg, Fla.
1927 W	Charlie Davis, Columbus, O.			
1927 S	Charlie Davis, Columbus, O.	64.8		Duluth, Minn.
1928	Charlie Davis, Columbus, O.	70.2		St. Petersburg, Fla.
1929	Blair Nunnamaker, Cleveland, O.	69.5		St. Petersburg, Fla.
1933	Ted Allen, Boulder, Colo.	73.5		Chicago, Ill.
1935	Ted Allen, Boulder, Colo.	75.5		Moline, Ill.
1940	Ted Allen, Boulder, Colo.	82.4		Des Moines, Ia.
1941	Fernando, Isias, Los Angeles, Calif.	82.9		Des Moines, Ia.
1946	Ted Allen, Boulder, Colo.	83.9		Des Moines, Ia.
1947	Fernando, Isias, Los Angeles, Calif.	83.2		Murray, Utah
1948	Fernando, Isias, Los Angeles, Calif.	84.2		Milwaukee, Wis.
1949	Fernando, Isias, Los Angeles, Calif.	83.3		Murray, Utah
1950	Fernando, Isias, Los Angeles, Calif.	83.5		Murray, Utah
1951	Fernando, Isias, Los Angeles, Calif.	85.7		Murray, Utah
1952	Fernando, Isias, Los Angeles, Calif.	83.5		Murray, Utah
1953	Ted Allen, Boulder, Colo.	83.2		Murray, Utah
1954	Guy Zimmerman, Danville, Calif.	84.8		Murray, Utah
1955	Ted Allen, Boulder, Colo.	86.5		Murray, Utah
1956	Ted Allen, Boulder, Colo.	83.4		Murray, Utah
1957	Ted Allen, Boulder, Colo.	85.1		Murray, Utah
1958	Fernando, Isias, Los Angeles, Calif.	84.3		Murray, Utah
1959	Ted Allen, Boulder, Colo.	84.4		Murray, Utah
1960	Don Titcomb, Los Gatos, Calif.	84.9		Muncie, Ind.
1961	Harold Reno, Sabina, Ohio	83.8		Muncie, Ind.
1962	Paul Focht, Dayton, Ohio	81 8		Greenville, Ohio
1963	John Monasmith, Yakima, Wash.	82.3		South Gate, Calif.
1964	Harold Reno, Sabina, Ohio	84.1		Greenville, Ohio
1965	Elmer Hohl, Wellesley, Ontario	84.6		Keene, N.H.
1966	Curt Day, Frankfort, Indiana	86.6		Murray, Utah
1967	Dan Kuchcinski, Erie, Pa.	84.4		Fargo, North Dakota

19

1968 National A.A.U. Horseshoe Pitching Championships

Mountain View Park, Middlesex, New Jersey

— FRIDAY, JULY 26th —

Qualifying from 1:00 P.M. to 11:00 P.M.

— SATURDAY, JULY 27th —

Qualifying from 8:00 A.M. to 10:00 A.M.

(Players who do not have established ringer average must qualify by pitching 100 shoes for class placement.)

Competition from 10:00 A.M. to 2:00 P.M.

Woman's Division
First half of Men's Championship Class
Men's Class "D"

Banquet at Bambo's from 2:00 P.M. to 5:00 P.M.
Welcome address by Mayor Charles S. Judson

Competition from 5:00 P.M. to 10:00 P.M.
Mayor Judson to pitch first shoe to start
final round of Championship Class
Men's Class "C"

— SUNDAY, JULY 28th —

Competition from 10:00 A.M. to 2:00 P.M.
Men's Class "B"
Men's Doubles

Exhibition from 2:00 P.M. to 3:00 P.M.

World Horseshoe Pitching Champion Danny Kuchcinski will present a display of trick pitching.

Farewell banquet for players at Bambo's & presentation of awards to winners

(Program subject to change without notice)

20

THE COMMITTEE

George R. Hoagland, Rahway, N.J., Director of the N.J.A.A.U.

Dr. Sol Berman, M.D., Elizabeth N.J., Program Chairman

Dr. Dale Eberhart, Middlesex, N.J., Program Book and Advertisements

Vince Yannetti, Bound Brook, N.J., Lodging and Information

Ronald Vogel, Middlesex, N.J., Schedule and Welcoming

Dr. Ralph Coleman, Middlesex, N.J., Scorekeeping and Grounds

Sgt. Hal Hanania, Middlesex, N.J., Local Publicity

George Cron, Elizabeth, N.J., N.J.A.A.U. Publicity Director

Paul Puglise, Clifton, N.J., Tournament Director

NEW JERSEY A.A.U. HORSESHOE PITCHING CHAMPIONS

Senior

1961	William Kolb, Belleville
1962	Sol Berman, Elizabeth
1963	Sol Berman, Elizabeth
1964	Sol Berman, Elizabeth
1965	Sol Berman, Elizabeth
1966	William Kolb, Belleville
1967	William Kolb, Belleville
1968	Not yet played

Junior

1961	William Kolb, Belleville
1962	Joseph McCrink, East Orange
1963	Joseph McCrink, East Orange
1964	Walter Haring, Middleville
1965	Walter Haring, Middleville
1966	Asa Brown, Butler
1967	Lee Davis, Ridgefield
1968	Jack Giddes, Martinsville

Note ! !   After a player has won the Senior AAU Championship, he is no longer eligible to compete in the Junior AAU Championship.

NATIONAL A.A.U.
HORSESHOE PITCHING CHAMPIONS and HOST (Location)

1960 Singles — Glenn Riffle, Dayton Ohio
   Doubles — Jack Stout, Melrose Park, Illinois & Roger Ehlers, St. Charles, Illinois
   Host — Dayton, Ohio

1961 Singles — Roger Ehlers, St. Charles, Illinois
   Doubles — Roger Ehlers, St. Charles, Illinois and Jack Stout, Melrose Park, Illinois
   Host — Winston-Salem, North Carolina

1962 Singles — Ira Jensen, Culbertson, Montana
   Doubles — Art Olsen, Helena, Montana and Ed Holmberg, Big Timber, Montana
   Host — Miles City, Montana

1963 Singles — Walter King, Asheboro, North Carolina
   Doubles — Walter King, Asheboro, North Carolina & Glynden Moore, Elon College, N. C.
   Host — Salisbury, Maryland

1964 Singles — Walter King, Asheboro, North Carolina
   Doubles — Walter King, Asheboro, North Carolina & Darrell Eller, Thomasville, N. C.
   Host — Elizabeth, New Jersey

1965 No Tournament

1966 Singles — Gurney York, Harmony, North Carolina
   Doubles — Walter King, Asheboro, North Carolina & Darrell Eller, Thomasville, N. C.
   Host — Winston-Salem, North Carolina

1967 No Tournament

1968 Singles —
   Doubles —
   Host — Middlesex, New Jersey

22

1968   [251]

(Continued from page 15)

Single Game — Both Players

Longest game, shoes pitched	96	Vicki Winston, Lamonte, Mo. &	
		Sue Gillespie, Portland, Ind.	1965
		Sue Gillespie & Lorraine Thomas	1965
Ringer Pct.	76.6	Sue Gillespie & Lorraine Thomas	1965
Total ringers	147	Sue Gillespie & Lorraine Thomas	1965
Double ringers	54	Sue Gillespie & Lorraine Thomas	1965
"Four Deads"	14	Sue Gillespie & Lorraine Thomas	1965
Consecutive "Four Deads"	5	Sue Gillespie & Vicki Winston	1964

Qualifying — 100 Shoes (Possible 300 points)

Total points	259	Sue Gillespie, Portland, Ind.	1964
Total ringers	86	Esther James, Hastings, Mich.	1935
Double ringers	34	Sue Gillespie, Portland, Ind.	1964

If you REALLY want to enjoy playing
— pitch in ORGANIZED competition.
Join the

NEW JERSEY STATE HORSESHOE PITCHERS' ASS'N.

for information call or write to:

PRESIDENT—Hal Hanania, 448 Runyon Ave., Middlesex, 968-2343
SECRETARY—Ron Vogel, 298 Lincoln Blvd., Middlesex, 356-2046
TOURNAMENT
    DIRECTOR—Paul Puglise, 200 Luddington Ave., Clifton, N. J., 478-3895

23

How the Game Began

No one knows who invented the game of horseshoes, or how or when it was first played. Several accounts of its beginning have been written, based on a few bits of information and a great deal of supposition.

The most likely origin of the game is that it started as a substitute for the Olympic game of discus throwing. The Greeks idolized the athletes who competed in the Olympic games and sought to imitate them.

The type of equipment used in the Olympic contests, including the discus, was too expensive for the average person to afford. It seems likely that poor people began to fashion substitutes for the discus and to hurl them for a distance. They eventually hammered out metal rings, shaped a great deal like a discus, and developed a game similar to quoits. The accent soon shifted from distance to accuracy, with pegs being placed in the ground as targets. They tried to encircle the peg for ringers, and thus was born a new game that was the predecessor of the game of horseshoes.

This game was being played before the birth of Christ. A few centuries after the dawn of the Christian era Greek and Roman armies began to attach metal strips to the feet of their horses to prevent the hooves from being torn to pieces on the rough terrain over which they moved. As these first horseshoes were discarded, they were gathered up by soldiers and camp followers and pitched. These shoes are thought to have weighed nearly four pounds.

The open side of the shoe brought out another interesting possibility. In addition to going over the peg as the quoit or metal ring had done, there would be occasional ringers when the peg slipped through the open side.

Whether the use of horseshoes instead of metal rings became popular because of more ringers is very questionable, however. It seems more likely that their use was more a matter of convenience. It was much easier to use them as they were than to hammer them into closed rings. As we shall see, it was a long time before any emphasis was placed on the open side of the shoe.

It is believed that the Roman armies brought the game to England when they invaded that country. Both horseshoes and quoits were played in England, with quoits being much preferred by the English. The nobles and aristocrats of England and many other nations played quoits for centuries. There are indications that horseshoes were first pitched in England by the women and children because they were lighter than quoits. Eventually, the men began to pitch them too. Both games were played in Europe throug'i the eighteenth century.

The early settlers in America brought along the games of quoits and horseshoes. By the time the Revolutionary War was fought, the game of horseshoes was played almost exclusively. Quoits was on its way to becoming extinct, and is now played almost nowhere. A link between the game of horseshoes and our early history is the often quoted observation of the Duke of Wellington that "the Colonial War of Liberation was won on the village greens by pitchers of horse hardware". Our forefathers were ardent players of the horseshoe game, and nearly every person in America today has played the game at some time or other in his life.

Horseshoe pitching has been played continuously from that time to the present in all parts of the United States. Our soldiers have played horseshoes in their leisure time in every war. In spite of this widespread playing of the game, there is no trace of organized play in the United States until an active local club was formed at Meadville, Pennsylvania, in 1899.

The game as we know it today is a very recent game, coming into its own about 1920. It is near this time that the "open shoe" became a deliberate scientific attempt, instead of a blind toss with merely a hope that it would be a ringer. Around this time many things happened that dramatically changed horseshoe pitching from a haphazard game with no standard rules to a well organized game, which can take its place alongside bowling, golf and other individual sports.

A few of the landmarks that changed the game were:

(a)   The formation of an organization or governing body.

(b)   Adoption of standard rules.

(c)   Development of the "open shoe".

(d)   Manufacture of standard pitching shoes with better hooks and balance.

Credit: Ottie W. Reno

24

1968   [253]

THE FUTURE OF HORSESHOES

The future of horseshoe pitching as a sport is bright. All sports are on the upswing in the United States, as more Americans continue to have more leisure time. There are many reasons why horseshoe pitching should grow.

One of the reasons is that the sport is very inexpensive. If you pitch at the city park or have a court available, all you have to have is a pair of shoes. With them you can pitch 10,000 games free of charge. If you compete in organized play, there will be some charge, but it is so small that it is only nominal. In so many sports, practice costs about as much as competition, and it is here that great savings are made.

Horseshoes are a family sport. Children and women can play in the same game with the men. It can be played as a group sport at reunions, picnics or company gatherings.

Horseshoes can be played all the year round. More and more indoor courts are being built, and they have proved to be very practical for local clubs.

The game is simple enough to be played by anyone, but difficult enough that no one can perfect it. No matter what your reason for playing a game, horseshoes should satisfy you. If you pitch for laughs, horseshoes is your game. If you are a man who tries to kill a game, be careful or horseshoes will kill you.

There is no game that can boast of better sportsmanship. With very few exceptions, horseshoe pitchers will give you the points rather than question them.

Horseshoes provide as much healthful exercise as you need. There is plenty of walking, throwing and bending. Outdoor pitching exposes you to the sunshine just like all other outdoor sports.

Horseshoes are beginning to get more publicity now. Several pitchers have appeared on television programs, and more and more newspapers and magazines are writing about horseshoe pitching. Roy Smith observed in the February 1949 issue of The Horseshoe Pitcher that "the greatest need in the horseshoe game today is that of proper and intelligent promotion." Men had said it often before him, and men have releated it often since. There are more and more who are doing something toward that end now.

Horseshoes are being added to the sports program of certain schools. The game is slated to be made part of the Olympic games, and there are other signs of its growth in every part of the United States. The membership in local clubs is jumping every year.

Scoreboards, neater batteries of courts, bleachers, more neatly dressed pitchers, and better organization on all levels have increased the game's attraction as a spectator sport.

If the officers in charge of the national organization and of the local clubs continue to work as hard as they are working at the present time, there is no way the game can go but forward.

Credit: Ottie W. Reno — The Story of Horseshoes.

WE WELCOME YOU TO MIDDLESEX

It is with great pleasure that we, the committee, the Middlesex Horseshoe Pitchers' Club and the New Jersey Horseshoe Pitchers' Association, welcome the National A.A.U. horseshoe pitchers, their friends and families.

Middlesex and the Middlesex Horseshoe Club are to be congratulated. They have gone to considerable expense, time and effort in creating the largest and one of the best sites for a large tournament.

We, the committee, and the New Jersey Horseshoe Pitchers' Association will do all we can to help Middlesex and the Middlesex Club in their quest of the World Horseshoe Pitching Championship Tournament.

The Committee wishes to thank the many friends, patrons, boosters, advertisers and subscribers for their help in making this event a success.

Our "Good Luck" wishes to all participants. We hope all our visitors will have a very pleasant and enjoyable stay.

Sincerely,
The Committee

"CLOSE ONLY COUNTS IN HORSESHOES"

The world's championship tournament of 1948 was conducted by the National Horseshoe Pitchers' Association at Milwaukee, Wisconsin, August 16 through August 21st.

During the long and gruelling contest, Casey Jones of Waukesha, Wisconsin gave what stands today as the greatest tournament, percentage wise, ever pitched. Casey hit 2159 ringers out of 2468 shoes in his 35 games for an amazing ringer percentage of 87.5. But this was not enough. Jones lost the tournament. Fernando Isais of Los Angeles, California won the world's championship, defeating Jones 50-49 in the deciding game. Isais' percentage for the entire tournament was 84.2.

As if losing the tournament after pitching a world's record ringer percentage were not enough, Jones hit a higher ringer percentage in the game he lost to Isais than did Isais. The game went 136 shoes with Jones getting 116 ringers for 85.2 percent while Isais got 114 ringers for 83.8 percent.

If ever there was proof that close ones do count in horseshoes, this should be it.

Admiral Chester K. Nimitz, a member of the Mosswood Horseshoe Club in Oakland, California, was an exponent of pitching horseshoes to keep physically fit, especially for those in the senior citizen age group. He maintained that it is an ideal exercise recreation.

Ex-president Harry S. Truman, a horseshoe pitching fan, had horseshoe courts built at the White House during his years in office.

26

NEW JERSEY STATE HORSESHOE PITCHING CHAMPIONS

1922	Henry Born	1943 - 1946	(No tournament held)
1923	Henry Born	1947	Lawrence Mahony
1924	No record available	1948	Lawrence Mahony
1925	Frank Boyce	1949	Douglas Fogal
1926	Frank Boyce	1950	William Kolb
1927	Frank Boyce	1951	William Kolb
1928	Frank Boyce	1952	William Kolb
1929	Frank Boyce	1953	William Kolb
1930	Frank Boyce	1954	William Kolb
1931	Frank Boyce	1955	Sol Berman
1932	Frank Boyce	1956	William Kolb
1933	Joe Puglise	1957	Sol Berman
1934	Lawrence Mahony	1958	Douglas Fogal
1935	Lawrence Mahony	1959	William Kolb
1936	Lawrence Mahony	1960	Lee Davis
1937	Lawrence Mahony	1961	William Kolb
1938	Lawrence Mahony	1962	William Kolb
1939	Lawrence Mahony	1963	William Kolb
1940	Lawrence Mahony	1964	Walter Haring
1941	William Kolb	1965	Sol Berman
1942	Anthony Scolari	1966	William Kolb
		1967	Jack Giddes

1968   [255]

The New Jersey State Horseshoe Pitchers' Association joins the Middlesex Horseshoe Pitchers' Club in saying "Thank You" to the governing body of the Borough of Middlesex for their interest and support of the game of horseshoe.

MIDDLESEX MAYOR AND COUNCIL: Left to right, Anthony Derwitz, Mayor Charles Judson, Anthony LaCamera, Charles Williams, John Sylvia, Charles Jennings, and Norman Seip.

32

1967 World Horseshoe Pitching Champion

At 18 years old, Danny is the youngest champion ever, winning the title in 1967 at Fargo, North Dakota on his third attempt. Danny broke into the Championship Class while only 16 years old at the 1965 World Tournament in Keene, New Hampshire where he placed 10th averaging about 82% ringers. In 1966 at Murray, Utah, Danny finished second and in 1967 won the title averaging over 84% ringers.

Left handed Danny will defend his title for the first time this year back in Keene, New Hampshire where he started his quest for it.

DANNY KUCHCINSKI

34

WELCOME

TO THE
NATIONAL
HORSESHOE
A.A.U.
Bambo's

651 Bound Brook Rd.   Middlesex, N.J.

1974

Hometown Winners

The 1974 National AAU event was destined to remain a lost tournament until I located the results of the 1977 National AAU tournament in an old edition of the AAU's magazine *Amateur Athlete*. The accounting of the 1977 event mentions that Clarence Daugherty, the year's winner, was also the 1974 champion. The article below appears to be describing a local or regional AAU competition; it makes no mention of being a national contest. But the 1977 narrative was part of an AAU annual report as a definitive national championship, so it seems unlikely it would indicate previous local or regional results as National AAU win. With some reservation, this chapter presents this 1974 event held in Terre Haute, Indiana, as a national championship, even though the participants hailed only from the states of Indiana and Michigan.

The September 30, 1974, edition of the *Terre Haute Tribune* reported:

Daugherty Wins Shoe Crown

Clarence Daugherty of Terre Haute is the new Amateur Athletic Union horseshoe pitching champion, taking honors yesterday at Collett Park on the city's north side.

Daugherty was followed by Jerry Washnidge of Coalmont, Hunter Dorman of Jasonville, John Roshel of Terre Haute, Lee Jacobs, the 1972 champion from Bellville, Michigan, and Elden Wells of Terre Haute.

Geraldine Jackson won the women's singles, followed by Kathleen Bridge, Margaret Shatos and Teresa Syjut, all of Detroit.

Michael Soria and Ricardo Martinez, both of Detroit, finished first and second in the 15 and under boys division.

Dorman and Washnidge won the men's doubles followed by Chester Nelson and Carl Weller of Terre Haute. Mixed doubles winners were Geraldine Jackson and Lee Jacobs, followed by Clarence Daugherty and Marty Boyke of Terre Haute and Margaret Shatos and Michael Sorta.

The event was sponsored by the city parks and recreation department, Terre Haute Amateur Sports Club and Terre Haute Horseshoe Club.

The article further complicates the question of whether or not the 1974 tournament in Terre Haute was a National AAU event. It names Lee Jacobs, aka Lee Rose, the self-proclaimed Rose of Detroit, as the 1972 National AAU champion. However, in a self-drafted bio Jacobs wrote for Ottie Reno's 1984 *American Directory of Horseshoe Pitching*, Lee noted his 1944 National AAU championship but made no mention of a 1972 title. Nor did he list a 1974 doubles championship. Also, research in Detroit newspapers of the time did not produce any corroborating information.

1975

No Information Available

No information could be found for a tournament held, or even scheduled, for that matter, in 1975. Odds are, no tournament was set up because there was no one to host or run the event. If a tournament had been held, some mention likely would have been made in the media coverage in 1976 or 1977.

This is a telling sign of what would come within a couple more years: the end.

1976

Far Away Traveler Wins

On July 23rd through 25th, 1976, Middlesex, New Jersey, hosted its third National AAU event in 12 years. New Jersey's horseshoe-pitching community remained more than other areas of the country and they continuously held State AAU competitions. Numerous New Jersey state tournament results were posted in *The Horseshoe Pitcher's News Digest*.

So far this book has not been in the practice of including detailed information on state-level competitions. The unusual story of the Class B results of the 1972 New Jersey state championships merit an exception, however. Here is how Class B was reported:

Class B		W	L	%
Vince Yannetti	Bound Brook	4	1	52.5
J. Segotta	Clark	3	2	52.5
Mary Lee	Brooklyn, N.Y.	3	2	53.1
B. Herrmann	Clark	3	2	48.0
Dale Eberhart	Middlesex	1	7	46.0
T. Skinner	Bloomfield	1	4	44.6

The results look rather routine until you notice that a gal, Mary Lee, was included in a traditionally all-male class.

Mary Lee was an exceptional young female horseshoe pitcher. She was the 1969 junior girls world champion. That in itself is not so remarkable—the unusual part is that she pitched from 40 feet, which allowed her to enter the National AAU competition with the men. The rules state that women (and junior girls) may pitch from 30 feet (which is actually 27 feet), though they can choose to pitch at a greater distance than the 30-foot mark. For what it's worth, men pitching from 40 feet are actually observing a 37-foot foul line.

Mary Lee pitched in four NHPA World Tournaments, all in the junior girls division. She was an World Champion in 1969, at age 13; placed third in 1970; and was runner-up in 1971, when she pitched 57.4 percent ringers, against competitors pitching 10 feet closer to the stake. To this date, Mary Lee is the only junior girls World Champion who won a world title pitching from forty feet. The reason for her unusual choice was that when she started pitching at an early age there were no young 30-foot pitchers in her region. So to enter competitions, she pitched from the 40-foot mark. She did not enter a World Tournament after her junior career, so for an historian of the sport, it was enlightening to see her name appear some five years later in an all men's competition.

Back to the 1976 National AAU tournament. A Middlesex newspaper printed the announcement, which informs readers of a last-minute switch in the host city:

Horseshoe Pitchers Club
To Host National Tourney

The Middlesex Horseshoe Club will be trying for a repeat performance of eight years ago. Back in 1968, in bringing the National AAU Champions to Middlesex, the AAU Association noted that "the most successful National AAU tournament ever held was the one hosted by the Middlesex Pitcher's Club in 1968."

Eight years later because of circumstances beyond the control of the Lafayette Indiana Horseshoe Club, the 1978 National AAU tournament will be staged at the 24-lighted courts in the Mountain View Park beginning Saturday. The championships will run through Sunday.

Individual competition will be played 10 a.m. to 2 p.m. on Saturday. The doubles competition is set to begin Sunday at noon.

"Our tournament back in 1968 was very successful," replied Middlesex Horseshoe Club president Hal Hanania. "This tournament generally moves across the country. At the last minute, after the club in Lafayette informed the association that they would be unable to hold the

tournament, we informed the AAU that we would accept. But," continued Hanania, "after we said we would, we told the AAU we wouldn't be
able to make many last-minute preparations."

Sgt. Hanania of the Middlesex Police Department said seven to eight
months of preparation is needed in handling a tournament such as this
national event. "We won't have all the color and pageantry as usual but
we will do our best. We're excited about having it again."

Without a pre-registration requirement, the number of participants
for this tournament is mere speculation at this point. "I expect there will
be somewhere between 75 to 100 contestants," Hanania said. The club
president anticipates representation from a great many states, "I expect
a great influx from Pennsylvania and a number of other states. Some as
far away as Ohio."

The world championship, for which the Middlesex Club bid for earlier, will be held in Levittown, Pa., this year. "Some of the players coming
here will be doing so with the world championship in mind."

The standard distances are 40 feet for men and 30 feet for woman.
Stakes stand 15 inches up right from the clay with a three-inch pitch.
The courts, constructed by members of the Middlesex Horseshoe Club,
have attracted the Middle Atlantic State Championships in addition to
the previous National tournaments.

Host of this competition include the Middlesex Horseshoe Pitchers' Club and the New Jersey State AAU Association. The tournament
is sanctioned by the National Amateur Athletic Union of America. Officers of the Middlesex club along with Hanania, include vice presidents
Dale Eberhart and Al Price, secretary Ronald Vogel and treasurer Ralph
Coleman.

While the final standings for the tournament appeared in the local paper, no
article was recovered. The anticipated number of entries for the tournament
was not realized, in fact, every participant was from either the New Jersey or
New York—with the exception of one entrant all the way from Albuquerque,
New Mexico. And, would you believe, he earned the top honors:

1976 National AAU Senior Men's Singles Championships

	Class A		Won	Lost	%
1.	Roger Vogel	Albuquerque, NM	15	0	69
2.	Joe Schultz	Brentwood, NY	13	2	68
3.	Art Tyson	Mt. Vernon, NY	11	4	65
4.	Lou Gancos	Brooklyn, NY	11	4	61
5.	Ted Lewis	Millville, NJ	9	6	58
6.	Sol Berman	Elizabeth, NJ	8	7	55
7.	Walter Pruiksma	Clifton, NJ	8	7	53
8.	Al Ward	Netcong, NJ	8	7	51
9.	Bill Kolb	Bellville, NJ	7	8	51
10.	Phil Zozzaro	Little Falls, NJ	7	8	49
11.	Jerry Nemschick	Medford, NY	6	9	51
12.	John Loughery	Bronx, NY	5	10	46
13.	Jim Reed	Oldwick, NJ	5	10	46
14.	Vince Yannetti	Bound Brook, NJ	3	12	41
15.	Bill Herrmann	Clark, NJ	2	13	40
16.	Tom Skinner	East Orange, NJ		Withdrew	

	Class B		Won	Lost	%
1.	Lee Marshall	Middlesex, NJ	5	2	39
2.	Tom Bailiff	Hawthorne, NJ	4	3	40
3.	Rocky Fithian	Bridgeton, NJ	4	3	38
4.	Ron Vogel	Middlesex, NJ	4	3	38
5.	Harold Christensen	Plainfield, NJ	4	3	34
6.	Al Price	Roselle Park, NJ	3	4	34
7.	Pete Albers	Nutley, NJ	3	4	33
8.	Jim Burd	Colifon, NJ	1	6	27

	Class C		Won	Lost	%
1.	Art Carson	Edison, NJ	7	0	37
2.	John Seland	Whiting, NJ	5	2	33
3.	Helmuth Ruesch	River Vale, NJ	4	3	37
4.	Tom Reutz	Brooklyn, NY	4	3	33
5.	Ed Brault	Middlesex, NJ	4	3	26
6.	Joe Payvis	Middlesex, NJ	2	5	27
7.	David Hall	Piscataway, NJ	2	5	17
8.	Robert Bradley	Paramus, NJ	1	6	28

1976 National AAU Senior Men's Doubles Championships

Class A		Won	Lost	%
1.	Al Cherry – Sol Berman	6	0	60
2.	Lou Gancos – Lou Stines	4	2	53
3.	Bill Kolb – James Reed	1	5	45
4.	Phil Zozzaro – Ron Vogel	1	5	42

Class B		Won	Lost	%
1.	Art Carson – Harold Christensen	4	0	38
2.	Al Price – Tom Bailiff	3	1	30
3.	Lou Ouellette – Tom Reitz	1	3	26
4.	Nick Simile – Lafe Collins	1	3	23
5.	Jim Burd – Andy Waisempacher	1	3	22

Some big names appear in the men's Class A finals. The third-place player, Art Tyson, who was pitching in his one and only National AAU event, is an NHPA National Hall of Fame member. Tyson won the 1977 New York state championship and he went on to earn another 12, but he was an amateur at this time. Tyson qualified for the men's championship class in NHPA Worl Tournaments 30 times throughout his career, and he ranks tenth on the all-time wins list, with 443 winning games. He was inducted to the New York State Horseshoe Pitching Hall of Fame in 1982 and the National Hall of Fame in 1993.

In second place was another New York star, Joe Schultz, who followed Tyson as the state champion in 1978 by pitching 75.5 percent ringers in the tournament. That was Schultz's only state title, but he qualified for the men's championship class in 11 World Tournaments and ranks 41st on the All-Time Wins List, with 173 games won. Schultz was inducted to New York's hall of fame in 1979.

The roster of the New York State Horseshoe Pitching Hall of Fame contains a couple of other 1976 National AAU participants: Lou Gancos, the 1968 National AAU champion was inducted in 1980, and John Loughery was a 1990 inductee.

The tournament champion, Roger Vogel, was conspicuous as the only player who wasn't from New Jersey or New York. He is the brother of Ron Vogel, one of the tournament directors and a long-time leader of the Middlesex Club. The family connection likely played a part in Roger Vogel's participation in the event. His pitching heroics began back in 1954, when he was an Illinois junior state champ and also a runner-up for the junior world title that same year. By 1958, he was qualifying for the men's championship class in NHPA World Tournament competition. In all, Vogel qualified 11 times for the championship class, and won 187 games to earn the 37th spot on the all-time wins list. On four occasions he averaged better than 75 percent ringers in World Tournament competition. We won't question whether or not he was an amateur in 1976.

Roger Vogel has the distinction of being the only pitcher ever to win men's state championships in five different states. Between 1970 and 1988, he won four titles in Illinois (1978, 1979, 1981, and 1982); three in Colorado (1972, 1973, and 1975); one in New Mexico (1976); one in Texas (1988); and one in Arizona (1970). He missed an opportunity for a sixth state title in 1959 as he was in the Navy and stationed in California. That championship was won by NHPA Hall of Fame member Jim Weeks.

The Vogels are the only family to count three generations of players among the qualifiers for men's championship classes in World Tournament competitions. Roger's father Nelson Vogel qualified for the final group six times in the 1950s, and his son Brett Vogel qualified in 2004 and 2011.

1977

End of a Forty-Year Era

In the later years of the National AAU Horseshoe Pitching Championships, the *Amateur Athlete* magazine did not cover the events well. In most cases, the magazine didn't even post the final results—at least not in as comprehensively as in the 1950s. 1977 was an exception, however. The final standings were printed that year and while they are not complete, the dates, location, and medal winners are listed. That information made it possible to obtain newspaper articles, which turned up another championship event (see the section on 1974) that was previously unknown.

The September 10th *Terre Haute Tribune* announced that the National AAU championship event was to be held that weekend, September 10th and 11th. The article does identify the event as a national competition, and the *Amateur Athlete* coverage confirms that it was. This is the article that led to uncovering information about the 1974 tournament, which was also held in Terre Haute:

AAU Horseshoes
Title Contested

The 1977 Amateur Athletic Union horseshoe pitching championships are being conducted this weekend at Collett Park, 7th Street and Maple Avenue. The event is co-sponsored by the Terre Haute Recreation Department, the Terre Haute Horseshoe Club and the Terre Haute Amateur Sports Club.

Regulation AAU national championship trophies will be awarded to the winners in the men's and women's singles, the men's doubles, boys' and girls' singles and mixed doubles of all ages.

Competition is scheduled to end Sunday among the participants who have traveled from different parts of the country to be here. Clarence Daugherty of the Terre Haute Club won the 1974 men's singles championship and is trying to regain that title this year.

And the final results were reported by the *Tribune*:

Daugherty Wins Title

The AAU horseshoe pitching championships concluded yesterday at Collett Park with Terre Haute's Chuck Daugherty winning the men's singles title, a feat he last accomplished in 1974.

He recorded 44 ringers in 50 throws to beat out another Terre Haute native, Carl Wefler. Daugherty was also part of the men's doubles and mixed doubles championship teams and every championship went to a Wabash Valley resident.

In Class B competition, Terre Hauteans John Wilson finished first and John Roshell third. The Class C winner was Mike Boswell of Brazil, with Don Jeffers of Clinton placing third. Finishing 1-2-3 in Class D was Donald Jenks of Terre Haute, Chet Melson of Terre Haute and Bill Robbins of Brazil. Tim Barton of Terre Haute captured the Class E title with Bob Eyre of West Terre Haute third.

John DeLisle of Terre Haute was named the top rookie pitcher.

And the final standings, as reported in a 1977 issue of *Amateur Athlete* magazine:

1977 National AAU
Horseshoe Pitching Championships
Terre Haute, Ind.
September 10–11, 1977

Men's Singles
Championship Class
1. Chuck Daugherty, Terre Haute, IN
2. Carl Welfer, Terre Haute, IN
3. Hunter Dorman, Jasonville, IN

Class B
1. John Wilson, Terre Haute, IN
2. Rex Swanson, Noble, IL
3. John Roshell, Terre Haute, IN

Class C
1. Mike Boswell, Brazil, IN
2. Lester Beasley, Bridgeton, IN
3. Donald Jeffers, Clinton, IN

Class D
1. Donald Jenks, Terre Haute, IN
2. Chester Melson, Terre Haute, IN
3. Bill Robbins, Brazil, IN

Class E
1. Tim Bartob, West Terre Haute, IN
2. Larry Tinnin, Indianapolis, IN
3. Robert Eyre, West Terre Haute, IN

Men's Doubles
1. Dorman Hunter – Chuck Daugherty
2. John Wilson – Bruck Aue
3. Jerry Washnidge –

Women's Singles
1. Vivian Kramer, Jasonville, IN
2. Mary Wilson, Terre Haute, IN

Girls Singles
1. Tanya Kramer, Jasonville, IN

Mixed Doubles
1. Vivian Kramer – Chuck Daugherty
2. Tanya Kramer – Hunter Dorman
3. Mary Brown – Jerry Washnidge

Mr. Horseshoe Award
Donald Jenks

Sportsman Award
Robert Gilmore

Outstanding Rookie
John DeLisle

The *Terre Haute Tribune* article remarked that players would be arriving from different parts of the country—well, that did not happen. Calling this a National AAU championship event is difficult. The final standings resemble a regional or a state AAU event far more than a National AAU competition. All the participants were from the host state of Indiana, except Rex Swenson, who was from neighboring Illinois. Most of the National AAU events in the 1970s show a similar trend, probably because the amateur horseshoe pitching was losing momentum.

In 1977, Tanya Kramer became the one and only National AAU girls junior national champion. There were other junior champs, but she was the only awarded as the girls junior champion.

CONCLUSION AND ACKNOWLEDGEMENTS

So a 40-year reign of national amateur horseshoe pitching championships came to a close. Back in 1937, when the initial arrangement between the AAU and the NHPA was made, no one could have foreseen the success and longevity that would be realized by the inclusion of horseshoe pitching in the National AAU's roster of events. Certainly there were highlights and disappointments along the way, depending on those in charge of individual events. The big-name pitchers and the winning champions are always the stars of the game, but also there are other less visible heroes—game promoters and organizers who plan, prepare, and host great events. Too often, the tournament directors and support staff go unnamed and unrecognized. In many of the events covered in this book, though, the promoters were included in the reports and articles, especially in the early years.

I have made several references to the difficulty of locating information about the old tournaments. If the event promoters made contact with the local media and if *Amateur Athlete*, the AAU magazine, reported the final results, the information was available for recovery. In the cases of lost years, many are probably unrecoverable because the promoters and directors simply didn't complete their jobs. In some cases, a tournament wasn't scheduled because no one was willing to step forward and accept the responsibility of hosting a National AAU event.

The first edition of this book is published with the knowledge that there very well may be some tournaments and champions yet to be recovered and reported. I hope my research so far will trigger more information to surface so a second edition can fill in many of the blank years or confirm the years no event was held.

My special thanks go out to Joe Crawford, who was my contact at the AAU Headquarters and who provided reports on many of the early events. I'd also like to thank George Rugg, curator of the Notre Dame Department of Special Collections, who provided access to archived volumes of *Amateur Athlete*. I'm indebted to library staff members across the country who assisted by providing roles of film of old local newspapers. While much information in this book is from the AAU and NHPA magazines, following is a listing of the newspapers and journals that through their courtesy supported some of the information provided in this book:

Resources

AAU's *Amateur Athlete*

Anderson Herald – 1938
Anderson Daily Bulletin – 1939, 1940
Arkansas Gazette – 1955

Baltimore Sun – 1949, 1950, 1951, 1953

Chicago Daily Times – 1941, 1943
Cincinnati Enquirer – 1937, 1942, 1945, 1946
Cincinnati Times Star – 1942, 1946
Cincinnati Post – 1946

Dayton Journal – 1956
Dayton Daily News – 1956

Elgin Daily Courier – 1959

Lee Rose journals – 1942, 1943, 1944

Marietta Daily Journal – 1954
Middlesex Mirror – 1968
Middlesex Chronicle – 1968, 1976

NHPA's *Horseshoe World*
NHPA's *The Horseshoe Pitcher's News Digest*

Richmond Times-Dispatch – 1942, 1952
Riffle family scrapbooks – 1954-1961

Salisbury Times – 1957, 1963
Staten Island Advance – 1938

Sports Illustrated – 1963

Terre Haute Tribune – 1974, 1977

Winston-Salem Journal and Sentinel – 1940, 1941, 1961, 1966

NATIONAL AAU HORSESHOE-PITCHING ALL-TIME MEDAL COUNT LEADERS

Player	Gold	Silver	Bronze	Total
Frank Breen	3	5	5	13
Glenn Riffle	7	2	3	12
John Lindmeier	5	1	5	10
Darrell Eller	2	4	3	9
Walter King	4	2	1	7
Alden Lindquist	3	2	2	7
Dorne Woodhouse	2	2	3	7
Hubert Trinkle	5	1		6
Chuck Daugherty	5	1		6
Rogers Ehlers	4	1	1	6
Floyd Toole	2	3	1	6
Albert Rumbold	3	1	2	6
Walter Lane Sr.	3	1	1	5
Charlie Sipple	3	1	1	5
Lee Jacobs	2	3		5
Conrad Murphy	1	4		5
James Garrison		2	3	5
Frank Garrison		3	2	5
Ray Griffin	2	1	1	4
Marion Shadley	2		2	4
Stan Manker		1	3	4
Clarence Stem	3		1	4
Woody Thomas	1	2		3
Charles O. Jones	1	1	1	3
Earl App		2	1	3
Hunter Dorman	1	1	1	3
Lou Gancos	1	2		3
Melvin Howard	1	1	1	3

NATIONAL AAU
HORSESHOE-PITCHING TOURNAMENTS:
CHAMPIONSHIP CLASS PLAYERS'
ALL-TIME CAREER LISTING

(Arranged alphabetically)

Player	City	Year	Division	Place	Won	Loss	%
Adkins, Wayne	Camp Lee	1942	Junior Doubles	3	0	1	
Anderson, Ellen	Fawn Grove, PA	1968	Women	4	0	3	11.4
Antleitner, Meril	Michign	1960	Men's Doubles	7	1	6	34.1
App, Earl	Flgin, Il	1954	Men's Doubles	5	4	3	
App, Earl	Elgin, IL	1956	Men's Doubles	2	6	2	
App, Earl	Flgin, Il	1957	Men	8	7	8	43.1
App, Earl	Elgin, IL	1957	Men's Doubles	3	5	2	
App, Earl	Elgin, IL	1958	Men	10	6	9	50.5
App, Earl	Elgin, IL	1958	Men's Doubles	2	6	2	
Aue, Bruck	Terre Haute, IN	1977	Men's Doubles	2			
Austin, Glenn	Anderson, IN	1940	Men	6	7	8	
Babusch, Edward	Chicago, IL	1941	Men	10	7	8	60.24
Bagley, Lester	Anderson, IN	1939	Men's Doubles	4	2	3	
Bagley, Lester	Anderson, IN	1939	Junior	3			
Baker, Edwin	Baltimore, MD	1953	Men's Doubles	6	0	5	
Ball, Tom	Michigan	1960	Men's Doubles	7	1	6	34.1
Bell, Michael	Peekskill, NY	1938	Men	2	6	3	50.9
Bell, Michael	Peekskill, NY	1938	Men's Doubles	6	6	3	41.0
Bell, Michael	Peekskill, NY	1938	Doubles Playoff		3	2	52.0
Bennett, Scott	Salisbury, MD	1953	Men	4	4	4	48.7
Bennett, Scott	Salisbury, MD	1953	Men's Doubles	2	4	1	41.1
Bennett, Scott	Salisbury, MD	1957	Men's Doubles	8	0	7	36.2
Berman, Dr. Sol	Elizabeth, NJ	1964	Men	8	8	7	62.5
Berman, Dr. Sol	Elizabeth, NJ	1964	Men's Doubles	5	6	3	51.8

Player	City	Year	Division	Place	Won	Loss	%
Berman, Dr. Sol	Elizabeth, NJ	1966	Men	6	9	6	
Berman, Dr. Sol	Elizabeth, NJ	1968	Men	5	2	3	65.7
Berman, Dr. Sol	Elizabeth, NJ	1976	Men	6	8	7	55.0
Berman, Dr. Sol	Elizabeth, NJ	1976	Men's Doubles	1	6	0	
Blake, George	Rahway, NJ	1964	Men's Doubles	9	1	8	31.1
Boles, Alan	Indianapolis, IN	1937	Men	7	1	1	54.62
Boles, Alan	Cincinnati, OH	1937	Men's Doubles	2	4		58.0
Boswell	Atlanta, GA	1954	Men's Doubles	7	2	5	
Breen, Frank	Elgin, IL	1939	Men	2	9	2	
Breen, Frank	Elgin, IL	1941	Men	2	13	2	69.83
Breen, Frank	Elgin, IL	1941	Men's Doubles	2	6	2	
Breen, Frank	Elgin, IL	1942	Men	6	8	4	63.0
Breen, Frank	Elgin, IL	1942	Men's Doubles	3	1	2	
Breen, Frank	Elgin, IL	1943	Men	3			65.5
Breen, Frank	Elgin, IL	1944	Men	5	10	5	60.14
Breen, Frank	Elgin, IL	1944	Men's Doubles	3	4	3	61.0
Breen, Frank	Elgin, IL	1945	Men	7			
Breen, Frank	Elgin, IL	1953	Men	1	7	0	63.9
Breen, Frank	Elgin, IL	1954	Men	2	7	2	63.8
Breen, Frank	Elgin, IL	1954	Men's Doubles	5	4	3	47.2
Breen, Frank	Elgin, IL	1956	Men	1	10	2	67.0
Breen, Frank	Elgin, IL	1956	Men's Doubles	2	6	2	54.6
Breen, Frank	Elgin, IL	1957	Men	3	13	2	62.6
Breen, Frank	Elgin, IL	1957	Men's Doubles	3	5	2	44.7
Breen, Frank	Elgin, IL	1958	Men	5	11	4	61.9
Breen, Frank	Elgin, IL	1958	Men's Doubles	2	6	2	52.5
Breen, Frank	Elgin, IL	1959	Men's Doubles	1 Tie	5	2	
Brock, Gust	Chicago, IL	1941	Men	15	2	13	49.41
Broughton, Mickey	Dayton, OH	1959	Men				
Broughton, Mickey	Dayton, OH	1960	Men				
Broughton, Mickey	Dayton, OH	1960	Men's Doubles	6	3	4	46.2
Brown, Asa	Butler, NJ	1964	Men	7	10	5	62.7
Brown, Asa	Butler, NJ	1964	Men's Doubles	3	7	2	57.2
Brown, Mary	Detriot, MI	1977	Mixed Doubles	3			
Burkhalter		1943	Men				
Burnett, Herbert	Richmond, VA	1952	Men	7	5	6	
Carson, Dale	Baltimore, MD	1949	Men	1			72.8
Carson	Baltimore, MD	1950	Men	1	7	0	71.8
Chatham, Grover	Salisbury, MD	1953	Men's Doubles	2	4	1	
Cherry, Al	Plainfield, NJ	1976	Men's Doubles	1	6	0	60.0
Chewning	Atlanta, GA	1954	Men's Doubles	8	1	6	

Player	City	Year	Division	Place	Won	Loss	%
Claus, Clyde	Tulsa, OK	1939	Junior	2			
Clift, Everett	Washington D.C.	1950	Men	5			44.2
Clift, Everett	Washington D.C.	1950	Men's Doubles	4			
Cloie Joseph	Cincinnati, OH	1957	Men's Doubles	4	2		30.0
Cogswell, Wilbur	New Albany, IN	1940	Men	3	13	4	
Colvin, Ronald	Montana	1962	Men	4	4	3	49.2
Colvin, Ronald	Montana	1962	Men's Doubles	5	4	3	43.3
Compton, Louis	Anderson, IN	1939	Men's Doubles	4	2	3	
Compton, Louis	Toledo, OH	1940	Men				
Conti, Paul	Greenwood, NY	1938	Men's Doubles	9	1	8	28.5
Corns, John	Winston-Salem, NC	1958	Men	15	1	14	45.3
Corns, John	Winston-Salem, NC	1961	Men's Doubles	3	2	2	
Corns, John	Winston-Salem, NC	1966	Men	8	7	8	
Cotton, John	Baltimore, MD	1950	Men	7			20.2
Cotton, John	Baltimore, MD	1950	Men's Doubles	5			
Couch, L.T.	Little Rock, AR	1954	Men's Doubles	6	2	5	
Couch, L.T.	Little Rock, AR	1955	Men's Doubles	6	0	5	
Danhauer, William	Chicago, IL	1939	Men	5			
Danhauer, William	Chicago, IL	1939	Men's Doubles	2	4	1	
Danhauer, William	Chicago, IL	1940	Men's Doubles	1	8	2	
Danhauer, William	Chicago, IL	1940	Men	5	11	5	
Danhauer, William	Chicago, IL	1941	Men's Doubles	6	2	4	
Danhauer, William	Chicago, IL	1943	Men's Doubles	4	5	3	
Darnell, G.B.	Roanoke, VA	1952	Men	8	5	6	43.3
Darnell, G.B.	Roanoke, VA	1952	Men's Doubles	4			42.5
Daugherty, Chuck	Terre Haute, IN	1974	Men	1			
Daugherty, Chuck	Terre Haute, IN	1977	Men	1			
Daugherty, Chuck	Terre Haute, IN	1977	Men's Doubles	1			
Daugherty, Chuck	Terre Haute, IN	1977	Mixed Doubles	1			
Davis, Lee	Ridgewood, NJ	1964	Men	13	4	11	51.2
Davis, Lee	Ridgewood, NJ	1964	Men's Doubles	6	4	5	
Dean, Cindy	McGaheysville, VA	1968	Men's Doubles	3	1	2	
Dean, Cindy	McGaheysville, VA	1968	Women	2	2	1	55.1
Dean, Robert	McGaheysville, VA	1968	Men	3	3	2	66.6
Dean, Robert	McGaheysville, VA	1968	Men's Doubles	3	1	2	
DeNuzzio, Neil	Staten, Island, NY	1964	Men	15	2	13	40.4
Doherty, Vince	Montrose, NY	1938	Men's Doubles	5	6	3	41.3
Doherty, Vince	Montrose, NY	1938	Doubles Playoff		1	3	36.9
Donovan, James	Clark, NJ	1964	Men's Doubles	10	0	9	30.0
Dorman, Hunter	Jasonville, IN	1977	Men	3			
Dorman, Hunter	Jasonville, IN	1977	Men's Doubles	1			

Championship-Class Players' All-Time Career Listing

Player	City	Year	Division	Place	Won	Loss	%
Dorman, Hunter	Jasonville, IN	1977	Mixed Doubles	2			
Douglas , Chuck	Helena, MT	1962	Men's Doubles	3	6	2	44.4
Dove, Linwood J.	Roanoke, VA	1952	Men	4	6	5	43.3
Dove, Linwood J.	Roanoke, VA	1952	Men's Doubles	4			42.5
Duncan, Fred B.	Richmond, VA	1941	Junior	3	5	3	
Duncan, Fred B.	Richmond, VA	1941	Junior Doubles	1	2	1	
Duncan, Fred B.	Richmond, VA	1942	Junior	2	6	1	47.4
Durham, Jene	Baltimore, MD	1949	Men	3			
Durham, Jene	Baltimore, MD	1951	Men	1			51.8
Dykes, Ralph	Lombard, IL	1941	Men	9	7	8	60.43
Dykstra, A.J.	Englewood, NJ	1964	Men	16	0	15	43.4
Eha, Charles	Bellevue, KY	1942	Men	12	1	11	52.0
Ehlers, Roger	St. Charles, IL	1959	Men's Doubles	1 Tie	5	2	
Ehlers, Roger	St. Charles, IL	1960	Men	2	12	1	
Ehlers, Roger	St. Charles, IL	1960	Men's Doubles	1	7	0	64.5
Ehlers, Roger	St. Charles, IL	1961	Men	1	6	1	65.9
Ehlers, Roger	St. Charles, IL	1961	Men's Doubles	1	3	1	
Ehlers, Roger	St. Charles, IL	1964	Men	3	11	4	65.7
Ehlers, Roger	St. Charles, IL	1964	Men's Doubles	4	6	3	
Eller, Darrell	Thomasville, NC	1957	Men	11	6	9	46.3
Eller, Darrell	Thomasville, NC	1957	Men's Doubles	6	3	4	39.2
Eller, Darrell	Thomasville, NC	1958	Men	2	13	2	63.8
Eller, Darrell	Jamestown, NC	1959	Men	2			
Eller, Darrell	Jamestown, NC	1959	Men's Doubles	1 Tie	5	2	
Eller, Darrell	Jamestown, NC	1960	Men				
Eller, Darrell	Durham, NC	1960	Men's Doubles	3	5	2	56.2
Eller, Darrell	Durham, NC	1961	Men	7	2	5	61.8
Eller, Darrell	Durham, NC	1961	Men's Doubles	2	2	2	
Eller, Darrell	Thomasville, NC	1963	Men	4			
Eller, Darrell	Thomasville, NC	1963	Men's Doubles	3			
Eller, Darrell	Thomasville, NC	1964	Men	2	14	3	66.1
Eller, Darrell	Thomasville, NC	1964	Men's Doubles	1	10	2	
Eller, Darrell	Thomasville, NC	1966	Men	3	11	4	
Endris, Arthur	New Albany, IN	1940	Men				
Endris, Louis	New Albany, IN	1940	Men				
Epperly, W.G.	Roanoke, VA	1952	Men	10	4	7	
Epperly, W.G.	Roanoke, VA	1952	Men's Doubles	6			33.3
Eutsler, Bob	Anderson, IN	1939	Men's Doubles	6	0	5	
Fagin, Joseph	Detroit, MI	1944	Men's Doubles	6	3	4	48.0
Favata, J.	New York	1938	Men's Doubles	10	1	8	23.4
Feeley, Feely	Chicago, IL	1959	Men				

Player	City	Year	Division	Place	Won	Loss	%
Ferguson, Myron M.	Columbus, OH	1937	Men	11	0	1	51.35
Fleming, Henry	Chicago, IL	1941	Men	12	7	8	57.54
Fleming, Henry	Chicago, IL	1941	Men's Doubles	4	4	4	
Fleming, John	Chicago, IL	1941	Men's Doubles	4	4	4	
Fleming, John	Chicago, IL	1941	Men	8	7	8	62.50
Flohr, Harry	Westminster, MD	1949	Men's Doubles	2			
Flohr, Harry	Westminster, MD	1951	Men's Doubles	2			50.0
Floyd, G.	Chicago, IL	1938	Men's Doubles	4	6	3	43.4
Floyd, G.	Chicago, IL	1938	Doubles Playoff		1	3	41.2
Ford, Randy	Helena, MT	1965	Junior	2			
Fox, E.	New York	1938	Men's Doubles	10	1	8	23.4
Freudenburg, Vic	Crystal Lake, NC	1959	Men's Doubles				
Gall, Edward	Baltimore, MD	1953	Men's Doubles	5	1	4	
Gancos, Lou	Brooklyn, NY	1968	Men	1	4	1	71.6
Gancos, Lou	Brooklyn, NY	1968	Men's Doubles	2	2	1	
Gancos, Lou	Brooklyn, NY	1976	Men	4	11	4	61.0
Gancos, Lou	Brooklyn, NY	1976	Men's Doubles	2	4	2	53.0
Garrison, Frank	Cramerton, NC	1952	Men	2	8	4	50.1
Garrison, Frank	Cramerton, NC	1952	Men's Doubles	2			46.4
Garrison, Frank	Cramerton, NC	1953	Men's Doubles	3	3	2	44.1
Garrison, Frank	Cramerton, NC	1954	Men	8	2	7	53.3
Garrison, Frank	Cramerton, NC	1954	Men's Doubles	2	5	2	
Garrison, Frank	Cramerton, NC	1955	Men	7	4	5	52.4
Garrison, Frank	Cramerton, NC	1955	Men's Doubles	3	3	2	47.4
Garrison, Frank	Cramerton, NC	1956	Men	8	3	6	
Garrison, Frank	Cramerton, NC	1957	Men	5	10	5	54.3
Garrison, Frank	Cramerton, NC	1957	Men's Doubles	5	3	4	
Garrison, Frank	Cramerton, NC	1958	Men	7	9	6	44.1
Garrison, James	Cramerton, NC	1952	Men	5	8		45.5
Garrison, James	Cramerton, NC	1952	Men's Doubles	2			46.4
Garrison, James	Cramerton, NC	1953	Men	3	6	3	45.2
Garrison, James	Cramerton, NC	1953	Men's Doubles	3	3	2	
Garrison, James	Cramerton, NC	1954	Men	7	3	6	49.6
Garrison, James	Cramerton, NC	1954	Men's Doubles	2	5	2	50.5
Garrison, James	Cramerton, NC	1955	Men	9	1	8	48.0
Garrison, James	Cramerton, NC	1955	Men's Doubles	3	3	2	
Getz, M.B	Ferndale, MI	1944	Men	15	2	13	45.47
Getz, M.B	Ferndale, MI	1944	Men's Doubles	8	1	6	
Giddes, Jack	Martinsville, NJ	1964	Men	10	7	8	52.3
Giddes, Jack	Martinsville, NJ	1964	Men's Doubles	8	2	7	
Giddes, Jack	Martinsville, NJ	1966	Men	12	6	9	

Player	City	Year	Division	Place	Won	Loss	%
Giddes, Jack	Martinsville, NJ	1968	Men	4	3	2	61.2
Giddes, Jack	Martinsville, NJ	1968	Men's Doubles	1	3	0	
Grace, Earl	Baltimore, MD	1949	Men's Doubles	3			
Grant, Louis	Cincinnati, OH	1937	Men's Doubles	5	1		48.0
Greene, James	Baltimore, MD	1953	Men's Doubles	5	1	4	28.1
Griffin, Ray	Atlanta, GA	1937	Men	9	0	1	59.21
Griffin, Ray	Atlanta, GA	1952	Men	1	11	0	59.6
Griffin, Ray	Atlanta, GA	1952	Men's Doubles	1			56.0
Griffin, Ray	Atlanta, GA	1954	Men	3	7	2	56.7
Griffin, Ray	Atlanta, GA	1954	Men's Doubles	7	2	5	50.3
Griffin, Ray	Atlanta, GA	1953	Men	2	5	2	50.9
Griffin, Ray	Atlanta, GA	1955	Men	6	4	5	59.1
Grosselin, Charles	Morgantown, WV	1945	Men's Doubles	1			
Grosselin, Charles	Morgantown, WV	1943	Men's Doubles	1			
Grosselin, Charles	Morgantown, WV	1944	Men	11	6	9	47.47
Grosselin, Charles	Morgantown, WV	1944	Men's Doubles	5	4	3	
Gulbranson, J.O.	Richmond, VA	1942	Junior	8	0	7	45.2
Gulbranson, J.O.	Richmond, VA	1942	Junior Doubles	1	2	0	
Gwynn, G.B.	High Point, NC	1958	Men	11	5	10	50.0
Hammerbacher, Gilbert	Baltimore, MD	1951	Men's Doubles	4			
Hammerbacher, Gilbert	Baltimore, MD	1953	Men's Doubles	6	0	5	21.0
Hangen, Ruth	Buffalo, NY	1968	Women	1	3	0	67.9
Haring, Walter	Middletown, NJ	1964	Men	11	5	10	49.5
Haring, Walter	Middletown, NJ	1964	Men's Doubles	6	4	5	47.1
Harlow, Clark	Cincinnati, OH	1937	Men's Doubles	6	1		42.0
Harmon, E.	Baltimore, MD	1951	Men's Doubles	4			30.9
Harris, Arlo	Indianapolis, IN	1937	Men	3	3	1	57.98
Harris, Arlo	Indianapolis, IN	1937	Men's Doubles	3	3		52.0
Harris, Orville	Indianapolis, IN	1937	Men	13	0	1	49.36
Harris, Orville	Indianapolis, IN	1937	Men's Doubles	3	3		52.0
Hartman, Herman	Dayton, OH	1956	Men	9	1	8	
Hauser, Roy	High Point, NC	1958	Men's Doubles	3	6	2	50.0
Hefner, Joe	Claremont, NC	1966	Men	16	0	15	
Heising, George	Little Rock, AR	1955	Men's Doubles	4	3	2	
Helton, Paul	Dayton, OH	1959	Men	3			
Helton, Paul	Dayton, OH	1960	Men				
Helton, Paul	Dayton, OH	1960	Men's Doubles	6	3	4	46.2
Helton, Paul	Dayton, OH	1961	Men	4	5	2	59.9
Henderson, Norman	Cincinnati, OH	1937	Men	12	0	1	50.00
Henderson, Norman	Cincinnati, OH	1937	Men's Doubles	2	4		58.0
Henn, Harry J.	Cincinnati, OH	1937	Men's Doubles	5	1		48.0

Player	City	Year	Division	Place	Won	Loss	%
Henn, Harry J.	Cold Spring, KY	1942	Men	11	3	9	53.0
Henn, Harry J.	Cold Spring, KY	1943	Men				
Henn, Harry J.	Cold Spring, KY	1946	Men's Doubles	6			
Herrmann, Bill	Clark, NJ	1976	Men	15	2	13	10.0
Hester, Howard	Winston-Salem, NC	1966	Men	14	5	10	
Higginbottom, Bill	Little Rock, AR	1955	Men's Doubles	5	1	4	
Higginbottom, Bill	Little Rock, AR	1957	Men	6	10	5	45.5
Higginbottom, Bill	Little Rock, AR	1957	Men's Doubles	2	5	2	
Higgins, John S.	Lexington, NC	1941	Junior	4	4	4	
Hill, Charles	Hamilton, OH	1937	Men	4	2	1	53.17
Hill, Leroy	Broadway, OH	1964	Men	12	4	11	51.9
Hirshman, R.	Saginaw, MI	1944	Men	14	3	12	44.80
Hoff, Charles	West Manchester, OH	1946	Men	5			
Hoff, Jacob	West Manchester, OH	1946	Men	6			
Hoffman	Baltimore, MD	1950	Men's Doubles	5			
Holman , Leslie	Sykesville, MD	1953	Men's Doubles	1	5	0	
Holman , Leslie	Sykesville, MD	1954	Men	10	0	9	45.5
Holman , Leslie	Sykesville, MD	1954	Men's Doubles	4	4	3	
Holman , Leslie	Sykesville, MD	1957	Men	13	4	11	39.2
Holman , Leslie	Sykesville, MD	1957	Men's Doubles	7	1	6	
Holmberg, Ed	Big Timber, MT	1962	Men	6	2	5	44.0
Holmberg, Ed	Big Timber, MT	1962	Men's Doubles	1	7	1	49.7
Hooker, R.R.	Winston-Salem, NC	1958	Men	12	4	11	50.0
Hoover, Al	Asheboro, NC	1957	Men	15	2	13	40.3
Hoover, Al	Asheboro, NC	1957	Men's Doubles	6	3	4	
Hoover, Al	Asheboro, NC	1958	Men's Doubles	4	3	5	52.5
Houldson, Everett	Sullivan, IN	1938	Junior Doubles	1			
Howard, Melvin	Jamestown, NC	1959	Men				
Howard, Melvin	High Point, NC	1960	Men's Doubles	3	5	2	56.2
Howard, Melvin	Jamestown, NC	1959	Men's Doubles	1 Tie	5	2	
Howard, Melvin	Jamestown, NC	1960	Men				
Howard, Melvin	Jamestown, NC	1960	Men's Doubles	8	0	8	26.6
Howard, Melvin	High Point, NC	1961	Men's Doubles	2	2	2	
Hull, E.	Cincinnati, OH	1937	Men	16	0	1	38.09
Hurley, Lowell	High Point, NC	1958	Men	6	9	6	60.3
Hurley, Lowell	High Point, NC	1958	Men's Doubles	3	6	2	
Hurst, Ken	Providence, RI	1937	Men	10	0	1	57.35
Hyzy, M/Sgt. Stanley	Camp Mead	1951	Men	7			32.9
Jackson, William	Staten Island, NY	1938	Men's Doubles	7	2	7	33.5
Jacobs, Lee	Detroit, MI	1942	Men	5	8	4	64.0
Jacobs, Lee	Detroit, MI	1943	Men				

Championship-Class Players' All-Time Career Listing

Player	City	Year	Division	Place	Won	Loss	%
Jacobs, Lee	Detroit, MI	1943	Men's Doubles	2	7	2	
Jacobs, Lee	Detroit, MI	1944	Men	1	14	1	69.33
Jacobs, Lee	Detroit, MI	1944	Men's Doubles	2	5	2	66.0
Jacobs, Lee	Detroit, MI	1945	Men	2	13	2	
Jacobs, Lee	Detroit, MI	1946	Men				
Jacobs, Lee	Detroit, MI	1974	Men's Doubles	1			
Jenkins, Benny	Richmond, VA	1941	Junior Doubles	2	1	2	
Jensen, Ira	Culbertson, MT	1962	Men	1	13	1	52.4
Jensen, Ira	Culbertson, MT	1962	Men's Doubles	2	7	2	52.1
Johnson, James "Pops"	Ludlow, KY	1942	Men	7	7	5	55.0
Johnson, James "Pops"	Ludlow, KY	1945	Men	1	14	1	58.5
Johnson, James "Pops"	Ludlow, KY	1945	Men's Doubles	3			
Johnson, James "Pops"	Ludlow, KY	1946	Men	2	16	3	
Johnson, G. Sr.	Indianapolis, IN	1937	Men	6	1	1	60.93
Jones, Charles O.	Richmond, VA	1941	Junior	5	3	4	
Jones, Charles O.	Richmond, VA	1941	Junior Doubles	2	1	2	
Jones, Charles O.	Richmond, VA	1950	Men	4			44.0
Jones, Charles O.	Richmond, VA	1952	Men	11	4	7	
Jones, Charles O.	Richmond, VA	1953	Men	6	3	4	35.0
Jones, Charles O.	Richmond, VA	1942	Junior	3	4	3	50.6
Jones, Charles O.	Richmond, VA	1942	Junior Doubles	1	2	0	
Jones, Tom	Winston-Salem, NC	1960	Men				
Jones, Tom	Winston-Salem, NC	1960	Men	8	0	7	26.6
Jones, Randall R.	Winston-Salem, NC	1957	Men	14	4	11	37.4
Jones, Randall R.	Winston-Salem, NC	1957	Men's Doubles	5	3	4	44.6
Jones, Randall R.	Winston-Salem, NC	1960	Men				
Keller, Joe	New York	1938	Men's Doubles	9	1	8	28.5
Kellog, Warren	Chicago, IL	1939	Men's Doubles	5	1	4	
Kelly, Joe	Detroit, MI	1944	Men	9	8	7	53.20
Kelly, Joe	Detroit, MI	1944	Men's Doubles	8	1	6	56.0
Killinger, R.	Westminster, MD	1951	Men's Doubles	2			
King, Walter	Asheboro, NC	1958	Men	3	12	3	57.9
King, Walter	Asheboro, NC	1958	Men's Doubles	4	3	5	
King, Walter	Winston-Salem, NC	1960	Men	4			62.4
King, Walter	Asheboro, NC	1960	Men's Doubles	4	4	3	53.1
King, Walter	Asheboro, NC	1961	Men	2	6	2	69.5
King, Walter	Asheboro, NC	1963	Men	1	15	0	68.3
King, Walter	Pleasant Gardens, NC	1964	Men	1	16	1	71.6
King, Walter	Pleasant Gardens, NC	1964	Men's Doubles	1	10	2	60.8
King, Walter	Asheboro, NC	1966	Men	2	12	3	
King, Walter	Asheboro, NC	1963	Men's Doubles	1			55.7

Player	City	Year	Division	Place	Won	Loss	%
Kirkpatrick, J.R.	Cincinnati, OH	1942	Men's Doubles	4	0	3	
Kirkpatrick, J.R.	Cincinnati, OH	1937	Men's Doubles	6	1		42.0
Kitterman, Lawrence	New Albany, IN	1940	Men				
Kolb, Bill	Belleville, NJ	1966	Men	13	5	10	
Kolb, Bill	Belleville, NJ	1968	Men's Doubles	1	3	0	
Kolb, Bill	Belleville, NJ	1976	Men	9	7	8	49.0
Kolb, Bill	Belleville, NJ	1976	Men's Doubles	3	1	5	45.0
Kolb, Bill	Belleville, NJ	1963	Men	5			
Kolb, Bill	Belleville, NJ	1964	Men	5	10	5	65.8
Kolb, Bill	Belleville, NJ	1964	Men's Doubles	5	6	3	
Konz, William	Toledo, OH	1940	Men				
Konz, William	Toledo, OH	1940	Men's Doubles	4	4	5	
Koppitsch, Frank	Detroit, MI	1944	Men's Doubles	2	5	2	
Kramer, Tanya	Jasonville, IN	1977	Girls	1			
Kramer, Tanya	Jasonville, IN	1977	Mixed Doubles	2			
Kramer, Vivian	Jasonville, IN	1977	Women	1			
Kramer, Vivian	Jasonville, IN	1977	Mixed Doubles	1			
Lackey, Ralph	Middletown, OH	1946	Men's Doubles	1			
Lackey, Ralph	W. Middletown, OH	1937	Men	8	1	1	51.78
Lackey, Ralph	Middletown, OH	1946	Men	4			
Lackey, Ralph	Middletown, OH	1937	Men's Doubles	7	1		44.0
Lackey, Ralph	Middletown, OH	1945	Men	5			
Lane, Walter Jr.	Anderson, IN	1938	Doubles Playoff		4	1	48.2
Lane, Walter Jr.	Anderson, IN	1938	Junior	4			
Lane, Walter Jr.	Anderson, IN	1938	Men's Doubles	2	6	3	45.7
Lane, Walter Jr.	Anderson, IN	1939	Men's Doubles	6	0	5	
Lane, Walter Jr.	Anderson, IN	1939	Junior	1			51.0
Lane, Walter Sr.	Anderson, IN	1938	Men	4	3	4	50.6
Lane, Walter Sr.	Anderson, IN	1937	Men	2	4	2	57.28
Lane, Walter Sr.	Anderson, IN	1940	Men				
Lane, Walter Sr.	Anderson, IN	1940	Men's Doubles	3	6	3	
Lane, Walter Sr.	Anderson, IN	1937	Men's Doubles	1	5		63.0
Lane, Walter Sr.	Anderson, IN	1938	Men's Doubles	1	9	0	60.0
Lane, Walter Sr.	Anderson, IN	1939	Men's Doubles	1	5	0	
Lane, Walter Sr.	Anderson, IN	1939	Junior	4			
Lane, Walter Sr.	Anderson, IN	1941	Men's Doubles	7	0	6	
Lange, Harold	Elgin, IL	1942	Men	10	4	8	52.0
Lange, Harold	Elgin, IL	1942	Men's Doubles	3	1	2	
Latzko, Joe	Flint, MI	1944	Men	2	13	2	68.13
Latzko, Joe	Flint, MI	1944	Men's Doubles	1	5	2	
Latzko, Joe	Flint, MI	1945	Men	4			

Player	City	Year	Division	Place	Won	Loss	%
Latzko, Joe	Flint, MI	1945	Men's Doubles	4			
Latzko, Joe	Flint, MI	1946	Men	1	18	1	
Latzko, Joe	Flint, MI	1946	Men's Doubles	2			
Leach, John	Columbus, OH	1966	Men	5	10	5	
Lewis, Ted	Milville, NJ	1976	Men	5	9	6	58.0
Limbaugh, Bud	Crystal Lake, NC	1959	Men's Doubles				
Lindmeier, John	Oak Park, IL	1937	Men	1	7	0	64.95
Lindmeier, John	Oak Park, IL	1938	Men's Doubles	4	6	3	43.4
Lindmeier, John	Oak Park, IL	1938	Doubles Playoff		1	3	41.2
Lindmeier, John	Oak Park, IL	1940	Men's Doubles	2	7	3	
Lindmeier, John	Oak Park, IL	1938	Men	3	5	2	60.5
Lindmeier, John	Oak Park, IL	1939	Men	3	9	3	
Lindmeier, John	Oak Park, IL	1939	Men's Doubles	3	3	2	
Lindmeier, John	Oak Park, IL	1940	Men	1	16	1	
Lindmeier, John	Oak Park, IL	1941	Men	1	14	1	67.01
Lindmeier, John	Oak Park, IL	1941	Men's Doubles	1	5	1	
Lindmeier, John	Oak Park, IL	1942	Men	3	8	4	68.0
Lindmeier, John	Oak Park, IL	1942	Men's Doubles	1	3	0	
Lindmeier, John	Oak Park, IL	1943	Men's Doubles	3	5	3	
Lindmeier, Walter	Chicago, IL	1942	Men	13	1	11	44.0
Lindquist, Arner	Morgantown, WV	1945	Men	6			
Lindquist, Arner	Morgantown, WV	1945	Men's Doubles	1			
Lindquist, Arner	Morgantown, WV	1940	Men's Doubles	3	6	3	
Lindquist, Arner	Morgantown, WV	1940	Men	4	11	5	
Lindquist, Arner	Morgantown, WV	1941	Men	4	9	6	61.23
Lindquist, Arner	Morgantown, WV	1941	Men's Doubles	5	2	4	
Lindquist, Arner	Morgantown, WV	1942	Men	1	11	1	66.5
Lindquist, Arner	Morgantown, WV	1942	Men's Doubles	2	2	1	
Lindquist, Arner	Morgantown, WV	1943	Men	2	14	2	67.4
Lindquist, Arner	Morgantown, WV	1943	Men's Doubles	1			
Lindquist, Arner	Morgantown, WV	1944	Men	3	11	6	61.60
Lindquist, Arner	Morgantown, WV	1944	Men's Doubles	5	4	3	50.0
Lockwood, Florence	Montrose, NY	1938	Women	1			
Lockwood, Frank	Montrose, NY	1938	Men	6	3	4	47.5
Lockwood, Frank	Montrose, NY	1938	Men's Doubles	5	6	3	41.3
Lockwood, Frank	Montrose, NY	1938	Doubles Playoff		1	3	36.9
Lockwood, Harold	Montrose, NY	1938	Men's Doubles	6	6	3	41.0
Lockwood, Harold	Montrose, NY	1938	Doubles Playoff		3	2	52.0
Loerzel, Leonard	Chicago, IL	1939	Men	4	8	4	
Loerzel, Leonard	Chicago, IL	1939	Men's Doubles	2	4	1	
Loerzel, Leonard	Chicago, IL	1940	Men				

Player	City	Year	Division	Place	Won	Loss	%
Loerzel, Leonard	Chicago, IL	1940	Men's Doubles	1	8	2	
Loerzel, Leonard	Chicago, IL	1941	Men	6	8	7	61.22
Loerzel, Leonard	Chicago, IL	1941	Men's Doubles	6	2	4	
Loerzel, Leonard	Chicago, IL	1943	Men's Doubles	1	5	3	
Longtin, Don	High Point, NC	1963	Men's Doubles	3			
Loughery, John	Bronx, NY	1976	Men	12	6	9	48.0
Loy, Tyler	Chicago, IL	1941	Men	13	6	9	59.52
Loy, Tyler	Chicago, IL	1941	Men's Doubles	3	5	3	
Luck, Tom	Ft. Thomas	1942	Men's Doubles	4	0	3	
Lundgren, Carl E.	Detroit, MI	1943	Men	1	15	1	63.8
Lundgren, Carl E.	Detroit, MI	1943	Men's Doubles	2	7	2	
Lundgren, Carl E.	Detroit, MI	1944	Men	4	10	5	62.14
Lundgren, Carl E.	Detroit, MI	1944	Men's Doubles	4	4	3	
Lundgren, Carl E.	Detroit, MI	1945	Men's Doubles	2			
Lunsford, Howard	Winston-Salem, NC	1961	Men's Doubles	3	2	2	
Lutter, Frederick	New Freedom, PA	1951	Men	8			57.6
Lynch, Charles	Charleston, SC	1952	Men	12	3	8	
MacPhearson, Harold	Covington, KY	1945	Men's Doubles	3			
MacQueen, D.	New York	1938	Men's Doubles	7	2	7	33.5
Maki, Atnold	Hibbing, MN	1937	Men	15	0	1	46.87
Malinowsky, Joseph	Linden, NJ	1964	Men's Doubles	7	3	6	
Manker, Stanley	Chillicothe, OH	1942	Men	4	8	4	67.0
Manker, Stanley	Chillicothe, OH	1942	Men's Doubles	2	2	1	
Manker, Stanley	Chillicothe, OH	1944	Men	10	7	8	59.07
Manker, Stanley	Chillicothe, OH	1944	Men's Doubles	3	4	3	
Manker, Stanley	Chillicothe, OH	1945	Men	3			
Manker, Stanley	Chillicothe, OH	1946	Men	3			
Marcum, June	Hamilton, OH	1946	Men's Doubles	1			
Markarian, Pete	Chicago, IL	1941	Men	7	8	7	60.3
Martin, Everett L.	Norwood, OH	1942	Men	9	5	7	52.0
Masencup, J.C.	Winston-Salem, NC	1941	Junior	6	3	4	
McChesney, Walt	Sidney	1962	Men's Doubles	3	6	2	44.4
McKinnon, John	Montana	1962	Men's Doubles	4	4	3	37.4
McCrink, Joesph	W.Orange, NJ	1964	Men	14	3	13	51.1
McCrink, Joesph	W.Orange, NJ	1964	Men's Doubles	3	7	2	
McPhearson, Harold	Covington, KY	1942	Men	8	5	7	54.0
Means, Robert	Baltimore, MD	1951	Men's Doubles	5			21.5
Michael, Elizabeth	West Augusta, VA	1968	Women	3	1	2	19.5
Middleton, Ray	Flint, MI	1944	Men	16	1	14	41.17
Middleton, Ray	Flint, MI	1944	Men's Doubles	7	2	5	55.0
Miller, J.H.	Camp Lee	1942	Junior Doubles	2	0	1	

Player	City	Year	Division	Place	Won	Loss	%
Moore, Glynden	Burlington, NC	1961	Men	6	2	5	63.0
Moore, Glynden	Burlington, NC	1963	Men	6			
Moore, Glynden	Burlington, NC	1963	Men's Doubles	1			55.7
Moore, Glynden	Elon College, NC	1966	Men	15	3	12	
Morgan, Arthur	Middletown, OH	1937	Men's Doubles	7	1		44.0
Morgan, Guy	Hamilton, OH	1946	Men's Doubles	6			
Morris, Chet	Anderson, IN	1938	Men	7	2	5	48.4
Morris, Chet	Anderson, IN	1938	Doubles Playoff		2	2	48.3
Morris, Chet	Anderson, IN	1938	Men's Doubles	3	6	3	45.0
Morris, Chet	Anderson, IN	1938	Junior	2			
Morris, Marion	Pendleton, IN	1938	Men	5	3	4	50.5
Morris, Marion	Pendleton, IN	1938	Doubles Playoff		4	1	48.2
Morris, Marion	Pendleton, IN	1938	Men's Doubles	2	6	3	45.7
Morris, Marion	Pendleton, IN	1938	Junior	3			
Morris, Marion	Pendleton, IN	1941	Men	5	9	6	60.3
Morris, Marion	Pendleton, IN	1941	Men's Doubles	7	0	6	
Mosness, Ron	Big Timber, MT	1965	Junior	1			38.0
Murphy, Conrad	Winston-Salem, NC	1954	Men	9	2	7	48.2
Murphy, Conrad	Salem, NC	1956	Men	7	4	5	
Murphy, Conrad	High Point, NC	1957	Men	16	0	15	34.2
Murphy, Conrad	High Point, NC	1957	Men's Doubles	4	4	3	
Murphy, Conrad	Winston-Salem, NC	1961	Men's Doubles	4	1	3	
Murphy, Conrad	Winston-Salem, NC	1963	Men	2			
Murphy, Conrad	Winston-Salem, NC	1963	Men's Doubles	2			
Murphy, Conrad	Winston-Salem, NC	1964	Men	9	7	8	57.4
Murphy, Conrad	Winston-Salem, NC	1964	Men's Doubles	2	9	3	54.0
Murphy, Conrad	Winston-Salem, NC	1966	Men	11	6	9	
Murphy, Conrad	High Point, NC	1954	Men's Doubles	1	6	1	
Murphy, Conrad	Winston-Salem, NC	1955	Men	5	5	4	54.6
Murphy, Conrad	Winston-Salem, NC	1955	Men's Doubles	2	4	2	53.2
Murphy, Conrad	Winston-Salem, NC	1958	Men	8	9	6	50.4
Murphy, Conrad	Winston-Salem, NC	1960	Men				
Murphy, Conrad	Winston-Salem, NC	1960	Men's Doubles	5	3	4	50.0
Nardiello, James	Roselle Park, NJ	1964	Men's Doubles	10	0	9	
Naylor, Ed	Winston-Salem, NC	1941	Junior	1	7	0	
Neilson, William	Dugger, IN	1938	Junior	1			
Neilson, William	Dugger, IN	1938	Junior Doubles	1			
Nellis, Willard	Washington D.C.	1950	Men	2			41.7
Nellis, Willard	Washington D.C.	1950	Men's Doubles	2			
Nelson, Grant	Camp Lee	1942	Junior	1	7	0	62.1
Nelson, Grant	Camp Lee	1942	Junior Doubles	2	0	1	

Player	City	Year	Division	Place	Won	Loss	%
Nemschick, Jerry	Medford, NY	1976	Men	11	6	9	51.0
Nichols, George	Westminster, MD	1950	Men's Doubles	3			
Nichols, George	Westminster, MD	1951	Men	6			36.7
Nichols, George	Westminster, MD	1951	Men's Doubles	3			32.9
Oakely, Eugene	Salisbury, MD	1953	Men's Doubles	4	2	3	27.4
Olson, Art	Helena, MT	1962	Men	2	5	2	41.2
Olson, Art	Helena, MT	1962	Men's Doubles	1	7	1	49.7
Otto, Jonas	Ann Arbor, MI	1944	Men	6	10	5	57.87
Otto, Jonas	Ann Arbor, MI	1944	Men's Doubles	4	4	3	65.0
Otto, Jonas	Ann Arbor, MI	1945	Men's Doubles	2			
Oyler, J.B.	Ronoke, VA	1942	Junior	4	4	3	44.5
Pekkale, Alfred H.	Detroit, MI	1944	Men	13	3	12	49.14
Pence, Robert	Chicago, IL	1941	Men	16	1	14	47.43
Pence, Robert	Chicago, IL	1941	Men's Doubles	3	5	3	
Perrott, Edward	Baltimore, MD	1949	Men's Doubles	3			
Perrott, Edward	Baltimore, MD	1950	Men	6			31.4
Perrott, Edward	Baltimore, MD	1951	Men	5			39.0
Perrott, Edward	Baltimore, MD	1951	Men's Doubles	5			
Poff, Kenneth	Centervillle, OH	1955	Men	8	2	7	51.1
Poff, Kenneth	Centervillle, OH	1955	Men's Doubles	1	5	1	
Poff, Kenneth	Centervillle, OH	1956	Men's Doubles	1	7	1	
Poppe, Martin	West Hempstead, NY	1966	Men	10	6	9	
Prescott, Phil	Poplar, Montana	1962	Men	5	3	4	45.0
Prescott, Phil	Poplar, Montana	1962	Men's Doubles	2	7	2	52.1
Pruiksma, Walter	Clifton, NJ	1976	Men	7	8	7	53.0
Rademacher, Gene	Plant City, FL	1968	Men	6	0	5	49.6
Rademacher, Gene	Plant City, Fl	1968	Men's Doubles	4	0	3	
Rademacher, John	Plant City, FL	1968	Men	2	3	2	72.6
Rademacher, John	Plant City, FL	1968	Men's Doubles	4	0	3	
Rambo, Bob	Jeffersonville, IN	1962	Men	3	5	2	44.1
Rambo, Bob	Jeffersonville, IN	1962	Men's Doubles	5	3	4	43.3
Reed, James	Oldwick, NJ	1976	Men's Doubles	3	1	5	
Reed, James	Oldwick, NJ	1976	Men	13	5	10	46.0
Reitdorf, Paul	Fort Wayne	1940	Men				
Riffle, Glenn	Dayton, OH	1954	Men	4	6	3	57.7
Riffle, Glenn	Dayton, OH	1954	Men's Doubles	3	4	3	52.8
Riffle, Glenn	Dayton, OH	1955	Men	1	10	2	64.6
Riffle, Glenn	Dayton, OH	1956	Men	3	7	2	
Riffle, Glenn	Dayton, OH	1957	Men	2	14	3	55.5
Riffle, Glenn	Dayton, OH	1957	Men's Doubles	1	7	0	61.2
Riffle, Glenn	Dayton, OH	1958	Men	1	15	0	67.8

Player	City	Year	Division	Place	Won	Loss	%
Riffle, Glenn	Dayton, OH	1958	Men's Doubles	1	8	0	64.7
Riffle, Glenn	Dayton, OH	1959	Men	1			
Riffle, Glenn	Dayton, OH	1959	Men's Doubles	1 Tie	5	2	
Riffle, Glenn	Dayton, OH	1960	Men	1	13	0	68.9
Riffle, Glenn	Dayton, OH	1960	Men's Doubles	2	5	2	59.9
Riffle, Glenn	Dayton, OH	1961	Men	3	5	3	66.0
Riggle, John	Bicknell, IL	1939	Men's Doubles	5	1	4	
Riggs, James	Jacksonville, AR	1955	Men's Doubles	5	1	4	25.1
Riggs, James	Jacksonville, AR	1956	Men	10	0	9	
Riggs, James	Jacksonville, AR	1956	Men's Doubles	3	5	3	
Rollick, Lee	Chicago, IL	1941	Men	14	5	10	55.38
Rollick, Lee	Chicago, IL	1941	Men's Doubles	5	2	4	
Ruby, Irving "Jack"	Sykesville, MD	1953	Men	5	4	4	42.6
Ruby, Irving "Jack"	Sykesville, MD	1953	Men's Doubles	1	5	0	43.7
Ruby, Irving "Jack"	Sykesville, MD	1954	Men's Doubles	4	4	3	47.3
Ruby, Irving "Jack"	Sykesville, MD	1957	Men	12	4	11	42.0
Ruby, Irving "Jack"	Sykesville, MD	1957	Men's Doubles	7	1	6	39.0
Rumbold, Albert	Westminster, MD	1949	Men's Doubles	1			
Rumbold, Albert	Westminster, MD	1950	Men's Doubles	1			
Rumbold, Albert	Westminster, MD	1951	Men	2			44.2
Rumbold, Albert	Westminster, MD	1951	Men's Doubles	1			50.4
Rumbold, Albert	Westminster, MD	1952	Men	3	7	5	
Rumbold, Albert	Westminster, MD	1952	Men's Doubles	3			42.5
Rumley, Louis	Lexington, NC	1938	Men's Doubles	3	6	3	45.0
Rumley, Louis	Lexington, NC	1938	Doubles Playoff		2	2	48.3
Rumley, Luke	Lexington, NC	1940	Junior	1	7	0	
Santilli, Joe	Staten Island, NY	1938	Men's Doubles	8	2	7	23.0
Santilli, James	Staten Island, NY	1938	Men's Doubles	8	2	7	23.0
Sarullo, James	High Bridge, NY	1938	Men	8	0	7	42.8
Schmoldt, Edgar	Elgin, IL	1941	Men's Doubles	2	6	2	
Schneckloth, Norm	Montana	1962	Men	7	2	5	33.4
Schneckloth, Norm	Montana	1962	Men's Doubles	4	4	3	37.4
Schreiber, Bernie	Baltimore, MD	1953	Men	8	0	7	7.6
Schultz, Joe	Brentwwod, NY	1976	Men	2	13	2	68.0
Schuyler, A.J.	Roanoke, VA	1941	Junior	8	0	7	
Schuyler, A.J.	Camp Pendleton	1942	Junior	5	4	3	41.8
Scotten, James	High Point, NC	1961	Men	8	1	6	61.4
Scotten, James	High Point, NC	1966	Men	4	11	4	
Shadley, Marion	Dayton, OH	1954	Men	5	5	4	55.6
Shadley, Marion	Dayton, OH	1954	Men's Doubles	3	4	3	
Shadley, Marion	Dayton, OH	1955	Men	3	7	2	66.6

Player	City	Year	Division	Place	Won	Loss	%
Shadley, Marion	Dayton, OH	1955	Men's Doubles	1	5	1	53.4
Shadley, Marion	Dayton, OH	1956	Men	6	4	5	
Shadley, Marion	Dayton, OH	1956	Men's Doubles	1	7	1	52.5
Shepherd, N.E.	Flint, MI	1944	Men's Doubles	7	2	5	
Shepherd, N.E.	Flint, MI	1944	Men	12	6	9	46.40
Shytle, Robert	Lexington, NC	1952	Men's Doubles	1			56.0
Sipple, Charlie	Dayton, OH	1956	Men	4	5	4	
Sipple, Charlie	Dayton, OH	1957	Men	4	12	3	53.6
Sipple, Charlie	Dayton, OH	1957	Men's Doubles	1	7	0	
Sipple, Charlie	Dayton, OH	1958	Men	4	11	4	62.2
Sipple, Charlie	Dayton, OH	1958	Men's Doubles	1	8	0	
Sipple, Charlie	Dayton, OH	1959	Men				
Sipple, Charlie	Dayton, OH	1959	Men's Doubles	1 Tie	5	2	
Sipple, Charlie	Dayton, OH	1960	Men	3			
Sipple, Charlie	Dayton, OH	1960	Men's Doubles	2	5	2	56.9
Skinner, Tom	E. Orange, NJ	1976	Men	16		Withdrew	
Smith, Howard	Salisbury, MD	1953	Men's Doubles	4	2	3	
Smith, Howard	Salisbury, MD	1957	Men's Doubles	8	0	7	
Spencer, Oliver	Westminster, MD	1949	Men's Doubles	2			
Spencer, Oliver	Westminster, MD	1950	Men's Doubles	3			
Spencer, Robey	Westminster, MD	1951	Men	3			40.9
Spencer, Robey	Westminster, MD	1951	Men's Doubles	3			
Spencer, Robey	Westminster, MD	1953	Men	7	1	6	31.6
St. Jean, Arthur	Camp Lee	1942	Junior Doubles	3	0	1	
Stancik, Ed	Durham, NC	1963	Men	3			
Stancik, Ed	Durham, NC	1963	Men's Doubles	2			
Stancik, Ed	Durham, NC	1960	Men				
Stancik, Ed	Durham, NC	1960	Men's Doubles	4	4	3	53.1
Stancik, Ed	Durham, NC	1957	Men	10	6	9	47.7
Stephenson, Hugh Jr.	St. Louis, MO	1950	Men	8			23.0
Stern, Clarence	Westminster, MD	1949	Men's Doubles	1			
Stern, Clarence	Westminster, MD	1950	Men's Doubles	1			
Stern, Clarence	Westminster, MD	1951	Men	4			43.1
Stern, Clarence	Westminster, MD	1951	Men's Doubles	1			
Stern, Clarence	Westminster, MD	1952	Men	5			44.6
Stern, Clarence	Westminster, MD	1952	Men's Doubles	3			42.5
Stewart, Clinton	Toledo, OH	1940	Men				
Stewart, Clinton	Toledo, OH	1940	Men's Doubles	4	4	5	
Stewart, Warren	Burlington, NC	1958	Men	14	3	12	50.2
Stines, Lou	Brooklyn, NY	1976	Men's Doubles	2	4	2	
Stone, Woodrow	Richmond, VA	1941	Junior Doubles	1	2	1	

Player	City	Year	Division	Place	Won	Loss	%
Stone	Richmond, VA	1941	Junior	2	6	1	
Stone	Richmond, VA	1942	Junior	7	1	6	39.6
Stout, Jack	Melrose Park, IL	1960	Men's Doubles	1	7	0	64.5
Stout, Jack	Melrose Park, IL	1961	Men	5	3	4	60.6
Stout, Jack	Melrose Park, IL	1961	Men's Doubles	1	3	1	
Stout, Jack	Melrose Park, IL	1964	Men	6	10	5	63.1
Stout, Jack	Melrose Park, IL	1964	Men's Doubles	4	6	3	56.0
Stylte, Robert	Lexington, NC	1952	Men	9	4	7	
Swartz, Elmer "Dutch"	Annandale, MD	1949	Men	2			
Szurley, Otto	Elizabeth, NJ	1964	Men's Doubles	9	1	8	
Terry, Jim	Rural Hall, NC	1958	Men	13	4	11	47.7
Thomas, Woody	High Point, NC	1954	Men	6	5	4	53.4
Thomas, Woody	High Point, NC	1954	Men's Doubles	1	6	1	54.5
Thomas, Woody	High Point, NC	1955	Men	4	6	3	58.6
Thomas, Woody	High Point, NC	1955	Men's Doubles	2	4	2	
Thomas, Woody	High Point, NC	1956	Men	5	5	4	
Thomas, Woody	High Point, NC	1957	Men	9	6	9	42.0
Thomas, Woody	High Point, NC	1957	Men's Doubles	4	4	3	42.9
Thomas, Woody	High Point, NC	1958	Men	9	7	8	51.9
Thomas, Woody	High Point, NC	1960	Men				
Thomas, Woody	High Point, NC	1960	Men's Doubles	5	3	4	50.0
Thomas, Woody	High Point, NC	1961	Men's Doubles	4	1	3	
Thomas, Woody	High Point, NC	1964	Men	4	11	4	61.3
Thomas, Woody	High Point, NC	1964	Men's Doubles	2	9	3	
Thomas, Woody	High Point, NC	1966	Men	9	7	8	
Toole, Floyd C.	Little Rock, AR	1954	Men's Doubles	6	2	5	37.3
Toole, Floyd C.	Little Rock, AR	1954	Men	1	8	1	63.0
Toole, Floyd C.	Little Rock, AR	1955	Men	2	9	3	63.5
Toole, Floyd C.	Little Rock, AR	1955	Men's Doubles	4	3	2	44.4
Toole, Floyd C.	Little Rock, AR	1956	Men	2	9	3	
Toole, Floyd C.	Little Rock, AR	1956	Men's Doubles	3	5	3	57.1
Toole, Floyd C.	Little Rock, AR	1957	Men	1	16	1	63.4
Toole, Floyd C.	Little Rock, AR	1957	Men's Doubles	2	5	2	56.1
Trinkle, Hubert	Anderson, IN	1937	Men	5	1	1	63.71
Trinkle, Hubert	Anderson, IN	1937	Men's Doubles	1	5		63.0
Trinkle, Hubert	Anderson, IN	1938	Men	1	8	1	72.1
Trinkle, Hubert	Anderson, IN	1938	Men's Doubles	1	9	0	60.0
Trinkle, Hubert	Anderson, IN	1939	Men	1	11	0	
Trinkle, Hubert	Anderson, IN	1939	Men's Doubles	1	5	0	
Trinkle, Hubert	Anderson, IN	1940	Men	2	14	3	
Tyson, Art	Mt. Vernon, NY	1976	Men	3	11	4	65.0

Player	City	Year	Division	Place	Won	Loss	%
Utt, Chester	Winston-Salem, NC	1941	Junior	7	1	6	
Van Sickle, Paul	Anderson, IN	1938	Junior	5			
Vogel, Roger	Albuquerque, NM	1976	Men	1	15	0	69.0
Vogel, Ron	Milville, NJ	1976	Men's Doubles	4	1	5	
Vogel, Ron	Milville, NJ	1964	Men's Doubles	8	2	7	36.0
Walsh, Sid	Winston-Salem, NC	1958	Men	16	1	14	43.5
Washnidge, Jerry	Jasonville, IN	1977	Men's Doubles	3			
Washnidge, Jerry	Jasonville, IN	1977	Mixed Doubles	3			
Webb, Ed	Little Rock, AR	1955	Men	10	0	9	30.5
Webb, Ed	Little Rock, AR	1955	Men's Doubles	6	0	5	27.4
Wefler, Carl	Terre Haute, IN	1977	Men	2			
Weil, C. Fred Jr.	Cincinnati, OH	1937	Men's Doubles	4	2		50.0
Whalin, Clive	Murray, UT	1952	Junior	1			
Wier, Art	Elgin, IL	1957	Men	7	8	7	53.2
Wilson, Charles	Peeksville, NY	1968	Men's Doubles	2	2	1	
Wilson, John	Terre Haute, IN	1977	Men's Doubles	2			
Wilson, Mary	Terre Haute, IN	1977	Women	2			
Wilson, Walter	Washington D.C.	1950	Men	3			50.2
Wilson, Walter	Washington D.C.	1950	Men's Doubles	4			
Woodhouse, Dorne	Chicago, IL	1939	Men's Doubles	3	3	2	
Woodhouse, Dorne	Chicago, IL	1940	Men				
Woodhouse, Dorne	Chicago, IL	1940	Men's Doubles	2	7	3	
Woodhouse, Dorne	Chicago, IL	1941	Men	3	12	3	67.56
Woodhouse, Dorne	Chicago, IL	1941	Men's Doubles	1	5	1	
Woodhouse, Dorne	Chicago, IL	1942	Men	2	9	3	65.0
Woodhouse, Dorne	Chicago, IL	1942	Men's Doubles	1	3	0	
Woodhouse, Dorne	Chicago, IL	1943	Men				
Woodhouse, Dorne	Chicago, IL	1943	Men's Doubles	3	5	3	
Woodley	Washington D.C.	1950	Men's Doubles	2			
Woodward, Ed	Flint, MI	1946	Men's Doubles	2			
Woodward, Ed	Flint, MI	1944	Men	8	9	6	58.53
Woodward, Ed	Flint, MI	1944	Men's Doubles	1	5	2	68.0
Woodward, Ed	Flint, MI	1945	Men's Doubles	4			
Word, Al	Netcong, NJ	1976	Men	8	8	7	51.0
Worsham, Charles	Fanwood, NJ	1964	Men's Doubles	7	3	6	34.1
Wright, Ray	Covington, KY	1937	Men	14	0	1	47.91
Wright	Atlanta, GA	1954	Men's Doubles	8	1	6	12.2
Yannetti, Vince	Bound Brook, NJ	1976	Men	14	3	12	41.0
York, Gurney	Harmony, NC	1966	Men	1	14	1	
Yorkison, Andrew	Detroit, MI	1944	Men	7	9	6	53.73
Yorkison, Andrew	Detroit, MI	1944	Men's Doubles	6	3	4	

Player	City	Year	Division	Place	Won	Loss	%
Young, Carl	Columbus, OH	1966	Men	7	8	7	
Zimmerman, E.R.	Chicago, IL	1941	Men	11	7	8	57.76
Zozzaro, Phil	Little Falls, NJ	1976	Men	10	7	8	49.0
Zozzaro, Phil	Little Falls, NJ	1976	Men's Doubles	4	1	5	42.0